The
Immortalist

Distributed by
Inspiration University
POB 1026 - Staunton VA 24402
Ph 540/885-0551/Fax 1230

THE
IMMORTALIST

ALAN HARRINGTON

Celestial Arts • Millbrae, California

Acknowledgment is hereby made to the following for permission to reprint from their works:

Dover Publications, Inc., and Macmillan & Co. Ltd.: *Tragic Sense of Life*, by Miguel de Unamuno, translated by J. Crawford-Flitch.

The Macmillan Company and The Macmillan Company of Canada: "The Tower" from *Collected Poems*, by William Butler Yeats. Copyright 1928 by The Macmillan Company; renewed 1956 by Georgie Yeats.

The Washington Post: a column by Victor Cohn in the May 24, 1968 edition.

Village Voice: a column by Don McNeill in the May 4, 1967, edition. Copyright © 1967 by the *Village Voice*.

Doubleday & Company, Inc.: *The Prospect of Immortality*, by R.C.W. Ettinger. Copyright © 1964 by R.C.W. Ettinger.

Library of Congress Catalog Card Number 69–16432

To PEGGY

All or nothing! . . . Eternity, eternity! . . . that is the supreme desire! The thirst of eternity is what is called love among men, and whosoever loves another wishes to eternalize himself in him. Nothing is real that is not eternal.

MIGUEL DE UNAMUNO
Tragic Sense of Life

CONTENTS

PART I

I

PRESENTATION OF THE IMMORTALIST ARGUMENT

Death is an imposition on the human race, and no longer acceptable. Men and women have all but lost their ability to accommodate themselves to personal extinction; they must now proceed physically to overcome it. In short, to kill death; to put an end to mortality as a certain consequence of being born.

Our survival without the God we once knew comes down now to a race against time. The suspicion or conviction that "God is dead" has lately struck home not merely to a few hundred thousand freethinkers but to masses of the unprepared. Ancient orthodoxies may linger, but the content of worship has begun to collapse. This is what makes our situation urgent: around the world people are becoming increasingly less inclined to pray to a force that kills them.

The most imaginative philosophical and religious answers to the "problem of death" have become precisely irrelevant to the fact that we die. Humanity's powers of self-deception seem to be running out. Modern theological word-games may be pleasing to seminarians. Let jazz and rock music be permitted in the old spiritual gathering places. Such developments must be understood as gallant but altogether pathetic holding operations.

Emotionally, growing millions of us are in crisis. "Men are so necessarily mad," wrote Pascal, "that not to be mad would amount to another form of madness." Three hundred years later, with the mass-communication of anxiety, and new weaponry and drugs in our possession, we need only open the morning paper or sit down to television, or look into our own lives, to observe signs of a growing spiritual insurrection. Life as it used to be seems in the process of slowly exploding. We wonder at the bursts of "senseless" violence that seem likely at any moment to invade our days and nights. Yet is this sort of behavior necessarily irrational? If sanity now calls upon us to accept death without hope, perhaps such recent ceremonials as smashing pianos and guitars on stage may be viewed as expressions of maddened realism.

We ought to say immediately that these outbreaks of distress for the most part afflict those who have time to think beyond the problem of barely staying alive. When economic misery exhausts the psyche, horizons draw in. The meaning of existence? God, as Gandhi pointed out, must reveal himself to the destitute in the form of food.

Nor will oppressed people who have yet to win or regain their dignity suffer overly much from thoughts of death and meaninglessness, since for them death lives, remains present everywhere, and therefore speculating about it is redundant. In particular, the revolutionaries of today or any time—while the revolution is in prospect or actually going on—rise above this condition.

One of the advantages in having a cause is that it saves you from worrying about what life means. (Indeed, this is what attracts many people to communal action.) Just as during World War II "anti-fascism" seemed a sufficient excuse for living, so the fight against one injustice or another has tended to deliver present-day activists from such maladies of privilege as intellectual doubt, cosmic weariness and boredom. While the revolution assaults any given establishment, the fact that an abyss waits at the end of life does not for the time being bother the rebel. Hatred of the system and concern with advancement of the war gives a man enough to think about. Only when the battle has ended does the freed soul turn and face the cosmic menace.

Who, then, has come to live "in fear and trembling"? I am talking about the great bulk of the rest not actively at war, within the reach of print and television; people of the city, town and suburb getting along reasonably well, who except during vacations walk on pavement. Among this currently decisive majority, an unmistakable phenomenon may be observed.

Civilized humanity is signaling. It seems to be both an S.O.S. and a warning. In many languages and forms the coded sign repeats: "Change this scene, or *we* will!" The message has by no means gone unnoticed. Governments, the professions, universities, the clergy and social agencies of every description have paid close attention to the semaphore. (When they don't, as we started to learn in the 1960s, their sanctums are frequently invaded by large crowds carrying signs and shouting obscenities.)

What do outbreaks portend? A revolution of some kind, beyond the political (though including it) would seem to have started then. Young people at that time carried most of the signs. They seem about to take over everything, determined, in Saul Bellow's phrase, to seize the day, and possibly the world. But there has been something desperate as well as knowing in the way they are going about it, for theirs has, once more beyond political causes, really been a revolt against meaninglessness — which at the present time they are attempting to cover up by mass-action, but which they covertly fear will outlast that action. And this mood is not confined to the young. Mature, wearying, old — so many of us are conducting our affairs in a peculiarly nervous fashion, as though time were short.

Quite evidently the people of our time are reporting an emotional displacement; a condition not new but, some say, "aggravated by the complexities of modern life." The diagnosis, roughly speaking: angst, alienation. The treatment? Any public library catalog offers an assortment of prescriptions. Also a host of new preachers and messiahs. Their life-plans usually involve one or a combination of these choices: spiritual uplift; psychiatric consultation; group action; drunkenness; embracing the outdoors; making love as often as possible to the very edge of consciousness and forgetting about anything else; burying oneself in work, games and large families; trying to follow the complicated religio-philosophical excuses for what Reinhold Niebuhr describes as man's "natural contingency," and in more recent years the skillful employment of narcotics, blowing your mind, and seeking rebirth in the psychedelic voyage.

Unfortunately, these panaceas have a single fault in common: they are all varieties of self-hypnosis. Without exception they aim to cover up our condition rather than change it. Tiptoing around like the old man with a young bride, they dare not come to grips because the bride is death.

Meanwhile, frightened, vulnerable and increasingly angry civilized men continue to signal their warnings. Though coded, the message is that of a grown-up child, and childishly easy to read. The "problem" expressed in whatever form—feelings of isolation; aggressive behavior toward one another; massive paranoia, and the common inability to believe, commit or care—derives, going back to the beginning, from a single cause.

At the heart of this distress, the illness may be identified, simply and without sham, as the fear of aging and death. All else is peripheral and finally unimportant. Hence, no therapeutic treatment, however inspirational,

can do more than apply a coating of salve to our concern.
The problem causing civilized men to semaphore frantically and strike out in all directions is ultimately neither social nor philosophical, not religious or even psychiatric. Rather, it is based solidly on an intolerable recognition only now emerging to general consciousness; with protective myths and orthodoxies having been stripped away, not merely the knowledge but the gut-realization that the void is waiting for everybody and that each of us is going to vanish into it. The gloomiest projection of this awareness comes from a master scientist and mathematician, the seventeenth century Jansenist, Pascal:

. . . that death, which threatens us every moment, must infallibly place us within a few years under the dreadful necessity of being for ever either annihilated or unhappy. There is nothing more real than this, nothing more terrible. Be we as heroic as we like, that is the end which awaits the noblest life in the world. . . . I know not who put me into this place rather than in another, nor why the short time which is given to live is assigned to me at this point rather than at another of the whole eternity which was before me or which shall come after me. I see nothing but infinities on all sides, which surround me as an atom, and as a shadow which endures only for an instant and returns no more. . . .

In our era Paul Tillich updates the same idea:

We are a generation of the End and we should know that we are. . . . Death has become powerful in our time. . . . For nearly a century this was concealed in Western Civilization. . . . We forgot that we are finite, and we forgot the abyss of nothingness surrounding us.

We need not detail any more such pronouncements. The point is not that philosophers feel this way, but that insight into doom, once the privilege of certified thinkers, has now been brought home to nearly every-body who can read. It is the "something new" of our day. All around us we have the spectacle of overflowing millions no longer praying but grasping for salvation, behind all façades of sophistication and toughness, each in his own style, every man for himself. Salvation by whatever means—and quickly. It has become the central passion that drives us, a need rapidly turning into an imperious demand to be rescued from nothingness.

This is not to deny that life can be sunny and lusty, packed with fascinating hours; that everybody has the chance to turn his span into an adventure filled with achievement and love-making, and that we dance, sky-dive, float in space, build marvelous computers, and climb mountains under the sea. Admit too that we have never had such music, and proliferating excitement, and varieties of challenge. Still . . .

After the exuberance of being young, as young men and women grow only a little older, there begins to intrude on all our scenes a faint disquiet. At first it visits intermittently. The occasional feeling of a shadow seems not too important, perhaps an illusion. Then it reappears. In the beginning the shadow may be mistaken for doubt, about certain values such as justice; about the prosperity of brutes, a child with leukemia, death to the volunteer, safety for the malingerer. But then the uneasiness grows into something more important than doubt.

An old Marxist cartoon showed languid dancers at a ball. A great worker-fist has rammed up through the dance floor. Death to the aristocrats! But there has always been this larger fist bringing death to all classes. The great fist of death appears sooner or later to every-one, at first in dim outline, not necessarily brandished in our direction, often in repose, but still there. It becomes a strange, inconstant vision; sometimes the fist recedes and appears to vanish, but then on another day returns.

As the years advance it slowly grows larger. Why it should be poised over us becomes as much of a mystery as the menace of the fist itself. The vision intrudes unexpectedly, not only in the middle of the night: perhaps during a cocktail party, after the football game, while you watch your children on the lawn. Not that we think about it all the time; people have other things to do. Still, it remains just beyond our attention, waiting.

We do our best to put the vision off somewhere, make it remote. Or close it off with black jokes. Any new religion is eagerly grasped for a little while. We must *kick* the vision by whatever means; otherwise all experience dissolves in irony, since it and we will soon be gone. In this state of mind, love, which passes, can become too much trouble. Without faith compassion seems useless. But now, precisely at the wrong time, men by the millions are in danger of succumbing to the tremendous input of their own information which has all but destroyed faith.

In *Escape From Freedom,* Erich Fromm saw this: "The state of anxiety, the feeling of powerlessness and insignificance, and especially the doubt concerning one's future after death, represent a state of mind which is practically unbearable for anybody."

Freud perceived in this psychic state the Universal Neurosis of Mankind. As Norman O. Brown has expressed it in *Life Against Death:* "Neurosis is not an occasional aberration; it is not just in other people; it is in us, and in us all the time." Man has established in himself "a psychic force opposed to his own idea." The force grows from a will to self-destruction which he tries to resist. Unfortunately, "the death instinct is the core of the human neurosis." Therefore, "mankind, unconscious of its real desires and . . . unable to obtain satisfaction, is hostile to life and ready to destroy itself."

A pure insight certainly, but perhaps not deep enough. Would it be ingenuous to explore the possibility that the fact of death alone, *all by itself,* may be what is at the core of the human neurosis? Perhaps man is not in the least hostile to his own consciousness, but only to life with death at the end of it.

As for the death instinct, admitting a countercurrent to the life force, are we stuck with the label? It might be asked, for instance, whether the death instinct could not just as well be performing also as an instinct to be reborn by changing from one form to another, crossing the border of death in between. Do death and rebirth tend to merge in the imagination? If so, when the drive to dissolve oneself occurs, we may find evidence that a death wish and rebirth wish can be the same.

The surface of history makes this conjecture seem worthwhile. Our species has never been reconciled to the brutal circumstance that we must die. Through the centuries we have invented an incredible number of explanations to account for our individual forms' decomposing in agony and returning to the earth.

The mysterious happening of death has led humanity to expiate primal guilt in both monstrous and beautiful ways. Hope of setting things right with the gods has driven us to lunacies of self-denial, cruelties, persecutions, elaborate ceremonies with incense and smoke, dancing around totem poles, the thumbscrewing of heretics; from Mexico to India, the casting of shrieking innocents into pits, and all kinds of psychotic, shameful and ludicrous practices such as would make whatever gods might be watching hide their eyes.

In the East we have been more subtle, attempting to placate destiny by an elaborate pretense of not wanting to survive, or preferring nirvana to the eternal return. But elsewhere listen to the wails, songs, shouts, hymns and chants. The voices of Islam, Judaism, Christianity and atheism join as one. Massed units in Red Square as well as Vatican City combine their energies in a single mighty appeal: *Save Us.* For the beauty and cruelty in the world, the kindness and the murder; our art trying to illuminate this wilderness; speculations of philosophers; and the descent into drugs and drunkenness; today's wildly emotional crowds rushing around the world's streets—all are organized around death, and designed to protect each of us from annihilation here or elsewhere.

Dostoevsky penetrates our situation with one quick thrust. In *The Possessed,* Kirilov, the engineer, about to become his own god by committing suicide: "Man simply invented God in order not to kill himself. That is the sum of universal history down to this moment."

Tracking man's spiritual history, we can follow this path: from the beginning, human consciousness longs and plans to perpetuate itself. Out of individuated consciousness, which is original sin, what Miguel de Unamuno called the "hunger of immortality" is born. Man craves personal immortality, but observes that everyone dies. He then creates gods, and worships and placates them. Assuming that "we must have done something wrong," he constructs systems of self-punishment to pay for the primal crime. Still everybody dies. Then, since eternal life on earth obviously is not forthcoming, and placating divine authority hasn't worked, he more or less unknowingly resolves to knock down the gods or replace them, or to become God. Since this must be done warily, for fear of retribution, he informs himself of what he is doing through myths. In these dream-projections the Promethean and satanic types, or the "Foolish Women" such as Eve, always undergo a severe chastising, but the idea of rebellion is thereby passed along. No good; everyone goes on dying.

He attempts to trick fate, as in the Far East, by pretending that he doesn't want to come back to life. That doesn't accomplish anything either. Now he grovels before the gods, saying, All right, I won't eat or make love too often; I'll play half-dead in advance, refuse to enjoy, even die before I die, offer myself for wounding, expose my undefended belly, genitals, backside, anything, is that what you want? No help.

Thus men alternate between abject surrender and assertiveness. But whatever our tactics, we have always been in a state of Permanent Revolution against Imaginary Gods. Rephrasing and extending the Freudian conception, all culture has been a subtle and devious attempt to usurp divine authority, to conquer death—at the same time taking care not to excite the anger of the gods who inflict mortality on us until we are strong enough to overthrow them.

Man is a rebel, as Camus says, but he also resists himself, resists and sabotages his own rebellion. The Permanent Revolution is constantly being interfered with. Counter-revolutionaries in humanity's own ranks have always managed to slow down the centuries-old drive to remove death. Their counter-measures spring from an ever-changing set of superstitions.

A fifth column of superstition obstructs every advance against the citadel of death. Oddly enough, in an evolutionary context, the race's sabotaging of its own progress may turn out to have been functional. An innocent revolutionary spirit running ahead of scientific advances, without superstition to slow it down, might long since have killed itself off after prematurely looking death in the face.

To rein ourselves in, we invented primal guilt. Even if it has or once had evolutionary sanction, guilt is more than painful. The imaginary gods in our psyche exact a toll when they are threatened. They strike back, and sometimes cause us to panic, to twist and turn, and to become frightened of our own daring, and to hate and fear others who dare. Challenging the gods can estrange us from ourselves as well as from others, and make us odd and unconfident. It can reduce natural exuberance, and make this acceptable as payment for hubris. The rebel is at all times exposed, vulnerable, and afflicted by the suspicion that in his refusal to accept divine authority which leads to death he is somehow "wrong."

Above all, we conceal from ourselves the existence of our underground drive against the cosmic establishment. Men must keep it from themselves that they are in revolt against the gods, or "against Nature." Only by means of this hypocrisy has our species been able to keep the revolutionary program going. It has enabled man to plot against his gods while he worshipped them.

A disguised drive toward divinity, the creation of our own divinity, carries us forward. At certain times we advance too quickly, and the gods in our heads inflict a terrible revenge—sometimes on ourselves, more often on others. Galileo and Bruno move too far out in front of their day, and are cut down. But in another country, in Jung's phrase, "the godly sense of curiosity strives for birth." Man, in the person of Francis Bacon, sets up the scientific method to dominate his environment, to remove all mysteries (divine property), in order to find the base Archimedes sought, the place to stand from which he could move the world, and ultimately remove death.

In his recent study, *On Aggression,* Konrad Lorenz reminds us of an "inestimably important fact that by the process of phylogenetic ritualization a new and completely autonomous instinct may evolve which is, in principle, just as independent as any of the so-called 'great' drives, such as hunger, sex, fear, or aggression, and which—like these—has its seat in the great parliament of instincts." Dr. Lorenz emphasizes that "those other rites, which evolve in the course of human civilization, are not hereditarily fixed but are transmitted by tradition and must be learned afresh by every individual." Hence, a biological accounting for such activity is not required. "Among animals, symbols are not transmitted by tradition from generation to generation, and it is here, if one wishes, that one may draw the border line between the animal and man." And ". . . man's whole system of innate activities and reaction is phylogenetically so constructed, so 'calculated' by evolution, as to be complemented by cultural tradition."

From Dr. Lorenz's conclusions it would seem unnecessary to question whether the struggle for individual immortality, if such can be shown to exist, is derived from animal traits. Doubt whether activity of this kind can be filed under "instinct" or "drive" becomes equally irrelevant. It will be enough to show—from man's history and continuing behavior—that one of his consistently prevailing modes of activity, conceivably his project since time began, has been that of seeking ways to perpetuate his individual forms (ourselves). If we have a clue here, then the animal-originated drives or instincts can be supposed to have been redirected in the special interests of human survival.

Does the Darwinian struggle for existence continue unchanged in modern dress? Perhaps, but the principle of natural selection has obviously, to some extent, been countermanded in human affairs—for instance, by medical advances, computer technology and the range and destructive power of weaponry. By these and other means a soft, over-affluent culture which, biologically and historically, might be expected to succumb to a tough, oncoming barbarian group, retains the weapons to destroy the challenger, requiring only a highly-trained fraction of its people to do the job.

Where men are concerned, what we are dealing with for practical purposes is an inevitable response to life's intolerable ground rules. We have a condition: individual man's knowledge that some day he will die. Given the scope of human awareness, as well as our facility with tools, it may reasonably be assumed that moves to remedy the brutal situation will follow and persist.

Arrogance is not required to advance this thesis. Each

man's struggle for indefinite survival beyond time need not violate concepts based on sexual energy, the will to power or, more recently, the principle of territorial defense. (But the territorial concern must by its own definition be peripheral. Territory is simply what surrounds life forms. Even enlarging the area to be defended so that it includes emotional *Lebensraum,* one's good name, and so on, the king finally preserved from harm is identity itself. Territory remains the outer perimeter, an outer concern of being, not its citadel.)

Having lost faith, a great many men and women have returned to the old superstitions now cloaked in new disguises. God may have retreated, but the *gods* today are by no means dead. Though disposed to destroy them, we simultaneously bow down to some of the weirdest assortment of deities ever known, such as History, Success and Statistics. We worship purveyors of Luck, Fashion and Publicity. We follow shifting gospels based on journalistic graffiti passing for honest news. We humbly receive the word from makeshift divinities seated at the head of couches, sexual statisticians, psychological testers, polltakers, various merchants of paranoia, the manipulators of public relations and television personalities—the multiple gods of our quickening century.

This is to say that increasing numbers of civilized men and women are progressing, or retrogressing, to a pagan state of mind. The most sophisticated as well as humble people live in fear of these gods and, atheists most of all, are guided by the need either to live up to their examples or compete for their approval. What emerges, astonishingly, is that the old gods in new forms live on in our heads not metaphorically but for all practical purposes *alive,* and that they exert a dominating influence over the great bulk of modern affairs. One development is new here. For want of any other way, the publicizing of one's excellence (fitness for survival beyond death) —publicity great and small—has become the path to immortality. The lust for do-it-yourself immortality has produced an emotional transformation in which the ideal of Right Conduct (formerly the passport to heaven) is being replaced everywhere by the ideal of Printing One's Image on All Things.

Yet, seeking to remedy his condition, civilized man also wildly contradicts himself. Expending his energies at one and the same time to placate, impress, destroy and replace his gods, he also exhibits a craving to *share consciousness* with all other beings, including the divine. The attempt at spiritual fusion with others can take many forms—destructive, saintly (that is to say, charitable) and quiescent. Consider some recent effects.

Writing in the context of Nazism, Jacques Maritain heard "the voices of a base multitude whose baseness itself appears as an apocalyptic sign." These voices cry out: "'We have had enough of lying optimism and illusory morality, enough of freedom and personal dignity and justice and peace and faithfulness and goodness which make us mad with distress. Let us give ground to the infinite promises of evil, and of swarming death, and of blessed enslavement, and of triumphant despair.'"

In contrast—growing out of San Francisco and New York and spreading across the country — we have had, emerging in full flower back in 1967, the hippie subculture, based originally on the ideal of natural saintliness, or at any rate of free-form living. This was made possible by a union bringing together the Wisdom of the East and Western pharmacology, with LSD and other substances providing the means for prolonged and repeated escapes from time (which marks the minutes leading to extinction). The movement, some of whose street people and their younger brothers and sisters linger still, should have been understood — and generally was not — as an attempt to achieve *immortality now*: freedom from time, money, history and death. It also attempted to realize a general sharing of consciousness, in other words, collective immortality.

"The basic unit of the culture," one calling himself Billy Digger said, "would be the commune instead of a house with one man and one woman in it. The commune would not be owned by one person or one group but would be open to all people at all times, to do whatever they wish to do in it. . . ." (In a different way, searching for communal immortality through violence, California's Hell's Angels and the Red Guards of China were into the same thing, and may soon again be without notice: making the air roar around decent folks or knocking down the uncles of the world and putting dunce caps on them.)

If such movements appear to deny old-fashioned responsibility and traditional modes of achievement, it is not surprising. The ideal of achievement has to do with a *reach* for immortality, which, if you feel already in that state, even in simulation, is obviously no longer necessary.

Still, these starts at saintly living (including, glibly, saintliness through violence), whether genuine or make-believe, fail to hide the phenomenon of flight. Saintliness in our time will not be able to generate corrective measures against our one long-range problem, which is death. Lacking a dynamic principle beyond that of shattering present life forms, it can only turn into another short-term holding operation. Saintliness can further charity, farming and simple craftsmanship. It can create motorcycles for the road to nowhere. It can promote measures at least temporarily to restore dignity, such as mass-sweeping of refuse-strewn neighborhoods. It can sponsor brotherhood-happenings in the park; create sweet afternoons with flowers, balloons and kites, and encourage people to draw closer to one another. But finally the uses of saintliness are defensive. Resisting technological inroads on the soul, they represent an attempt to deal with a neurotic industrial society by dropping out of it. Possibly the goal of all these efforts is that of agrarian-return or return to the small machine-shop.

But with all the love and kindness in the world, no agrarian retreat or machine-shop rendezvous can prevail for long against the thought of death, except by encouraging the participants to ignore it—and as the body grows older this cannot be done. The enlarged or extended families of the *Now* people have already grown about a decade older. As many have discovered, the measures they have undertaken may not be wrong, but right before their time. Perhaps living outside of bourgeois time may, over the years, turn out to have been a practice run, with painful lessons that will prove valuable when we reach our Utopia Beyond Time, eternally right though temporally assaulted by hardships that caused many to give up or give out.

As for the psychedelic trip, no one should doubt that it can prove rewarding, if it is not taken too far and too often. But resorted to as a complete way of life, it may hurt you in mysterious ways, and achieve not much more than a temporarily helpful, and perhaps cowardly, cracking of identity. What makes widespread psychedelic dropping out as alarming as it can be is that—if the substances are used improperly—after a point, with each new voyage, return to the old identity and earthly purpose tends to seem increasingly less worthwhile. True, identity can become a cross when it is formed too rigidly. But ego-identity is also our main source of power in the world, and only by organizing the power of our protesting intelligence can we hope to bring about the death-free life man must have.

Finally, by blowing their minds young men and women hide from death. It is good sometimes to hide from death, and to go through simulated death and rebirth now and then. But too many trips, indiscriminately taken, can lead to an unearned passivity. If passivity takes hold, this society, undesirable as it may seem, will become far worse. Extremes of violence and mass-passivity will build up. When these two forces are polarized, disaster comes, and, contrary to myth, violence nearly always wins. It has already started to win again. The finest among us are shot in the head by half-crazed and above all lonely individuals. Not only assassins, but the most advanced elements of our younger society, can no longer stand being alone. Youth's quiescent and largely drug-oriented nihilism of a few years ago quickly gave way to the New Left's all-out freedom through violence. But — quite apart from the justice of all causes — the New Left, as evidenced by its massive shock tactics, its theater and enlarged family foundations, were clearly moving toward exactly the same goal as that of the Psychedelic Mutants — a collective and communal escape from time and death.

What happened is this: in the past quarter-century the public relations of death, as managed by theologians of all creeds and every secular orthodoxy, all but exhausted the ancient excuses for what Unamuno called "the running away of life like water." Interestingly, the atomic bomb, LSD and the Pill were developed at about the same time. Could this be the evolutionary crisis of our species? For centuries men and women were able to hold on to their peace of mind by repetitive prayer, chants, rhythms and psalms set to music. But repetition, beauty and music no longer possess the force to distract us from meaninglessness.

Today we are in a race against time, racing, as Maritain suggests, our own apocalypse. Our inexorable though hardly remorseless drive to divinity is taking new, non-institutionalized forms. This comes down to the simplest of propositions: the species must solve the problem of death very soon, blow itself up, or blow its mind.

Medical help is on the way. But so too are fire-power and despair. All have computer technology behind them. Any one of the three might win. Will medical advances to arrest the aging of human tissues prevail over weaponry and mass psychosis? That has become the question of our time and conceivably of all time.

The immortalist position is that the usefulness of philosophy has come to an end, because all philosophy teaches accommodation to death and grants it static finality as "the human condition." Art too, insofar as it celebrates or merely bemoans our helplessness, has gone as far as it can. The beautiful device of tragedy ending in helplessness has become outmoded in our absurd time, no longer desirable and not to be glamorized. The art that embellishes death with visual beauty and celebrates it in music belongs to other centuries.

It comes as no surprise that traditional forms of art are being shattered, with the editing and fixing of life no longer allowed. Our participation is demanded in these works; we cannot be spectators. The discotheque takes its place as an electric art form. We loosen our anxieties with the help of enormous guitars in a temple of fragmentation. Kinetic and luminous forms that reach out and bring us into the action; declaimed poetry now so often set to music; multiple screens, happenings that frequently involve orgy and obscenity—all have one purpose: to smash the *separateness* of everyone present; to expose feeling and break through thinking; to make us live, in the phrase Alan Watts has quoted from Ananda K. Coomaraswamy, "a perpetual uncalculated life in the present." And all this too amounts to one more attempt to hide from the end—by substituting Dionysian togetherness for romance, and a bombardment of the senses, lightworks of the soul, a sort of electronic Buddhism in place of sequential perception. The use of kinetic environment as an art form removes death, creating the illusion of an Eternal Now—an illusion in that it seems to guarantee eternal youth, which, of course, is what this generation is really after.

The immortalist thesis is that the time has come for the

race to get rid of the intimidating gods in its own head — grow up out of our cosmic inferiority complex (no more "dust thou art, and to dust thou shalt return . . ."), bring our disguised desire into the open, and go after what we want, the only state of being we will settle for, which is divinity.

We have long since gone beyond the moon, touched down on Mars, the moon, harnessed nuclear energy, artificially reproduced DNA, and now have the biochemical means to control birth; why should death itself, "the Last Enemy," be considered sacred and beyond conquest?

A new act of faith is required of us: the kind of faith that we might have had a few decades ago, and did not, when Dr. Goddard was bravely projecting his rockets into the atmosphere, and a band of futurists was insisting that not just in comic strips but in reality we could lift ourselves beyond any space that could be seen from the earth. This new faith we must have is that with the technology at our disposal in the near future death can be conquered. This faith must also weld Salvation to Medical Engineering.

We must drive away the gods of doubt and self-punishment. Our new faith must accept as gospel that salvation belongs to medical engineering and nothing else; that man's fate depends first on the proper management of his technical proficiency; that we can only engineer our freedom from death, not pray for it; that our messiahs will be wearing white coats, not in asylums but in chemical and biological laboratories.

With such faith we will stop shrinking into conformity, huddling in corporations and communes, and numbing our anxieties by means of network television. (Great corporations can, of course—in fact, must—contribute to this effort, but with much more imagination and daring than most of them exhibit now.) In this spirit, many young people will perhaps moderate their future dependency on the psychedelic simulation of death and rebirth, their escape into mob action, and such devices as the electronic scrambling of consciousness.

Does such a project seem quixotic now? Perhaps so, but it will not tomorrow. It is at least as practical as going beyond the moon, and conceivably, from an evolutionary standpoint, part of the same program.

Our conception of immortality now requires precise definition. What must be eliminated from the human situation is the inevitability of death as a result and natural end of the aging process. I am speaking of the inescapable parabolic arching from birth to death. But we must clearly understand that any given unit of life— my individual existence and yours—can never be guaranteed eternity.

Until such time as duplications of individual nervous systems can be grown in tissue cultures (at this point no one knows "whose" consciousness they would have), our special identities will always be subject to being hit by a truck or dying in a plane crash. A sudden virus or heart seizure, even in the body's youth, may carry us off. Statistically, looking ahead thousands of years, the chances are that every human and even inanimate form will be broken sooner or later. But the distress felt by men and women today does not arise from the fear of such hazards. Rather, it comes from the certainty of aging and physical degeneration leading to death. It is the fear of losing our powers and being left alone, or in the hands of indifferent nurses, and knowing that the moment must come when we will not see the people we love any more, and everything will go black.

Some would fear the opposite: living through a great blank eternity with our eyes open. This would be comparable to endless days without sleep. But no problem confronts us here. A state of indefinite living can be programmed through a succession of lives by means of designed sleeps or hibernations to last for years, decades or centuries. We will see that family ties can be renewed and dropped like options from one life to another. People can be phased, perhaps psychedelically, out of one life, and then, reactivated according to their own desire, briefed back into the next. Those who find the opportunities for future existences insupportable will be welcome to decline rejuvenation. For others who prefer a life not risk-free, the zero and double-zero of accidental death can provide the spice of chance in the living continuum. In the society that some day will live beyond time what is now called the Absurd will undoubtedly turn into our saving grace.

In our conception immortality is *being alive now, ungoverned by span, cycle* or *inevitability.* Civilized man's project will no longer be as Freud suggested to recover his lost childhood, but rather to create the adult equivalent: an immortal present free from the fear of aging and death. Our aim (against the counsel of nearly all wise old men) will be to fix our immediate environment so that, puny as we like to tell ourselves we are (still placating the old gods), the environment puts itself at our service.

"The world is made for Consciousness. Each Consciousness," wrote Unamuno. ". . . A human soul is worth all the universe. . . . " Our project—at least as worthy as the Manhattan Project that produced the atomic bomb and the National Space Program—can be to individualize eternity, to stabilize the forms and identities through which the energy of conscious life passes.

An "Immortality Program" would not be nearly as expensive as the atomic energy and space projects. At the beginning, it would involve intensive work in basic biology, since the first principles of the aging process are only dimly understood, and have not yet been satisfactorily formulated. We will find that a full-scale assault on death begun in this manner is by no means impractical, and that, even if it were, men and women (still unbeknown to themselves) have already decided to undertake it.

The case for the immortalist point of view will rest on evidence that since the beginning of recorded time man has engaged in a disguised drive to make himself immortal and divine, and that this overriding motive which accounts for much of his significant action, is now driving him toward his evolutionary crisis. The time has come for men to turn into gods or perish.

II

THE LONGING
FOR REBIRTH

The idea of a second birth is found at all times and in all places.

JUNG

In his unconscious every one of us is convinced of his own immortality.

FREUD

Man is a finite, limited creature but he holds infinity within him, and he demands infinity as an end.

BERDYAEV

The hope of rebirth or returning to consciousness after death, or between deaths, has always obsessed us. Freud calls belief in a future life "the oldest, strongest, and most insistent wish of mankind." According to Jung: "Rebirth is an affirmation that must be counted on among the primordial affirmations of mankind."

Tribal societies of the plains; mountain, desert and valley dwellers; inhabitants of jungles, forests and remote spits of land—all have independently created mythic systems guaranteeing return to consciousness. The idea of an indestructible, traveling soul springs up everywhere.

The Dakota, Huron, Mohave and Natchez Indians of North America; Eskimos; the Carib, Mayan, and Patagonian tribes of Central and South America; Okinawans, Papuans, Melanesians, Fijians, and the Dyaks of Borneo, react to the prospect of oblivion with the same overriding faith that they will live on in some fashion. So do the tribes of Australia and islands nearby: Aruntas, Kadhirs, Warramunga, Tasmain; the Druses of Lebanon, and millions in Bengal and Burma; in Africa, the Mandingo, Yoruba, Zulus, Bantus and Baritse. In Europe the idea of reincarnation came up against the Mediterranean orthodoxies which hold out the prospect of saving the single existence rather than continuing on through a succession of rebirths. Still, in the north, there may be found among the Finns, Lapps, Danes, Norse, the Celts of Gaul, Wales, England and Ireland, old Prussians and early Teutons, the conviction that they have lived other lives and will be born again.*

Jung lists five types of rebirth imagined by mankind:

1. *Metempsychosis.* Transmigration of souls. Continuity of personality not guaranteed.
2. *Reincarnation.* Rebirth in bodily form.
3. *Resurrection.*
4. *Renewal,* in our lifetime, sometimes by means of ceremony.
5. *Participation in the Process of Transformation.* This "indirect rebirth" is achieved in ceremonies like the Mass.

---

* Several examples of the world-wide preoccupation with rebirth cited in this chapter are taken from *Reincarnation, An East-West Anthology,* compiled and edited by Joseph Head and S. L. Cranston, the Julian Press Inc., New York 1961.

The roll call of genius responding to these various forms of revival is virtually endless. At random, begin with Plato's account of Socrates' death in the *Phaedo*. About to take the hemlock, Socrates will not envision the end of his own being: "There comes to mind an ancient doctrine which affirms that [the souls of men after death] go from hence into the other world, and returning hither are born again from the dead."

Centuries later St. Augustine asked: "Say, Lord, to me . . . say, did my infancy succeed another age of mine that died before it? Was it that which I spent within my mother's womb . . . and what before that life again, O God my joy, was I anywhere or in any body?"

In the Koran, it is written: "God generates beings, and sends them back over and over again."

The Egyptians, more obsessive than anyone in their pursuit of resurrection, filled the *Book of the Dead* with such boasts as "Homage to thee, O Governor . . . who makest mortals to be born again, who renewest thy youth. . . . I am Yesterday, Today and Tomorrow, and I have the power to be born a second time. . . . I have knit together my bones; I have made myself whole and sound; I have become young once more; I am Osiris, the Lord of Eternity."

Of the great orthodoxies, the Jewish religion has the least to say about rebirth. But in Judaism's underground stream of thought carried forward in the Kabalistic works, the theme recurs, as set forth in the Zohar: "All souls are subject to the trials of transmigration; and men do not know the designs of the Most High with regard to them; they do not know how they are being at all times judged, both before coming into this world and when they leave it. They do not know how many transformations and mysterious trials they must undergo; how many souls and spirits come to this world without returning to the palace of the divine king."

For Luther, in the words of Norman Brown, "hell . . . is not a place, but is the experience of death. . . . It is the hope of a joyful resurrection that alone saves Luther from the dominion of death. . . ."

Unbelievers too voice their longing to live on.

In *Thus Spake Zarathustra*, Nietzsche vowed: "Oh, and could I not be ardent for Eternity, and for the marriage ring of rings—the ring of the return."

The most ironical have found some excuse on which to base their hopes for continued consciousness. Voltaire, for one: "The doctrine of metempsychosis is, above all, neither absurd nor useless. It is not more surprising to be born twice than once; everything in nature is resurrection."

One of the coolest atheists who ever lived, the Marquis de Sade, has his dying man mock an attending priest, but coming out from behind the irony we hear: "Nothing dies, my friend, nothing in this world is destroyed. Today a man, tomorrow a worm, the day after a fly, is that not always existing?"

The transcendentalists, of course, are open to any suggestion. Thoreau passed along the story of a strong and beautiful bug which was said to have eaten its way out of a tree hundreds of years old and "hatched perchance by the heat of an urn." The report "has gone the rounds of New England," and hearing it: "Who does not feel his faith in a resurrection and immortality strengthened . . . ?"

At all times, personal immortality is what we are after. Unamuno suggested to a peasant that there might be a God in the form of a universal consciousness, but that man's soul may not be immortal. The peasant replied: "Then wherefore God?"

Why fight death? All the advanced thinkers keep telling us not to. Advice comes from such counselors as Alan Watts to accept our disappearance into the void as part of life. But with what complacency this counsel can be offered! Watts argues, for example, that "the attempt to triumph over death by the miracle of resurrection is the failure to see that these pairs are not alternatives but correlatives." In another passage, our unfortunate destiny, personal annihilation, is disposed of as meaningless: "Now this is what we fear—the loss of human identity and integrity in a transient stream of atoms." Anxiety results from nothing more than "the frustration of not being able to have life without death. That is, of not being able to solve a nonsensical problem."

Such assurances have the ring of wisdom. They may even be momentarily consoling. Yet somehow the cool view of approaching oblivion seems a bit unreal. Death *is* nonsense, but it will not be experienced as a "nonsensical problem" by you or me, or by the philosopher himself who probably moans when he has a toothache like anybody else, and who, when his time comes, will in all likelihood struggle just as frantically to keep his head out of the black sack.

In contrast to the general run of wise men, Unamuno cried out with no reservation or shame: ". . . for me the becoming other than I am, the breaking of the unity and continuity of my life, is to cease to be who I am—that is to say, it is simply to cease to be. And that—no! Anything rather than that!"

There are, of course, loftier philosophical positions. From the vantage point of the Himalayas we of the West who cannot stand flies resting on our eyelids seem hopelessly ego-ridden. Alan Watts sets forth this view (italics added) :

. . . during the era in which Christianity arose both the Hebrew and Graeco-Roman cultures were much preoccupied with a craving for salvation in terms of individual immortality. Both cultures had developed in such a way as to increase that vivid sense of the ego, of individual isolation which—ever since—has been so *peculiarly characteristic of the Western mentality.*

But the fear of death can hardly be imagined as peculiarly Western. If this were true, why would tribal societies on every inhabited continent invent all kinds of rebirth systems? And was it not primarily the thought of his own mortal condition that turned the Buddha away from the world? "Promise me that my life will not end in death," he is said to have asked his father, "that sickness will not impair my health, that age will not follow my youth, that misfortune will not destroy my property." Since his father could not promise these things, the young Buddha decided: "The world is a prison," and resolved to seek means of leaving it.

Since then derivations of Buddhist thought have emphasized that clinging to existence is the source of pain. To avoid pain, give up craving life here. The goal is to exist out of time, beyond life and death, free from craving, suffering and sorrow. Do not fear death: what dies is only the world of *maya* centered about one's more or less illusional feeling of separate identity.

But for all its subtlety this ingenious rationalization of nothingness is a thought-game like all the others. Finally, in Lhasa, Jerusalem and Little Rock everyone pursues the same dream. Reincarnation, resurrection, the arrival of a Messiah, *nirvana*, it hardly matters which: East and West have simply come up with varying means of evading oblivion. The difference is that the Asians and their followers give death a judo twist, enabling Eastern Man to fling the void over his shoulder by seeming to embrace it. Around the Wheel of Being survival has been generally anticipated in one way or another.

In the *Bhagavad-Gita* Krishna declares: "I myself never was not, nor Thou, nor all the princes of the earth; nor shall we hereafter cease to be." Also: "the man whose devotion has been broken off by death goeth to the regions of the righteous, where he dwells for an immensity of years and is then born again on earth in a pure and fortunate family."

And in China, 6th century B.C., from Chwang Tzu, the disciple of Lao Tzu: "To have attained to the human form must always be a source of joy . . . then, to undergo countless transitions, with only the infinite to look forward to—what incomparable bliss is that!"

"It is nature's kindness that we do not remember past births," writes Gandhi to his disciple, Madeleine Slade. "Where is the good either of knowing in detail the numberless births we have gone through? . . . The form ever changes, ever perishes, the informing spirit neither changes nor perishes. . . . " But then from Gandhi, (italics added) : ". . . Both birth and death are great mysteries. *If death is not a prelude to another life, the intermediate period is a cruel mockery.*"

Freud has said that the unconscious does not believe in its own death: "it behaves as if immortal." Jung finds archetypal patterns collectively to *be* immortal, reaching down to our carbon origins. In *Modern Man and Mortality,* Jacques Choron cites the observation made some years ago by psychiatrists Walter Bromberg and Paul Schilder that dreams following an epileptic attack have one specific content: the patient experiences a simulation of death "in some form or other." The most common "death" is followed by a sensation of being reborn. "The authors conclude that the rebirth fantasy is part and parcel of the fantasy life of every human being, and that the idea of reincarnation, represented by this birth fantasy, may be considered as the basic factor in our representation of death."

Epileptic outbreaks, therefore, may be understood as violent and faulty reproductions of a natural rhythm. This rhythm is always with us: a continuum of dissolution and renewal, expressed in both dramatic and hardly noticeable forms.

The most routine human life (even going to sleep and waking up) moves in obeisance to at least faintly-experienced simulations of death and rebirth. The longing to be reborn rises from the body; it dictates our pleasures, and seems recognizably indispensable to emotional health. One senses the presence of an overwhelming, cellular need. Failure to move with the death-rebirth rhythm makes us feel out of sorts, despondent, vicious. Apparently, at regular intervals, mortal being must go through the reenactment of the dissolving, dying process in order to maintain a zest for life. In combination with this, the involuntary pilgrim puts up with mortality by every now and then *knocking himself out of time*. But simulated death is the key—or rather the doorway—to resurrection and the life. Christ, too, arose out of the rhythm of our desire.

Repeated imitations of dying and rising once more help recharge our energies. The need to repeat this process over and over makes demands on every kind of human relationship. The aim of sexual love: simultaneous death and transfiguration, completely out of control. The little death in what Unamuno calls "the genetic spasm" makes all things new again. Or the spiritual equivalent of this release: making a clean breast of things. Pray, confess, unload sorrow by giving up all dignity and pretense. "Die" to your pride, as in the Roman Catholic rite, and gain a new beginning by means of absolution. More slowly, psychoanalysis too aims to break apart, to "kill" the unit of resistance lying on the couch, forcing it to die to itself before healing can begin.

What compels us at intervals to move into a different kind of time, and to dissolve and reassemble the self, accounts, as will be seen, for humanity's world-wide dependence on plays, film and games. Members of an audience, Aristotle knew, vicariously die, purged and then renewed by pity and terror—and also laughter. In the same way, small deaths and rebirths occur in the imagination depending on whether we win or lose a game, on how our team fares, or whether the ball lands on the red or the black.

Through history the sensation of being reborn has been achieved in spectacular fashion by *violence,* between individuals and gangs, and by tribes and nations in violence's massive form, war. Aggression forces men to "die a little" in risking disaster. The conflict will naturally have other reasons-why. Sometimes it will be thrust upon us when, at the moment, we ourselves have no need for such cleansing action. We attack others—or violently defend ourselves—to preserve integrity, to extend power and being, to possess their turf, wealth, women, to protect ours, and so on. Yet as often as not persons and tribes may be found inventing a threat, picking a fight, for no special reason. This arbitrary malevolence can be understood only if it is seen that, quite apart from motives of self-protection and conquest, the combative man is also driven by the compulsion to be born again.

Violence will do it, shaking and disarranging the psyche. The risk can make all of life seem fresh and thrilling. For example, black riots in Detroit, Johannesburg, and other cities have been motivated by a hierarchy of reasons: resistance to injustice; retaliation for damaged manhood; tactical aims; to crowd and press the white establishment; sheer frustration, and, on a Dionysian level, the joy of running wild. But behind the proud and gleeful faces of the rioters, the raging countenances, the expressions of abandon, greed and hatred, the contempt and derisive laughter, can be detected the face of people desperate to be reborn.

An unfortunate awareness has overtaken our species: masses of men and women everywhere no longer believe that they have even the slightest chance of living beyond the grave. The unbeliever pronounces a death sentence on himself. For millions this can be not merely disconcerting but a disastrous perception.

Like accident victims showing no visible abrasion, those who have lost the dream of immortality sustain a grave internal injury. Viscerally, and in the very impulses of the nervous system, they have always felt rebirth waiting on the other side. Now that it no longer waits there, the rhythmic "imitation of immortality" lived out from day to day is being disrupted. With the prospect of survival denied him, the unbelieving man—who may outwardly, perhaps to fool himself, still be professing some kind of faith—tends to become emotionally cornered and thrown back into his doubtful self.

Sexual and confessional release still help, but are harder to come by. Without hope of rebirth, confession is far less satisfying. One dissolves before a blank universe and returns to it. There will be no authority for renewal except another's heart, which may be somewhere else with its own troubles.

The prospect of oblivion has also resulted for many in an impairment of sexual grace, loss of faith in the body. Hence, mass-atheism troubles the sensuality of millions. Rhythms of desire that assume everlasting life now break against the new unbelief—and sexual energy takes contrived and lunging forms, seeking to force eternity. Loving eternity becomes more important than loving another. Sensuality may turn off altogether, continue half-heartedly, or begin a feverish hunt for rebirth. In carrying on this search, men and women depend increasingly on sexual symbolism. The sexual partner turns into a stand-in for various dream figures, phantasms in a stage-managed resurrection. These figures—father, mother, brute, victim, amazon, master, slave, child, disciple—are all agents of immortality to be conquered or succumbed to many times over, in order that the pilgrim without faith may symbolically die and live again. In consequence, the lover whose once-immortal soul is gone does not so much possess his companion as his own dreams. The loved one's role becomes less that of being loved than one of assisting the other's desire to live on—a sort of sexual travel agent helping to arrange divine trips.

For this reason, staged sexuality with props and fetishes has become commonplace. Orgies, husband and wife swaps, and the like, more popular than ever among groups of quite ordinary people, represent a mass assault on the mortal barrier. Similarly, the rituals of sadism and masochism can be viewed as pseudo-religious ceremonies. The sadist plays a god; the masochist seeks renewal he cannot obtain otherwise through carefully-arranged violence, worshipping an earthly god or goddess with absolute power over him. Each is trying to break through to lost immortality, and the same may be said of all our sexual experimenters and outlaws.

Anxiety increases with education. As we grow more sophisticated, which is to say more "unnatural," ever more ingenious rationalizations are needed to explain death away. Faith survives among intelligent people, but not so easily now. The devout must somehow manage to embrace absurdity or ignore it. The second comes much more naturally. *Mens sana* is still best maintained by not thinking about possibilities. Unhappily, with the immense input of information at our disposal today, a certain number of ideas destructive to peace of mind will be almost bound to penetrate one's protective screen.

Meanwhile a man's, a woman's, blind desires have no idea of what has happened to the spirit. They persist, again in Freud's expression, "behaving as if immortal." But the waking intelligence knows at this evolutionary moment that we have been self-hoaxed; that we will not in fact be reborn in another world or return to this one. The confrontation between unbelief and desire has turned into an emotional *High Noon.* Irresistible cellular push to live on meets brute, unmoving fact: you will not; vision of immortality falls apart.

Deprived of the rebirth vision, men suffer recurring spells of detachment, with either violence or apathy to follow. And so the twin detachments of violence and apathy, side by side, are growing stronger and advancing within us.

Institutionalized violence—not only against others but against all of nature, the bringer of death—multiplies everywhere. Bombing and polluting, men commit massive aggressions against everything—earth, air, water, countryside—as if hoping to bring existence itself down on their heads. Violence against our own mortal nature leaps out of the television screen, into the living room, out the door and into the neighborhood. At the smallest provocation people spill out on the streets, overturning all forms in the way. Their message is: since life has let us down, smash it.

Between man and man aggression has changed markedly in character, becoming more frequently random, fluky, and even, as laughter attends killing, a source of amusement. Atheism without hope has fathered this viciously creative effort—to try divine privilege on for size by reducing or destroying another for no particular reason.

The mild twin, apathy, grows from a deliberate reduction of consciousness which doesn't care to deal with the unknown any more. One finds solace and safety in repetition, hours of torpor in front of a television set, and the like. The much-despised reflexes of conformity still prevalent in middle-class American life are part of this withdrawal. In extreme form, apathetic reactions to life's uncertainty and pain lead to the narcotic refuge, a horrible miscalculation since narcotics set one free of city-time but adrift without rebirth. Worse, on the other side of the dissolve and the nods there awaits nothing but a further craving.

Into the wasteland came riding, about twenty years ago, Eastern Wisdom (passing en route Western philosophy going the other way to inspire the newly-materialistic Asians). Buddhist thought offered new hope to what were at first relatively small groups of younger Americans. Asian masters taught the disciplines that lead to serenity. Yield up the frightened, grasping self, that which suffers. For resurrection and the hope of eternal life substitute cyclic existence within the great Wheel of Being. Live with all our senses wide awake, particularly, eternally, *now*.

The Buddhist outlook, acquired as it must be by profound effort (the effort not to try), would probably have remained with a few thousand adepts had it not been for Dr. Albert Hofmann's accidental discovery, in 1938, of the mind-opening properties of lysergic acid and ergot, synthesized in 1943 as LSD_{25}. In the 1950's there followed banker Gordon Wasson's researches with Mexican mushrooms. Reports of wondrous visions led to the production of LSD and psilocybin; publicity for peyote; the rise of Timothy Leary, prophet of psychedelic revelation; inevitable prohibition of the materials; then, of course, bootlegging. All at once it became possible for any American high-school boy to gaze into mysteries visible before only to sages, saints and madmen. Visions once earned by going without sleep, fasting and motionless contemplation could now be summoned up chemically by real estate salesmen and grocery clerks.

Today's proclaimed revolution of consciousness among the young middle-class masses has only just begun. It is going to continue—indefinitely. There will be no way to halt the distribution of psychedelic chemicals, because these substances are the stuff of what passes for revelation. They have provided a new means of attaining simulated rebirth just at a time when the old ones were giving out.

In sufficient strength, LSD and similar preparations (assuming, say, with LSD, a dosage of 300 micrograms) nearly always, on one trip or another, recapitulates the process of having a fall, coming apart and being put together again. Although experiences along the way are different each time, and unique for each traveler, the *form* of the voyage is likely to follow a predictable flight plan, with a symbolized reenactment of death-and-rebirth occurring at some point.

Authorities laboring to control the misuse of LSD should understand this: the acid trip is a quest for instant renaissance in a society whose orthodox avenues to immortality are all but closed. Whether realizing it or not, the psychedelic rebel turns his back on death. Confronted by meaninglessness, he blows his mind, the apparatus that perceives death.

The startling correlation between mysteries of the Himalayas (such as the soul's journey described in the Tibetan *Book of the Dead*) and those uncovered by psychedelic materials supports the possibility that an incessant and rhythmic propulsion toward rebirth may be mankind's strongest motivating force.

The chemically-released journey also reveals not merely a flaw but a horror at the center of unformed existence, where the cosmic soul is supposed to be. Eastern wisdom holds that a return to individual consciousness is undesirable. In the LSD rerun of the soul's orbit, those who are not synthetically reborn, who fail to complete chemical *samsara,* do not come back, and in many instances, remain permanently out of their minds. In short, the only way not to be reborn is to split, fragment and remain in pieces.

But if the pieces of your mind do not come together

again, the currently fashionable ideal of "fragmentation" resolves into a horrible condition. The unreborn individual remains inside a wrapping with cracks in it. There can be nothing much more terrible than to remain in this diffuse state of being. Only the sensation of being born again brings the victim or the remote, smiling child back to unitary consciousness. The psychedelic lesson informs us that rebirth is all. Supposedly profound men who glorify the diffusion of consciousness, with no reemergence of the self in view, are recommending that humanity conquer death by going mad.

A recent example of the depth of this longing, even among sophisticated medical practitioners, may be seen in the publicity given to the findings of Dr. Elizabeth Kubler-Ross—"I know beyond the shadow of a doubt that there is life after death"—and of Dr. Raymond A. Moody, University of Georgia Medical School, in their studies of the dying, and particularly life's last moments.

Both cite out-of-body experiences reported by patients returning from the edge of death. Feelings of bliss, peace and relief appear to be common. And also, Dr. Kubler-Ross declares, the encountering of a divine light: "That light is God. God is the light and love these people experience. They are entering His presence. . . ." Further, such patients exhibiting no vital signs report later having an overview of, say, the operating room, and can report exactly what has gone on around them. Beyond this, "often, the transition out of body was accompanied by the experience of being rapidly drawn through a dark tunnel."

It is consoling to learn that during the final hours and minutes before death the dying person can leave the world blissfully, with his or her agony gone. Still, it must be said that the experiences related by Dr. Kubler-Ross are quite familiar to anyone who has had an LSD trip to any depth. LSD also removes pain, putting it "off there." (As Aldous Huxley, dying, experienced through injections in 1963.)

Out-of-body experiences may be had by any of us from nitrous oxide, which prompted a friend to observe in the 1960s that "your best guru is your dentist."

In short, it is likely that the departing persons studied by Dr. Kubler-Ross are many of them tripping out on death, and mercifully so. As during an acid trip, they pass through the death and rebirth fantasy. We have here then, perhaps the soul's desire from our common memory pool, but as yet no release from oblivion.

If men and women long and plan to live forever, how to explain suicide? In part, as a rebirth project, an attempt to reach an exalted state of being, and also, as Dostoevsky revealed through Kirilov, an act of god-imitation. Thoughts of suicide begin to occur when accustomed patterns of death-rebirth simulation break down or go awry. The depressed individual no longer has the means to shed his fatigued, used-up self. Hope and enthusiasm, which can only be made new by repeated imitations of rebirth, no longer carry him forward. He imagines splitting off, getting away from the old self he can't be reborn from. He may then reach the stage of being "beside himself," in emotional fission. The action need not be purely mental; for instance, a physically-afflicted man may be moved to split off from himself by form-breaking and identity-breaking pain. Suicide will then be a way to kill the pain, but not necessarily the self now enduring it.

Doctors identify gradations of contemplated suicide. Some distracted individuals really intend to take their lives, others partly intend it, while still others have in mind only the form of self-destruction.

Contrary to Camus, suicide has never been "the one truly serious philosophical problem." It is not a problem, but a commitment, and commonly beyond that an act of faith. For those who really intend to close out their identities, this commitment is the most despairing in the human psyche: the willingness to act on an utter loss of faith in the possibilities of rebirth. Suicide as a positive act of faith, though physically amounting to the same thing, springs from hope: a last-ditch measure to destroy mortality; to rise above your condition; to dissolve life here before it dissolves you and, in terminal defiance, to realize the fantasy of continuation elsewhere.

Killing oneself in this way takes place within the framework of resurrection. In *The Logic of Suicide*, Edwin S. Shneidman and Norman L. Farberow discover in the suicidal state of mind a confusion of selves. They distinguish "I_o," the self imagined as seen by others, from "I_s," the inward I:

The suicide says in effect, "I_o will get attention, that is, certain other people will cry, go to a funeral, sing hymns, relive memories, and the like." But he also implies or states that even after death, I_s will go through these experiences, that is, "I will be cried over; I will be attended to"—as though the individual would be able to experience these occurrences. . . .

In *Suicide and Scandinavia*, Dr. Herbert Hendin notes that "the act of dying itself can be conceived as pleasurably incorporated into [a] reunion fantasy. Most frequently the emphasis is not placed on the dying but on the gratification to follow. . . ." He recalls a 47-year-old woman whose fantasy of being united with her first lover could only be realized by an attempt to kill herself. Another man sought to "join" his wife who had just died. A woman failed in her attempt at suicide, but lost her leg under a train. Hypnosis shortly after the event brought out the dream of a long, narrow tunnel with light at the end of it, her father and mother standing in the light as Joseph and Mary, and she as the Christ child, reborn a boy.

Gregory Zilboorg found varied immortality-fantasies among suicidal patients. Don D. Jackson summarizes Zilboorg's view that "suicide is a way of thwarting outside forces that are making life impossible. . . . Another aspect . . . is the paradoxical effect of living by killing oneself. This is one method of gaining immortality and fame, thus maintaining the ego rather than destroying it."

Finally, suicide results from an excess of isolation, the inability to reach out and touch another, or be touched, and have it mean anything. One of two states of mind precedes the act. First, the sharpening of the moment, an intolerable sharpening of perception which reveals edges to all things, and which, in turn, leads to intensified awareness of things being separated. As if enlarged by a microscope, life before one's eyes takes on unbearable clarity, and one is suspended in that clarity with no means of escape.

The impulse may also come from precisely the opposite visual distortion, frequently precipitated by drinking. This is a sensation of miasmic glory. The inner and outer world become misty and seem to merge. According to Dr. C. A. Wahl ("Suicide as a Magical Act"), this dispersion of consciousness reproduces the outlook of all-powerful infancy, a state in which all problems are solvable. The suicide "achieves, as does the infant, a kind of cosmic identification."

Killing oneself in this way is selective and arranged death, looking forward to transfiguration. Suicide sheds the body, the dying part, enabling the distressed person to break free from an impossible scene. He or she aims to lose consciousness and have it at the same time. Suicidal men and women claim the privilege of overseeing their own total loss. Remaining superior to the act, they can project the fantasy of being able to live beyond the earthly self. The ribbon of fantasy unreels beyond the prospect of death.

Thus the voluntary ending of life begins as an assertion. It implies godlike control over both exit and subsequent reentry. Suicide controls and dictates death, as if to a stenographer. Master-minding one's end assumes mastery of some future renaissance. The Dionysian self-destroyer envisions a round-trip ticket and, since death intervenes, he will not be disappointed.

A third element can be found in the suicidal passion. In an interview with Jean Stein for the *Paris Review* series, "Writers at Work," William Faulkner said, "Life is motion. . . ." He went on:

The aim of every artist is to arrest motion, which is life, by artificial means and hold it fixed so that a hundred years later, when a stranger looks at it, it moves again since it is life. Since man is mortal, the only immortality possible for him is to leave something behind him that is immortal since it will always move. This is the artist's way of scribbling 'Kilroy was here' on the wall of the final and irrevocable oblivion through which he must some day pass.

But this compulsion drives others as well as professional artists. In clumsy ways it can be the project of all kinds of people: to give their lives some kind of dramatic form so that—life being motion—they will move again. Every suicide then, in all its attendant despair, attempts a final work of art. The conquering victim—in the planning, duration and execution of his project—plays the role of an artist seeking immortality. Therefore, the interior processes governing suicide will never be "explained" any more than the imaginative breakthroughs of an artist can be accounted for. We only know that each is striving to live again in his own way.

Berdyaev, the Russian Orthodox mystic, has a disturbing conviction: that the death of the body assures everlasting life of the soul, and that life of the body, if eternal, would assure death of the soul.

Does this help account for the willingness of so many men and women to cripple and kill themselves and others in order to live forever?

III

WE MUST HAVE DONE SOMETHING WRONG

The Book of Genesis represents the act of becoming conscious as the breaking of a taboo, as though the gaining of knowledge meant that a sacred barrier had been impiously overstepped.

JUNG

I shall speak to my Lord though I be dust and ashes . . . if I vilify myself and bring me to naught and fail from all manner of proper reputation (thought of myself) and make me dust as I am, thy grace shall be merciful to me.

THOMAS À KEMPIS

Wherever the religious neurosis has appeared on the earth so far, we find it connected with three dangerous prescriptions as to regimen: solitude, fasting and sexual abstinence.

NIETZSCHE

We must have done something wrong; otherwise there wouldn't be death. This reasoning has led the races of mankind to make a cruel and foolish, and sometimes beautiful spectacle of themselves courting a higher authority which exists only in their own heads. Imagine how mystifying our behavior would seem to a task force of interplanetary explorers from Alpha Centauri, especially if they had no idea of death. From their viewpoint, gazing down on us from the windows of their saucers, members of the strange colony below would seem periodically to go mad, with the outbreaks taking both weirdly personal and ceremonial forms.

Consider the neurotic circus we put on. Earth people are forever falling into agonized postures, extending their arms in supplication and knocking their heads on the ground. They gather regularly listening to one of their number talk, or speak in unison, ring bells, blow mournful horns, light candles and fall down. Then they lift their heads and, with a blending of voices, give utterance to strangely beautiful outcries.

In these states, are the inhabitants suffering or enjoying themselves? Does some sort of gain result? Impossible to tell. Earth people may also be observed bursting into others' holy places; running around and flailing one another with whips; killing goats; spreading out victims on crosses; kissing big rings; dousing each other in the water; bowing to a distant heap of buildings; jumping up and down, waving little red books at other people and forcing them to their knees; weighting the legs of bonneted housewives and tossing them in the river; in solitude, sitting for years on top of pillars in the desert, twisting their bodies and spirits into crooked shapes and holding the position until it becomes permanent.

Other figures shuffle around under bejeweled head pieces, red hats, black hats, tall and little flat hats, and suddenly drop down on their knees, singly or together, talking to themselves. Still others dance around huge poles with faces painted on them; spin in dust clouds; fall down; eat dirt; kiss trees, and moan and chant at sunset.

This vaudeville of despair, performed so far as we know before no audience but the players themselves, might be judged a terrible waste of time and energy. But until now it has served to ward off mass-suicide. In our tragic and also stupid situation, the worship of imaginary forces has been essential. Without false gods to console and torment us, the haphazard nature of existence could not have been borne. After all, our working conditions are impossible. At the end of a short life, the gift of self, which the individual never asked for but now desperately treasures, is torn from him. Sometimes this happens violently; more often in the process of "natural" death which, as George Orwell has said, "almost by definition, means something slow, smelly and painful." In whatever way the end comes, our identities are summarily dissolved like over-boiled turnips, with no explanation or excuse given. How to account for this appalling cosmic whim?

From the start, we countered annihilation simply by refusing to believe in it. Death in this world, which requires that we survive in the next, is imagined by a great many peoples as an unnatural state of affairs visited on man by mistake, or as the result of some primordial misunderstanding.

". . . and all the world may become guilty before God," warned St. Paul in the Epistle to the Romans. Guilt in its oppressive form belongs largely to the Jews and Christians, but tribally rough equivalents to explain death exist almost everywhere.

Rationalizations of mortality are commonly based on one or more of three mythic misfortunes: 1) Primal

Crime, Original Sin, etc. 2) a Misunderstood Message from On High, and 3) an Improper Response to some Divine Command. A variation to be taken up later is that 4) man himself, in his individual form, is a sort of mistake spun off from central consciousness and seeking to rejoin it.

Superstitious Man looks back, musing: "This jungle must once have been a garden. What went wrong?" Now-familiar excuses follow, represented mythically in a downfall. Somebody (like Prometheus, Eve) stole something (fire, knowledge), presumptuously crossed a line, failed to recognize a deity come down to earth, accidentally or purposefully attacked the descending god, blasphemed, failed to get the message, peeked from the bushes at forbidden mysteries—and so we are mortal.

These examples taken from *The Golden Bough,* Part VI, The Scapegoat, can be multiplied many times:

. . . the Arauaks of British Guiana say that man was created by a good being whom they call Kurumany. Once on a time this kindly creator came to earth to see how his creature man was getting on. But men were so ungrateful that they tried to kill their maker. Hence he took from them the gift of immortality and bestowed it upon animals that change their skins, such as snakes, lizards and beetles. Again, the Tamanchiers, an Indian tribe of the Orinoco, tell how the creator kindly intended to make men immortal by telling them that they should change their skins. He meant to say that by doing so they should renew their youth like serpents and beetles. But the glad tidings were received with such incredulity by an old woman [!] that the creator. . . changed his tune and said very curtly, 'Ye shall die.'

Similarly:

In Annam [Viet Nam] they say that Ngoc hoang sent a messenger from heaven to inform men that when they reached old age they should change their skins and live for ever, but that when serpents grew old, they must die. Unfortunately for the human race the message was perverted in the transmission so that men do not change their skins, and are therefore mortal, whereas, serpents do cast their old skins and accordingly live forever.*

Anthropological literature is filled with stories of this kind—as well as gotterdammerungs and apocalypses. All such accounts relate to one primal transgression. The myths that sustain mighty orthodoxies and wistful folk tales combine in a flow of guilt deriving from the impudence of being human. Put another way, in nearly every culture, humanity has always felt that it must pay for being itself. We pay for having dared achieve separated consciousness. This is the crime of becoming, in our own imagination, a threat to the gods. Understandably, we have been frightened by our boldness. Resisting death, even by mentioning the failure to overcome it, our race dimly fears that the gods will uncover the seedling of insurrection and react angrily by crushing our survival project.

The revolt against oblivion was preceded by centuries of petitions. We apologized for existing. Ceremonially and in solitude, we pleaded: "Gods, pardon me for being, but if there is any way to arrange it, though I am unworthy, let me be!"

Attempts to resist death by placating the gods invariably begin with the principle of sacrifice. This is a form of spiritual bribery, as explained in the *Bhagavadgita*:

---

* The "magic skin" theme carries forward the hope of eternal life in many tribal societies. As will be seen in Chapter V, the snake is often involved in the fantasy. Balzac uses a wild asses skin as a symbol of shrinking immortality. The Aztecs, according to Frazer, believed so firmly in the immortal properties of a new surface covering that they would flay their enemies alive and wear the bleeding skin "like garments thrown over their own."

The Creator, the lord-of-progeny (Prajapati), created at the same time the sacrificial ritual and man. And he said to man: through this ritual shalt thou progress; it will fulfill thy desires. Thou shalt please the gods with its help, and in return the gods will protect thee. Thus, helping one another, thou shalt gain true happiness. Pleased with thy worship, the gods will grant thee all enjoyments.

Sacrifice crops, ears of corn, vegetables, and so on. This may seem to help bring on richer harvests, but obviously does nothing to preserve the body from death. Offer up animals, and still we die. To save ourselves for eternity, offer up a captive *human* life: "If this is what you want, here, take it!" Throw some alien into the pit—five, ten, a hundred strangers. At last, this having failed, we begin to understand. What the authorities want is a piece of our selves, and specifically our pleasure.

Now the spirit of *self*-sacrifice comes into being, and Self-Punishing Man walks about large areas of the earth, animated by the conviction that unrestrained enjoyment without a balance of suffering will displease the gods. Knowing this, Navajo cowboy, Boston security analyst and Nagasaki fisherman pay before or after pleasure; also bow down; pay regularly self-imposed tribute to the celestial authority so that compensatory misfortune will not be due.

We pay small or severe dues. Knocking on wood, for instance, costs nothing. Refusing to eat meat on Friday is a somewhat greater inconvenience. The day-long fast during Ramadan, the Moslem period of atonement, can result in prolonged and gnawing discomfort. Most devices to even up fortune involve at the very least the sacrifice of comfort or pleasure. All follow the rules of a Divine Mathematics which promises that the less you live now the more you will live later. If you restrict exuberance now (or take a little off the top, prudently tithing it), that much, and more, will be credited to your survival-account in the Bank of Heaven. Under this system, pain and self-denial becomes money in the bank. They gather a compound interest, in the form of voluntary non-being, that the gods must pay back by granting you being after death.

Faith in this double-entry bookkeeping of the spirit is made possible by civilized man's *neurotic devotion to symmetry*. Many of us who think we believe in nothing conduct our affairs as though a symmetrical balance sheet of retribution and reward actually were being kept somewhere. Without knowing it, even atheists may find themselves obeying an economics of immortality. This encourages us to bank on abnegation or suffering, and to bill providence later. Through a system of pre-paid punishment, we establish credit to cover the future beyond time.

A type of ascetic individual hopes to discount death by thinking about it at all hours, and in some instances pretending to want it. For example, the English monk Thomas à Kempis:

If it be dreadful to die peradventure it is more perilous to live long: blissful is he that hath the hour of his death ever before his eyes and that every day disposeth himself to die. When it is morning think that thou shalt not come to the even; and when even cometh be not bold enough to promise thyself the morning. Wherefore be ever ready and live so that death find thee never unready.

He, of course, the exponent of this fearful philosophy, lived to be ninety-one (1380–1471). Still, the life-denying appeal to Refrain Now, Live Later does not seem very attractive. Is there not something dishonest in making a virtue of withdrawal? Or in elevating what may be nothing more than abject fear of experience to the status of holiness?

One hundred years ago, in Massachusetts, the moral

mathematics of Self-Punishing Man produced this classic caricature of misery. From *The Story of a Bad Boy* by Thomas Bailey Aldrich:

And then I had a cloud at home . . . It was Sunday . . . the deep gloom which has settled over everything set in like a heavy fog early on Saturday evening. At seven o'clock my grandfather comes smileslessly downstairs. He is dressed in black and looks as if he has lost all his friends during the night. Miss Abigail, also in black, looks as if she was prepared to bury them . . . (Breakfast) progresses in silence . . . My grandfather sits in a mahogany chair reading a large Bible covered with green baize. Miss Abigail occupies one end of the sofa and has her hands crossed stiffly in her lap. I sit in the corner, crushed . . . My grandfather looks up, and inquires in a sepulchral voice if I am ready for Sabbath School . . . I go to meeting . . . Our minister holds out very little hope to any of us of being saved. Convinced that I am a lost creature, in common with the human family, I return home behind my guardians at a snail's pace. We have a dead cold dinner. I saw it laid out yesterday . . .

More recently, in *Report to Greco,* Nikos Kazantzakis tells how, during his first trip to Florence, he felt so joyful that he became terror-stricken:

For, as I well knew, the gods are envious creatures, and it is hubris to be happy and to know that you are happy. In order to exorcise their evil eye, I had recourse to comic schemes for diminishing my happiness. I remember being so elated in Florence that I realized the rights accorded to humans had been overstepped. I had to find some way of suffering, so I went and bought a pair of shoes much too narrow for me. I put them on in the morning and I suffered so much that I could not walk—I hopped about like a crow. All that morning, until midday, I was miserable. But when I changed shoes and went out for a walk in the afternoon, what joy.

The economics of immortality lead men and women to keep books of virtue which they look forward to opening up for Olympian credit investigators. Thoreau, with his meticulous expense accounts at Walden Pond, was really proclaiming to heaven that he had cost little, that he was a modest, inexpensive man, a bargain. At times he wrote like an accountant of the spirit:

Goodness is the only investment that never fails. In the music of the harp which trembles around the world it is the insisting on this which thrills us. The harp is the traveling putterer for the Universe's Insurance Company, recommending its laws, and our little goodness is all the assessment that we pay. Though the youth at last grows indifferent, the laws of the universe are not indifferent, but are forever on the side of the most sensitive.

Thoreau being among the sensitive, this translates: "I and my kind qualify for eternal life."

Work, without enjoyment, for its own sake, is one of the more unhappy measurements of virtue that Superstitious Man has imposed on himself. It may not only be caricatured as the curse of the drinking classes and the opiate of the people, but also summed up more seriously by Durkheim as "for most men a punishment and a scourge" and by Norman Brown as "pure self-punishment, and therefore . . . a pure culture of guilt."

Until lately mercantile groups have remained under the spell of the pronouncement in Genesis that because Adam and his mate sinned we must earn our bread with the sweat of our faces. Or, in modern office terms, we must at least put in time, *seem* to work. For this reason, proposals to establish a guaranteed annual income cannot help but inspire fear and anger among business people. The awful thought arises that a passage to happiness is possible *without* paying off the gods by "going through the mill." If this is true, then sacrifices-through-toil merely waste us. We have been tricked; suffering is a waste of man-hours. Once the law enables loafers to spend the day happily strumming guitars, the structure of symmetrical retribution tumbles down, and the expiating power of labor stands exposed for what it is: a dismal superstition.

Of all the tribulations men have visited on themselves to gain or regain immortality, the most grievous has been that of interfering with their own sexual enjoyment. Evidently those who fear death most, fear the body most—and what Herbert Marcuse defines as "the universal guilt which is life itself, the life of the body" quite naturally fixes on the body's greatest pleasure.

Self-Punishing Man hit on the idea that the act most pleasurable to us must be the one that offends the lords of death, because in the midst of it we pay no attention to them. Lustful coupling makes us forget death, fate and the gods. For in our thrashings we are creating a little immortality of our own. Members of all religious establishments tend to regulate this sort of thing. In the presence of sexual anarchy they become apprehensive, fearing that such heedless delight, unless paid for, will irritate our divine overseers.

To avoid retribution, Self-Punishing Man has tried for centuries to enclose lust within the framework of sacraments. The idea was, and among the orthodox still is, to make all such pleasure a divine gift. Lust is considered proper only within a "legal" setting. This sometimes leads to disconcerting outbreaks. For those who think they have withdrawn from the flesh, sensuality may rush in at sacred moments. John of the Cross laments ". . . Satan, who in order to disquiet the soul during prayer . . . causes the filthy movements of our lower nature . . . some persons not only relax in their prayers through fear of these movements . . . but even abandon them altogether for they imagine that they are most liable to these assaults than at other times."

Exactly so, because prayer is an interlude of approved ecstacy, a devotion beyond reproach. Within communion, all feelings are sanctified, and it ought not to be surprising that previously blocked-off sexual excitements come pouring through without fear.

"For two thousand years or more," Norman Brown observes, "man has been subjected to a systematic effort to transform him into an ascetic animal." This tendency has been inspired across the centuries by a strung-out band of prophets and disciples—themselves seized and dominated by overwhelming visions of immortality.

Prophets are curious individuals, highly sensitive to personal extinction and more afraid of it than the general run of men. At once god-imitator and god-fearer, the prophet intends to lead the rest of us along the right path. He does this in order to win the favor of the gods in his own mind, so that he himself will become divine, thus taking the high road to his own rebirth. The man shouts, hoping to be overheard by heaven, confident that a gold star will be placed next to his name on the Olympian bulletin board.

Most successful holy men with a long-range influence on history have tended to preach restraint. They and the disciples and orthodoxies following them have two reasons to rein in pleasure. Suspecting that play without compensating pain or homage leads to death, they also darkly and contrarily wonder whether devotees of open-ended excitement (with no dues to be paid) just might know something about life and death that the more docile elements on the hillside have forgotten or never knew. The prophet and his eventually orthodox followers must reject all extreme experiences not in accord with the original vision. This is true not only for the reason that the gods might become angry with the sinners (and kill man's immortality-dream) but also, paradoxically, because they might not be angry at all.

Sinners of every description—lovers, wild dancers and singers, orgiasts, drinkers, hashish smokers and more recently psychedelic voyagers—get out of time on their own. Escaping the consequences of primal crime by means of ecstacy, they knock out our moral mathematics. This affronts the worshippers of symmetry. Unabashed sin threatens the orthodox seekers after heaven in two ways. If the unruly among us are in the wrong, the hubris of their unpaid-for ecstacy will rub off on everyone (as in Sodom and Gomorrah) ruining the community's chances for eternal life. But worse, if the sinners, the ecstatic dancers, are right, and closer to the gods than we are; if ecstacy *endears* them to the gods, then our orthodox restraint has been a fool's game, and our cherished Right Conduct—far from bringing us closer to heaven—has kept us farther away from the immortal state than all those heedless revelers who haven't even been forced to pay!

The same double-edged fear accounts for the violent reaction to heresy characteristic of all orthodoxies. Sade urged that "no law should be passed against religious crimes—for he who offends against a myth offends against no one." But in practice this is not so. He who offends against a myth frightens everyone who has been trying to believe in it. The heretic's approach to immortality threatened others' hope of survival. By bringing the wrong approach to the gods into the open, the heretic or infidel jeopardizes *our* standing with Higher Authority. We go after him, just as we would throw overboard a man boring a hole in our lifeboat.

Origen of Alexandria offered just such a threat. He earned the condemnation of the Church by hoping out loud that God would not persist in his vengeance forever, but after a time release the damned souls from torture. The modest hope that merciful Christ would not accept the eternal damnation of a single soul was enough to cast Origen out. The fathers who condemned him feared that mercy-carried-to-excess would unbalance the immortality equation, which—because of our neurotic devotion to symmetry—awards or denies eternal life in accordance with the Moral Mathematics of Retribution.

There was also the fear that the Almighty would become incensed if He thought we presumed to anticipate His mercy. In fact, Origen's hope must be everyone's innermost hope, even that of the authorities who excommunicated him. But magic has always required that we pretend to expect worse from the gods than we suspect they will deal out—as a prisoner when asked by a cruel barbarian chieftain: "What do you think is going to happen to you?" may reply in a despondent and hopeless tone that he expects a horrible fate. He does this in the hope that, placated by his premature terror, the chief will not carry out the punishment the captive has already "gone through" by a suitable show of fear. Similarly, a criminal may tell the judge that he deserves the electric chair, with the hope that by admitting this he will excite a sort of appreciation and obtain a reduced sentence. But a plea that he does not deserve the chair will very likely cause the judge to find him unrepentant, hence more eligible than ever, as a recent sex murderer put it, to "ride the lightning."

Heresy-hunters are also driven to emotional extremes by another, equally important concern: the notorious *imprecision* of the gods when it comes to distributing punishment en masse. We imagine that divine justice meted out to individuals will be precisely symmetrical, but retribution brought down on large numbers has always been sloppy.

Disasters inflicted by fortune (the gods) all too frequently sweep away the just along with the unjust; the rain of fire descends on many harmless citizens. (Job's retainers were wasted for no reason they knew; there must have been some good people in Sodom.) The prophet fears that through divine negligence God will not distinguish him from other mortals; will drop flames on him as well on as the unrighteous. Therefore, he and his followers demand that we demonstrate before heaven that our heretical neighbor is offensive to us, that we have nothing to do with his way of thinking; that retribution should wipe him out, not us—and that if retribution does not manifest itself, *we* will wipe him out.

Finally, vengeful pursuit of the heretic—as with the traditional persecution of those advocating open-ended ecstacy—is intensified by the outside chance that he may have the ear of the gods, may even be influencing them by his charm. Thus, heresy advances no mere difference of opinion. Even if in the wrong, heretical magic and charm may amuse the gods and win their favor, and thereby, summoning up divine intervention, alter reality.

If I am orthodox, heresy threatens my claim to immortal being. Since there can be no more frightening threat to my superstitious nature, heretical charm (unless I have a stake in it) must be destroyed as soon as possible, and all memory of it made contemptible. The urgent measures required to accomplish this have brought into being what Nietzsche describes as "a great ladder of religious cruelty." The ladder reaches toward heaven, and cruelty comes down.

Even in mythic times, Superstitious Man secretly doubted that the authorities would respond to his appeasement techniques by granting him eternal life. He continued—sometimes prudently, sometimes passionately—to worship one set of gods or another, but meanwhile began taking steps to win his freedom from death, with or without their consent.

IV

THE DISGUISED DRIVE
TO BECOME DIVINE

If a mass death sentence defines the human condition, then rebellion, in one sense, is its contemporary. At the same time that he rejects his mortality, the rebel refuses to recognize the power that compels him to live in this condition.

CAMUS

. . . if you keep the opposition between God and man, then you finally arrive, whether you like it or not, at the Christian conclusion . . . that all good comes from God, and all evil from man. With the absurd result that the creature is placed in opposition to its creator and a positively cosmic or daemonic grandeur in evil is imputed to men.

JUNG

Men and women have always half-knowingly plotted against their own gods, even while worshipping them. Evidence of an elaborately camouflaged rebellion against the divine order (which allows us to die) is revealed in large areas of the world among cultures unaware of one another's existence.

Our species may be described as living in a state of Permanent Revolution Against the Gods. It would have been impossible for such resistance not to develop. Given *a*) the persistent longing for individual immortality and *b*) fear of divine retribution, *c*) a disguised drive to usurp the privileges of Divinity (principally the Immortal state that goes with it) must sooner or later animate all concerned.

This prototype of all revolutions takes passive and active forms of varying intensity. It has led since our mythic dawn to a "politics of immortality" similar in form and character to earthly politics. The struggle against the tyranny of death has been waged—as it is against every tyranny—by conservative, moderate and extreme factions of the human spirit, with heresies bedeviling each of these forces.

In the drive to share or take over divine power, our species has proposed to deal with its imaginary gods in four ways: to *placate, impress, imitate* or *destroy* them. The politicians of immortality split and wrangle, as do earthly politicians, over the best ways to get around the Establishment and set up a new order of things. Hence, the groups hoping to win immortality by different techniques continually struggle against one another as well as against death.

Advocates of the "soft line" approach to divine authority—in the main, more fearful primitives and the great orthodoxies—set out to propitiate the gods rather than knock them down. As seen in Chapter III, they rest their hopes on celestial justice or some kind of everlasting mercy. Death can be avoided by Right Conduct, demonstrations and celebrations of love and fear, systematic pleading with the authorities, ostentatious sacrifice, self-denial, and, at the extreme, groveling before heaven and mutilation of one's being through such means as self-torture, vows of silence, etc.

A second, more "practical" group, hopes to earn eternal life by individual enterprise: impressing the absentee lords by existence by good or mighty works, showing off one's achievements before an All-Powerful Presence or Jury in order to qualify for the life to come.

A third revolutionary wing is convinced that the best means of becoming a god is to act like one; to build, create or destroy like one; to pass for a god now, and thereby pass unchallenged into the immortal state later on.

Humanity's radical wing, growing stronger by the decade, has devoted its energies for more than five hundred years not to joining the company of imagined gods but rather to overthrowing the celestial ruling class, replacing these deities and even finally *becoming* them. The slow-working universal solvent developed to accomplish this end has been inductive research.

Probings into every corner of knowledge carry forward the race's enduring project: to gain complete dominance (divine power) over all processes that might affect the human form. This effort represents the boldest self-assertion of our species, our supreme aggression against the death-dealing environment. Camouflaged by outward humility, what we call pure science serves as the arm of pure rebellion. It aspires to nothing less than supreme being. In theory, the race's radical wing moves ahead disinterestedly searching, but in the end—beyond the succession of limited objectives along the way—the quarry being hunted down is death.

In only one respect does the rebellion against death differ greatly from all others. Earthly plotters think they know what they are about. They can readily identify their objectives: to blow up the arsenal, overthrow the king or the system. But the plot against the gods, though race-wide, moves forward on a conscious level *unshared*.

It evolves in each earthling's spiritual underground. To deceive celestial authority the plotters must also deceive themselves in order to dare carry on their project. In short, the drive to become immortal and divine involves such enormous hubris that the final goal has remained unnameable, revealed only a little here and there, most of the time being shrouded from the perception of the revolutionaries themselves.

As unconscious plotters, we may have shown good sense here. Perhaps we half-realized the undesirability of premature revelation. So long as, technologically, the race was in no position to do anything about death, the revolutionary goal revealed too soon would have been unbearable to contemplate. In these circumstances the creation of gods, and all superstitions based on their existence, answered a tactical need. Such superstitions have helped the species avoid summoning up the unthinkable to consciousness: that the gods' most devastating vengeance on us may take the form of a revelation that they do not exist; that no life-rescuing force exists. Hope of immortality would then have been thrown back on what were until recently our small scientific talents. Only now with the state of the medical art making our liberation from mortality at least imaginable has the thought that we can actually become gods, free of time, been permitted to surface.

The Permanent Revolution against death has always taken place in a wilderness of symbols. Disguising the dangerous project, keeping it below the level of consciousness, we necessarily obstruct our own advancement toward the divine state. Peoples of the earth not only trample on others for misbehaving before the gods but also, individually, persecute themselves when they feel dangerous thoughts coming on. Negotiations with the imaginary powers, and our own powers, must be conducted with the most delicate hypocrisy. In the manner of Mao Tse-Tung and Ho Chi Minh, we negotiate while fighting. This is done by making deals with the prevailing superstitions. In effect, as a race, we intrigue against our own neuroses.

The four lines of action—to placate, impress, imitate or destroy the celestial establishment—contend with one another, as groups or individuals with different life programs collide. The same conflicting tendencies are also likely to exist together in one person, frequently setting him at cross-purposes with himself. In fact, it is rare for any one of us not to follow several or all of these approaches to the gods at one time or another. We are several kinds of revolutionaries at once, and the drive toward immortality advances amid confusion through wildly superstitious country.

A religious naturalist, Charles Darwin, undercuts the structure of faith, formulating the evolutionary hypothesis. An industrialist, in brutal displays of power, imitating god on earth, may alternately bully his associates and give them unexpected presents, but on Sundays he gets down on his knees in church. Genuises and others devoted to building new forms and shattering old ones (assuming the godlike power to create and destroy); those engaged in pure research (breaking down the gods' mysteries one by one); discoverers of a new vaccine (reducing the province of death)—all compete with childish jealousy for the attention of a God they may not think they believe in, to make sure that their achievements make a greater impression on the recording angel than those of a rival. The middle-class conformist placates heaven and earth, begging not to be unduly singled out, but secretly he plans to perpetuate his consciousness, slipping into immortality unnoticed on a group ticket. The Red Guards of China some years ago (and who knows, may do it again) slashed ancient scrolls and defaced statues of the Buddha (knocking down gods who have outlived their usefulness) and at the same time, intoxicated by the illusion of timeless youth, roamed the countryside putting dunce caps on their seniors in a mass exercise of god-imitation.

Functional hypocrisy still governs the project to overcome death, in that we deliberately keep ourselves ignorant of what we are doing. This is never more noticeable than in public ceremonies (which presumably the gods are watching more closely than private ones). Startling cultural lags are likely to be in evidence at such affairs. Gatherings of people suddenly become religious. For instance, in formal dedications of new schools, medical laboratories, telescopes, space ships and computers, speakers usually invoke the blessing or inspiration of some deity: God, Buddha, Allah, Lenin, Mao, etc. In other words, tools designed to break apart the "miracle, mystery and authority" that Dostoevsky's Grand Inquisitor deemed essential to man are regularly dedicated to miracle, mystery and authority. Why should this be so? Why are the gods summoned forth at this point, blown up like nodding balloons and presented to us? Because, although we are inventing the tools to destroy authority, we are still afraid of them. Out of an old ancestral memory, we fawn on what we propose to attack. (True, this may be nothing more than "a matter of form"; yet lip service is given only to what we think possesses at least vestiges of power.)

Thus the rebellion against mortality proceeds along crisscrossing lines of action, shot through with neurosis, resisting its own discoveries, interfering with itself in every possible way. We have never been able to decide, for instance, whether to seek earthly or heavenly paradise—whether to earn immortality in this world or the next. Even though the two drives, move in the same direction, they must always conflict. One destroys mystery; the other preserves or celebrates it. Again, both tendencies, can be found within each of us.

The plotters of earthly and heavenly paradise have fought, slandered and sabotaged one another for hundreds of years. One stands accused of unbridled hubris (risking divine retaliation, jeopardizing everybody's chances) ; the other of superstition (cringing before mystery) ; and each finds the other obstructing the road to eternal life.

The drive to join or replace the gods has often been masked in fables which ostensibly make the point that any such effort is foolish. Here, slightly abridged, with italics added, is a classic example of this masked desire, the Tower of Babel story from Genesis.

And the whole earth was of one language, and of one speech. And it came to pass, as they journeyed from the east, that they found a plain in the land of Shinar; and they dwelt there. And they said to one another . . . "Go to, let us build us a city and a tower, whose top *may reach unto heaven;* and *let us make a name,* lest we be scattered abroad upon the face of the whole earth."
And the Lord came down to see the city and the tower, which the children of men builded. And the Lord said, "Behold, the people is one, and they have all one language; and *this they begin to do:* and now *nothing will be restrained from them,* which they have imagined to do. Go to, let us go down, and there confound their language, that they may not understand one another's speech."
So the Lord scattered them abroad from thence upon the face of all the earth: and they left off to build the city. Therefore is the name of it called Babel; because the Lord did there *confound the language of all the earth.* . . .

The chronicler dutifully sets down a parable which frustrates his people's desire. But the failure to build the tower disguises a warning. The desire to create such a structure that "may reach unto heaven" remains very much alive, and we are not to forget it.

The Lord speaks dryly. You can hear his weary impatience: ". . . and this they begin to do: and now nothing will be restrained from them . . ." Obvious enough but still easy to forget: all these observations, such as that "nothing will be restrained from them," are man-made. The story-teller imagines a not-too-severe punishment for the challenging desire to erect a tower. In a sardonic mood, the Lord sets the foolish builders to cackling incomprehensibly among themselves. The thrust of the tower is considered foolish rather than wicked.

The disguised message in the Tower of Babel story is that if we get together and talk in one language we *can* erect a structure that will reach heaven—in other words, become gods ourselves and attain immortality. Knowing his own ambition, man (in the person of the chronicler) guesses that God must be nervous. He has the Lord read man's intentions accurately and put them down humorously. No one suffers in this story. We have simply placed on the record our plan of action, which is some day to win a share in heaven. Yet, as in all such myths, we do our best to deceive the authorities by cloaking an early venture in failure.

Neglecting to cover up our project can be dangerous. When the desire to become immortal and divine is revealed in undisguised form it usually meets with angry or scornful resistance. Paul found this, as Unamuno pointed out, in Athens, "the noble city of the intellectuals." In the Areopagus, home of free discussion, "Paul stands . . . before the subtle Athenians . . . men of culture and tolerance, who are ready to welcome and examine every doctrine. . . . But when he begins to speak of the resurrection of the dead their stock of patience and tolerance comes to an end, and some mock him, and others say: 'We will hear thee again of this matter!' intending not to hear him."

Open, as opposed to suitably veiled, discussion of life after death was what irritated the loungers of Athens. The crude vision of resurrection expressed the desire in too direct fashion for the sophisticates of that time. Similarly, today, the idea of aiming toward and at some time attaining immortality on earth has been angrily or derisively rejected by most highly educated people.

Yet once this same dream of immortality is suitably disguised, every vision is permitted. In the war against death hypocrisy continues to be our secret strength. See, for example, how the race's drive to live forever has been carefully projected onto the image of Man's Great Enemy.

V

SATAN, OUR STANDARD-BEARER

It's I myself speaking, not you. . . . You are myself, myself, only with a different face.

IVAN KARAMAZOV

Cultures in every part of the Western world have created Luciferian figures to serve notice of our primary, if hidden, desire, to replace the gods and seize from them the power over life and death. "Ye shall not surely die" was Mediterranean man's first promise to himself, the promise he still intends to keep. Voiced by Satan in the guise of a serpent, this is followed in Genesis by the assurance: "Ye shall be as gods knowing good and evil."

We created the Devil to express our most radical and dangerous intent. Through history he has been the host, the standard-bearer of man's aspiration to become immortal and divine. In Hebrew, Satan means Adversary. He is also described as the Slanderer. Adversary to whom, slanderer of whom? Necessarily of the Divine Being whose plan seems not to have made provision for our conscious survival.

If God is the Establishment that inexplicably creates, loves, and kills, the Devil incarnates our desire to be independent of such a system, and to thwart it by becoming gods ourselves. Hence, the consciousness that dawned in the Middle East when we ate the apple came into being (we say) through satanic suggestion. Individual consciousness was the Devil's creation, and the act of becoming conscious original sin. As Jung supposes, "it must appear as a sin to the naive mind to break the law of the sacred primordial oneness of all-consciousness. It is a Luciferian defiance against the oneness. It is a hostile act of disharmony against harmony; it is separation against all-embracing unity."

The Devil in the mosaic of our imagination appears in all kinds of disguises, and performs every sort of role, but exists for one purpose only: to make sure that consciousness does not die. The activities attributed to him maintain our alertness to the main chance. Consistently, he nourishes our faith in the power of self-creation. To this end, satanic figures may be counted on at all times to push for immortality and our potential freedom from divine control.

In *The Devil,* Giovanni Papini cites the Muslim demon, Iblis, who damages himself because of his "exclusive love for the idea of divinity." Like other mythological favorite sons, he refused to bow down to man, complaining to Allah: "I am better than he. Thou createdst me of fire, while him thou didst create of mud." Decoded, this message is clearly addressed by us to ourselves; it says: "We have the right to be divine, and refuse to accept mud-like mortality."

Similarly, Loke or Loki, the satanic figure in Norse mythology, upbraids the gods at the banquet table. (The gods are having a party for the privileged who never die, and are not inviting us.) He sets forth his claim, and ours, in this arrogant challenge:

Why are ye silent, gods!
And sit so stubborn?
Have ye lost your tongues?
Give me a seat
And place at the banquet,
Or turn me away!

Pretending to disown the Devil, we shamelessly make use of him as a front man for our hidden rebellion. The best of men have resorted to this hypocrisy: Sir Thomas Browne, for one, in *Religio Medici:* "Were there not another life that I hope for, all the vanities of this world should not intreat a moment's breath from me: could the Devil work my belief to imagine I could never dye. . . ." No coward but a prudent man, this contained and civilized Elizabethan physician finds it necessary to shift the blame for his desire to the dark angel, when expressing the forbidden thought.

Thus, the Devil serves as our representative, enemy and victim. In Three Persons, he is Rebel, Tempter, and at times Collaborator with God, existing with divine consent. We punish the idea of him, even as he asserts our claim. We abuse and punish our desire, and ascribe heinous intentions and deeds to the Great Adversary who put the idea of immortality into our heads, thereby causing us to "fall." We are two-faced toward the Devil, always betraying him. In doing so we betray ourselves, since he *is* us, and in denouncing him man is the Judas of Satan.

The One we really long to speak up to is the Almighty, but few dare make our resentment explicit. A handful of poets have done it, among them Byron. In *Cain,* Lucifer exhorts man:

Thou livest, and must live for ever . . .

Souls who dare use their immortality—
Souls who dare look at the Omnipotent tyrant in
His everlasting face, and tell him that his evil is no
good! If he has made us—he cannot unmake:
we are immortal. . . .

Bold as it may seem, this outburst comes forth only within the framework of evil and failure. Rebel though he was and demonic too, Byron means the reader to assume, at least on the surface, that the Devil's counsel is false and futile.

The satanic figure never dies. Satanic god-challengers, carrying with them our dreams of immortality, are invariably brought down but never destroyed. At the end of the story, we leave the mythic incarnation of our desire, the troublemaker, staked out, under endless torture of some sort, in hell, darkness, exposed on a mountain top, but always with the form of his existence intact. The unfortunate rebel remains also, to his intense distress, in full possession of his senses.

Even in the vengeful Book of Revelation, Satan is carefully preserved:

And I saw an angel come down from heaven, having the key of the bottomless pit and a great chain in his hand. And he laid hold on the dragon, that old serpent, which is the Devil and Satan, and bound him a thousand years.

Following the millennium Satan will be allowed to emerge and "go out and deceive the nations." Whereupon in the vision the climactic battle ensues and the forces of evil are smashed once and for all:

. . . the devil that deceived them was cast into the lake of fire and brimstone where the beast and the false prophet are . . .

Yet after all this Satan will not be made to vanish. Rather he "shall be tormented day and night for ever and ever."

In *Paradise Lost,* a latter-day development of the story, Milton, as expected of all good Christians, curses his innermost desire but explicitly preserves the hope behind it. We encounter the evil one "with his Angels lying in the burning lake, thunder-struck and astonisht . . ." and he "with his horrid crew Lay Vanquisht, rowling in the fiery Gulf Confounded though immortal."

Our myths are exceedingly lenient in granting stays of execution to the malefactors. Coming back to the Islamic Satan, Iblis, who rebelled against Allah when man (mortality) was created, had his punishment put off until Judgment Day. Across the Mediterranean Typhon, who sought to turn the cosmos upside down, was struck by Zeus's thunderbolt and then buried, but lay by no means dead under a mountain, causing quakes to this day with his periodic writhings. Loki, after berating the Norse gods for not inviting him to the banquet, was chained to a rock. A serpent suspended over him drips venom onto his face. Loki too twists in agony creating earth tremors, but will live on like so many titanic evildoers until the Last Day. So will Prometheus, who stole the gods' fire, on his Caucasian rock with the eagle tearing endlessly at his liver (although some accounts permit the fire-stealer to be rescued by Hercules). Sisyphus also, whose crime was specifically that he tried to put death in chains, is still pushing his rock to the top of the crevice and watching it roll down again, but he will not perish.

With the "Last Day" concept, we brandish the fist of death at ourselves. But what we really anticipate is release from our death sentence, a pardon from the Governor. We created Judgment Day as a dramatic break out of time, a beginning. For good people, and even in some heresies, for evildoers who have suffered enough, the Last Day is envisioned as the moment beyond history when the survivors among us will become divine. The survival even of Judas Iscariot was imagined by Origen. He may have derived this hope from Persia. The Iranian myth looks forward to dark Ahriman being reconciled with Ormazd at the end of time, and the two, side by side, entering the kingdom of heaven. Among the Yezidi, an heretical Moslem sect, God forgives the fallen "peacock angel" and entrusts him with ministering to earth. Thus, men covertly admire their own pride and arrange for its survival.

The Last Day means the end of time, and the end of time means simply the end of death. So the punishment of god-challenging rebels put off until the Last Day will be no punishment at all, since this moment is foreseen as the start of a general amnesty.

Over the centuries the role of our Satan has changed greatly. Relieved of his agony, he was allowed to take on a new role. In the horrendous pit he becomes the custodian of our desire. He seems a wickedly humorous archangel demoted to janitor. Here he strokes the fire of our determination to live forever, even as he inflicts the most ingenious torments (only following orders) on suffering humanity.

In another guise, the Devil emerges as a sort of traveling salesman, agent and seducer of Faust. What the student necromancer really wanted was to achieve divine status. The debased satanic projection represented by Mephistopheles sardonically deceives him, as man's hope of immortality was then being painfully deceived. Mephistopheles is projected as a false guide. That is, man's program to become divine had apparently played him false. In the sixteenth century there was nothing to do but view this unfulfilled desire as being sinister and from hell.

Hell as we imagined it, derived from the genius of

Dante and Hieronymus Bosch, has now become a joke. We are amused by Satan and his imps prodding anguished sinners with pitchforks. But it was once serious, and today, under the comic disguise, the pitchforks still instruct men: "Keep awake!" Such punishments, it seems, are no more than contrivances to ward off obliteration. The suspicion grows that hell is only incidentally the destination of sinners. Its original terrors amounted to a form of optimism. "In Hell," says Camus, "we are still alive with this body—and this is better than annihilation." The psalmist pleads to be saved from the real terror: "In my death the coils of Sheol will not embrace me, but thy hand will grasp me. Thou wilt not leave my soul to Sheol."

Hell, then, is the picture of reassurance. If you commit the most terrible crime, you will still remain in one body. The Devil presides over us in hell. Our own desire presides over us. Sins are excuses for arranging pain, which is the coin we are willing to pay the Establishment in return for being allowed to remain in one body after death.

The depth and persistence of our longing for eternal life may be judged from the horrifying conditions we signal that we are willing to put up with, and the tortures we have envisioned for ourselves in our imagined underworld— to pay for the privilege of maintaining consciousness. A Bosch triptych reveals the marvelous lusts of the ungodly alongside ecstatically ghastly punishments. The overpowering effect—and the underground if unknowing intent of the artist—is to celebrate enduring lust. What smoulders below the surface here is not so much evil as a burning desire to survive. In medieval times and today, *sin* and the underground lust to survive appear to merge and become the same thing.

The race's hunger for eternity is readily admitted as evil, worthy of all retributive measures, if it can only be allowed to persist burning under the earth, just as our desire for eternal consciousness burns on under the psyche. The Devil is "evil" only to the extent that all unsuccessful revolutionaries may be considered so. Since there was and is death, and we are not yet gods, a goat was needed. Frightened by our own failed projection, we fix on Satan. But his crime, and ours, is simply that of being a loser; of raising false hopes of eternal life and then being unable to deliver.

In myth and history, the Devil, on whom we have projected our intent to become divine and live forever, is said to take as many forms as there are men and women. To Berdyaev, Satan "is an imposter, having no source of life or being of his own." In *The Mirror of Magic*, Kurt Seligmann summarizes this view: "The devil can be an actor. He can be whatever he chooses. He is everywhere, the contemporary demonologist Denis De Rougemont says. According to him, the Evil One wants to pretend that he does not exist. 'I am nobody,' he says. But he is legion . . . he makes us doubt the reality of the divine law; he is a liar, a tempter, a sophist and, though being nobody, he can impersonate as many beings as there are in this world."

In this way, to cover up our planned attack on the Divine Being, we insult ourselves, damning our own revolutionary desire in all its shapes. And we can go to the most fantastic lengths to hide from ourselves what we are doing. According to Seligmann, in the thirteenth century "Caesarius of Heisterbach informs us that the devil can appear in the shape of horses, cats, dogs, oxen, toads, monkeys, bears; at times, however, he favors the features of a 'decently' clad man, a handsome soldier, a husky peasant or a good-looking girl. Then again he assumes the form of a dragon, a Negro, or a fish. He is the ape of God, copying all forms with which the creator has endowed man."

Alan Watts has said that "in conceiving the image of the Devil there were no laws to be kept, and the creative imagination could run riot, emptying all its repressed and sensuous contents. Hence, the persistent allure of Satanism and the fascination of evil."

But to describe this persistent tendency as no more than an "allure" relating to a mysterious "fascination" is to explain nothing. What is so evil about evil finally? The "evil principle" manifests itself in two ways: plotting or moving against Divine Order, and injuring our fellow men and women. How do we injure a fellow man? By breaking his form in one way or another, and diminishing his immortality-potential in order to enhance our own.

Both aggressive actions involve an attempt to rise above the mortal condition. The supposedly mysterious "evil principle" derives simply and understandably from resistance to death. Hence, intriguing as "evil" may seem, there is really no problem of evil but only the problem of death. As long as death exists, so will the other. Conquer one, and conquer the other. In these circumstances evil emerges as being not particularly glamorous and also as oddly irrelevant—and, again, punishment for our sins, may be understood as coin to pay for our survival after death in one body.

The enduring confusion of sin with the pursuit of immortality accounts for the proliferation of satanic concepts and forms over the centuries. If our project to live forever had been free to go abroad in the daylight, satanic mysteries would never have come into being. But we remain superstitious. Since even today the pursuit of eternal life is considered dangerous and wrong, we continue to push our aspirations under cover, and the Devil still goes about in new disguises, exciting and disturbing us.

Our satanic self, as projected in the form of the devil, leaves us hopelessly ambivalent about our attractively evil creation of an Elder Brother. To each of us a different Devil appears. Noble, sinister and clownish—the evil one may be described in all these terms. Who is he? The Son of Dawn (Isaiah), once the brightest, most favored archangel; Great Cherub (Ezekiel); or a Pan-like winged monster, hoofed, blackened, smouldering, speaking with a forked tongue, having horns and a wicked, ridiculous tail, trickster, monkey, fox, satyr, Emissary of Man and scapegoat—remembering that goats are slaughtered and sacrificed, sometimes turn Judas, but leap upward from crag to crag as the loose rocks give way under their feet.

Through this ever-changing figure we view ourselves and our right to become divine with shifting reverence, narcissism, contempt and laughter. Seen as the Fallen Angel, the Devil affirms our nobility, reminding us of our lost eminence.

Papini has a Miltonian vision of the Great Adversary as "the stricken angel," and salutes his "dark grandeur" and "fearful sorrow." Berdyaev almost admires him: "Satan by dint of his superior spiritual powers has succeeded in leading men astray, by suggesting to them that they will become as gods." However to reconcile this proud captain with the sulphurous visitor to Faust? Perhaps De Rougemont has the key: "Satan is an Individualist. He upsets the commandments of heaven. . . . the devil is ever-changing in men's minds . . . [he] likes to be modern. . . ."

The answer seems to be that Satan represents all that is recalcitrant in us. He varies with the ages, and the way he appears tells something about the age and the strength of the disguised drive to immortality at given points in history. His impressiveness seems to rise and fall with our hopes for survival. Thus, some medieval mystery plays in which the Devil appears as a buffoon convey a low-grade hysterical reaction to the broken hope of life everlasting. In the latter part of the nineteenth century, with one scientific disclosure after another seeming to impoverish hope of personal survival, Dostoevsky's devil who materializes in the fever of Ivan Karamazov is portrayed as a rheumatic, down-at-the-heels "idle land-owner" who remarks good-naturedly: "You are really angry with me for not having appeared to you in a red glow, with thunder and lightning, with scorched wings, but [*sic*] have shown myself in such a modest form."

The Devil comes on as we come on, and reflects our own view of our general situation. What a long way from the huge glowering fallen angel smashed on the burning lake to the evil presence in the Book of Job who can be imagined sauntering in on the Almighty. He has been "going to and fro in the earth," and jeers at what has been accomplished. Jahveh asks, it can be inferred in a defensive tone: "Hast thou considered my servant Job . . . a perfect and upright man? . . ." Satan answers with little or no respect that Job has been overly blessed. But "put forth thine hand now, and touch all that he hath, and he will renounce thee to thy face." The voice speaking so derisively is, of course, our own; the protest is ours. The challenges voiced by Job, Eliphaz the Tema-nite and Bildad the Shuhite are all ours. What we manage here is aggression against God turned around and disguised in the form of rhetorical questions:

Are the consolations of God too small for thee? . . .
Shall mortal man be more just than God? Shall a man be more pure than his Maker?
Doth God pervert judgment? Or doth the Almighty pervert justice?
Yea, man giveth up the ghost, and where is he?

Again we find the eternal question tucked away:

If a man die, shall he live again?

After losing his oxen and cattle, having his servants slaughtered by the Sabeans; having lost sheep, servants and camels to the Chaldeans; his son killed by a tornado

Job falls down worshipping: "The Lord gave, and the Lord hath taken away." But this is acknowledged only as *so*, not as *right*.

The disguised indictment of life's unfair conditions, mingled with sobs of outrage, counterpointed by angry and unanswerable questions, along with pleas for resurrection and/or eternal life, have all come about through the intervention of the Devil delivering man's message. Our hostility is concealed by pious insertions, but resentment still breaks through: "In all this Job sinned not, nor charged God with foolishness." Charges that the wicked man "hath stretched out his hand against God" and "behaveth himself *proudly* against the Almighty" simply give currency to the thought that such resistance is possible. In the end naturally the revolt subsides. Job pays his spiritual dues: "Wherefore I abhor myself, and repent in dust and ashes."

The Book of Job has been described by Homer Smith as an apology for the existence of evil. Rather it seems that arbitrary evils are denounced as intolerable, and that an apology is demanded of God. The genius who created this revolutionary drama has Satan trap the Almighty in a philosophical ambush. The evil one, our older brother, sets in motion a dialogue which ends up, according to Jung, with Jahveh feeling guilty and desiring to become *more human*. (Which translated, means that we think He and humanity should be more on the same level.)

Satan then has consistently proven to be our unacknowledged leader in the pursuit of immortality. We turn to him and recoil from him, as we are at various times proud of and repelled by ourselves. He is grand and mean, tragic and comic, charming company and the embodiment of loathsome temptation, depending on our state of mind. He is what we are, want most, what

we admire and also most fear in ourselves when we con-
sider our qualifications for divinity. Hence his (our)
many forms and disguises.

But what persists through our relationship to this fig-
ure is a devotion to troublemaking. Lately this has taken
the form of a search for and identification with a low-
grade redeemer, today the *absurd savior*. In him we
pursue the incalculable, the principle of perverseness, in-
determinacy, anything to disrupt order. He is the sin-
ister, left-handed, insolent part of our nature that
refuses to acquiesce in the natural order of things leading
to death.

The Devil is our authority-baiter playing tricks on the
devout. Centuries ago these tricks came down to earth.
Impudently he catches Martin Luther on his stool. He
performs obscene dances in the mind's eye of St. An-
thony. This kind of humor is what distinguishes him from
his Greek cousins, Prometheus and Sisyphus. They serve
as fierce and noble symbols; he displays all our abrasive
and vulgar qualities. It is the difference between hubris
and *chutzpah,* nobility and gall. Satan is the Joker Against
God, the wild card in our deck. He is paradox, the
straw, chance for me, more than likely bad luck for
me too, but still promising release from the bondage of
mathematical certainty.

He is frequently pictured as a gambler. Those of us
who gamble with him invariably lose. Since, after all, he
doesn't exist except inwardly as the double of our re-
sisting nature, the "game" in fantasy is with death, and
for a while longer death must win. In obeisance to that
certainty, we invent frustrated heroes such as von Falken-
berg, the Flying Dutchman, condemned in the German
version of this legend to sail forever around the North
Sea in a ship without helm or steersman, playing dice
with the Devil for his soul.

Satan's mission is to weaken the sanction of death,

to postpone death, and sometimes as a clown to ridicule it away. When he turns into a mischief-maker, his holidays such as Halloween and *Walpurgisnacht* are likely to mean bad news for the authorities—orgies, promiscuous and irresponsible behavior on the streets, the defacing and smashing of property, and the like.

Among the Hopi Indians of our Southwest, Erna Fergusson has written in *Dancing Gods,* each pueblo has a society of sacred clowns. "Whenever they appear in a dance, these fun-makers (known as Koshare) are privileged to do and say anything, and nobody may resent it." These clowns represent the spirit of the dead, and irreverent laughter accompanies their return. The antics of the Koshare develop as a masked attack on all authority, whether that of the white man or elders of their own tribe—and sometimes if the occasion seems appropriate they will mock holy scripture. "On one occasion they were funny when they took off on a church service. One of them stood solemnly intoning from a mail-order-house catalogue, held upside down, while the others knelt in the dust before him. Then he closed the book, and began to thunder in wrath, waving his arms . . . The angrier he got, the more sleepy grew his audience, until they finally fell over, overcome with sleep. . . ."

At the end of the ceremony and of "all appearances of the Koshare, they utter a short prayer which is an apology to God for whatever offense they may have given Him, or anyone." The sacred clown apologizes to God, but the ritual has meanwhile allowed him to undermine celestial authority with laughter.

A characteristically satanic relationship may be noted here between the fun-makers' mingled function of *clowning* and *curing.* Mrs. Fergusson reports that among the Pueblo tribes members of the clown society "are able to cure certain diseases; and their membership is increased by those whom they have cured." Gwyneth Wulsin, a specialist in the affairs of the Papago in Southern Arizona, writes that this tribe also has a group of holy clowns who, apart from their sinister aspect, practice healing arts.

Clowning and curing alike are aimed at disrupting the natural order or reversing it, holding off the processes that lead to death. Clowning holds back death, in that nonsense takes us out of time. Equally the sick joke of recent years is meant simultaneously to shock and to heal, and is Satanic in origin. The tasteless shock of a joke which has Mary rushing forward to help Jesus with his burden, and he turning to her furiously: "Mother, I'd *rather do it myself!*" obviously helps fight off the fear of maternal envelopment. But this parody of a television commercial is also aimed at unhinging the majesty of all crucifixions and taking the glamor out of ritualized death.

In his serpentine aspect the Devil has always been a healer. As such, he resists god-given diseases and promotes the hope of immortality. His form wreathes the staff of the physician. Hospital operating rooms are known for the diabolical witticisms and humorously sensual by-play exchanged among the surgeons and nurses while the sedated patient is being opened up. The serpent frightens men, yet in folklore, according to Ramona and Desmond Morris, old superstitions have it that "the snake could prolong life, restore warmth to the sick, *revive the dead,* ensure fertility, and counteract poisons."

While we hunt for salvation, the Devil in us tells men to engineer it for ourselves, and—as we have created him —likes to boast that he can copy as well as destroy God's work. The holy clowns of the Pueblo tribes, in Erna Fergusson's account, say that "they can control waters by making floods recede or rains fall. Also they can create fertility in man and beast and plant; and therein lies their license to joke as obscenely as they wish."

We have made sure that the bringer of immortality is a multi-formed deceiver not stuck with one identity. Hence, he can never be stuck with death. As soon as death catches up and seems about to define him, he becomes something else. The snake sheds his tail or his skin; the Devil slips in and out of disguises; we dream of reincarnation. If we could only move in and out of many identities, death would never catch up with us. At the last moment we could always assume a new one (be reborn).

The Devil's numerous shapes are simply projections of our desire not to be trapped in a single, immovable self which can be extinguished. Most of all we would prefer to live in various incarnations and stay out of death's reach. To manage this, the Buddhists employ the ingenious trick of pretending to desire *nirvana* rather than the eternal return. This is the equivalent of Br'er Rabbit begging: No, no, whatever you do, don't throw me in that Ol' Briar Patch.

The Prince of Darkness is paradoxically Lucifer, bringer of light, slang for a World War I match. With the times his light has changed from once-heavenly radiance, which he possessed as the brightest angel, to a smoky, conspiratorial flare. We can see him properly in both lights, as conspirator and pursuer of knowledge. From the beginning, consciousness (the acquiring of light and fire) has belonged to wrongdoing. "Evil" has sought restlessly to gather information. The diabolical vision is that knowledge will sooner or later lead to divinity.

As things have turned out, this is being accomplished through the scientific method. Scientific research was carried forward in earlier centuries through alchemy, the devil's art. "Alchemy leads to chemistry," Frazer reminds us. The Evil One, the "Messenger of Knowledge," as Seligmann calls him, knew what he was about. Via alchemy the Devil's secret followers and adepts led future generations not only to chemistry but to the depths of biology and the breaking of the genetic code. The ancient effort to trap light and create gold in the laboratory led eventually to the laser beam and gold therapy for cancer.

Satan has always had a curious and persistent interest in flying above the earth. This ought not to be surprising, since flying was, and still is an aggressive and revolutionary act directed against the gods. We fly to imitate or replace God, and today we know that mastery of the air and outer space is essential to any immortality-program.

Early pagan visionaries, afraid of their own dream of flight, dutifully punished the mythic heroes who acted it out. But even though Phaeton's flaming chariot came apart and Icarus' wings melted in the sun, they fixed the vision in our minds, and the message that came down through the centuries to Kitty Hawk in 1903 was: *Try again.*

Traditionally we see Satan with great wings, appearing instantaneously followed by a whiff of sulphur, as though to remind faltering man that, if you have the secret, time and space mean nothing.

Papini maintains that "man's present dominance over gravity" leads to destruction and serves diabolical ends: "The dream of men from Icarus to Simon Magus has always been that of flight, of being able freely to roam the air in his own right without fear of falling. . . . Conquest of the material heavens is one of the symbols of power which most closely draw and inebriate men, and in this century yielding to diabolical temptation, man has finally achieved his dream."

The Devil's arguments fly too. Dostoevsky's shabby devil, while taunting Ivan Karamazov off-handedly (presumably sometime in the 1870s), anticipates the Soviet *Sputnik:*

What would become of an axe in space? *Quelle idée*. If it were to fall any distance, it would begin, I think, flying round the earth without knowing why, like a satellite. The astronomers would calculate the rising and setting of the axe. . . .

The Satanic preoccupation with flight connects in another way with our drive to achieve immortality. The principle could be that of the *mobility of evil*—remembering that "evil" and the hunger to survive are mythically close to one another.

Consider, for instance, the pleasure we take—often in formal debate—in confounding an earnest individual with flights of false logic. Playing this devil's game, one joyfully bewilders the plodding truth-teller, confusing the issue with specious arguments that jump from here to there. We take mischievous pleasure in the incalculable. In this satanic mood, one defies logical sequence and regard for "the truth," simply because the truth ends in death. Devil's Advocacy is the hope of living transformed into enjoyment of the might-be, enjoyment of the irrational and absurd, amounting to a delight in the destruction of what others take to be true and sure. Politically, Senator Joseph McCarthy played god in the cruel and fluky world of the absurd which the Devil loves. If satanic flights of thought correspond with our delight in flying, this relates to the Joker's chance to survive via a tricky airborne escape from the earth-truths we are to be buried under.

The Devil in his classic form has become passé. For most civilized people he no longer exists, or rather he lives on in new forms. Our imagined Satan will always shift identity with the changing times. He had brought us this far along the road to divinity. Resistance to death was what we asked him to preach to us. He pushed our survival claims. He helped us resist the orthodoxies that counseled men to accept and even embrace death without protest.

As scientific research grew and became respectable and the tools for the attack on death increased in number and variety, the Devil's image retreated and dimmed. The decision to overthrow the gods now had a method to carry it forward (and this is what the scientific method is, despite the inconsistency of "devout scientists," etc.). The Devil in his traditional role, it would seem, has little more work to do. The principles he stood for are firmly implanted, and his old field of action has become the province of respected men.

Today our demonic impulse has moved on, perhaps to discredit and mock the new orthodoxies that satanic energies originally helped to create. The satanic function today may be that of applying an evolutionary brake, employing feelings of alienation and absurdity to fight back against technological developments that increasingly leave the individual with a sense of helplessness. As we move into the last third of the twentieth century, the Devil in us is sick. This illness reveals itself in the form of emotional reservation. Lack of commitment could be the satanic game today. The devil we know is that of non-commitment and multiple choice not taken, and it leads to the psychiatric couch where the man labors to cast out the demon called alienation. What was formerly hell is now alienation. The thousand devils that afflict many are the neuroses of discontent. The Devil still jokes. His joke today is fashionably and quite anxiously publicized as the Absurd, and in presiding over this condition he becomes indistinguishable from God.

There is nothing mysterious in the evolution of the Devil within us. To reach our present state of consciousness we have had to go through a war with our own superstitions and terrors. Our advances to the frontiers of unbelief have cost us severely. We have moved up beyond the old fears and taboos, but now, even though we may think we are on the right track, without the gods' blessing life can seem empty, meaningless and frightening.

Life is to be enjoyed. But to enjoy life one must accept its rules—especially the parabolic aging to death. Therefore, those who, even without knowing it, are determined somehow to live forever must almost unavoidably fall victims to what Buber terms "primal doubt." This habit of doubt creates habitual reservations about entering fully into any emotional life that might be possible—because in the end there is death. And unfortunately a negative reflex comes into being; that the only way to hold off death is to refuse to jump into the life that leads to it. If you don't buy death you may refuse to buy life. The demon's question becomes: Will you accept life-unto-death and enjoy it, or hold out for more, thereby to some extent sacrificing enjoyment to an obsessive determination to survive some way in eternity. There always was a price that had to be paid to Satan, and this is ours.

We are caught between the desire to press home the final attack on the gods and the still-desperate need to placate them. We hang in doubt, because we are the transitional people. The palace of immortality glitters in the distance. Who can be sure that our grandchildren will not live in it? But the near-certainty is that we will die, with the prospect of eternal life just out of reach. In these circumstances it takes courage not to pray. But Satan has always demanded sacrifices of his children.

All forms of what we know as evil arise in one way or another from the competition for immortality. When death is finally conquered the reflexes created to resist the organism's demise will be redirected; earthly evil (reducing another's survival-potential) should become vestigial, or will be acted out only within the framework of games.

The world waits vainly for messiahs and second comings

—for whomever will deliver to us the longed-for eternal return. But the satanic spirit in man returns millions of times a day. It never dies; never has to give up any ghost; knows very well that we are forsaken; does not cry out and ask why; and came into being a long time ago to do something about forsakenness. In its perverse and deceitful forms, the satanic spirit inspired our resistance to annihilation, resisting God's truth, because God's truth instructs us to forgive death in this world.

The Devil in us will never quit. In our ever-recurring dream of overthrowing the Death-Giver, he reappears to monkey around with human destiny. We are unwilling to let him die. Execrable as our myths make him out to be, we know his imaginary rebellion was and is really ours, that sin and the lust for everlasting life are inextricably mingled together, and that if the Devil dies we die too.

PART II

VI

CONDITIONAL IMMORTALITY FOR THE ELECT

Immortality was a privilege of divinity. The man who was exempted from the common lot of his kind was therefore the equal of the gods; he had risen above his perishable condition to acquire the everlasting youth of the Olympians. . . .

Hermes Trismegistus explains that there are royal, that is to say divine, souls of different kinds, for there is a royalty of the spirit, a royalty of art, a royalty of science, and even a royalty of bodily strength. All exceptional men were godly, and it was not to be admitted that the sacred energy which animated them was extinguished with them. . . .

FRANZ V.M. CUMONT

In the history of man's religious thought," Unamuno observed, "there has often presented itself the idea of an immortality restricted to a certain number of the elect, spirits representative of the rest and in a certain sense including them; an idea of pagan derivation—for such were the heroes and demigods —which sometimes shelters itself behind the pronouncement that there are many that are called and few that are chosen."

Religious orthodoxy was invented to give everyone a chance to earn life everlasting. Talent and accomplishment were minimized. Righteousness was the way to God's love, and only divine approval could save you from hell or nothingness. The hierarchy, priests, rabbi or imam, or holy scripture, defined your right conduct, and—so far as the after life was concerned—staying on the good side of God was the only thing that made any difference.

This comforting arrangement for poor and mediocre people began to break down in the eighteenth century, and is now practically in shambles. We sing the old songs on cue, but almost no one really believes that goodness will help him continue beyond the grave. Instead, the old pagan conviction has come back full force: that personal survival after death can and must be earned by achievement, or failing that, publicity. Churchgoers and unbelievers alike are unknowingly caught up in this neo-pagan faith. The pursuit of status amounts to nothing but the pursuit of credentials for everlasting life. Even in a time when the search for collective immortality is on the rise, most men and women still mean to join the elect. They mean to qualify for survival by making an imprint on the scene, emulating the film players the imprint of whose hands, feet, lips and profiles may endure forever in the cement outside Grauman's Chinese theater.

Our best citizens struggle along with the others to enshrine themselves alive in great or miniature halls of fame. Loss of orthodox faith has completely unshackled them. New emperors show us the way. The Egyptian king's solar boat is now a yacht in the Mediterranean, a comedian's private train moving across the country with a dixieland band playing, or an industrialist's personal jet.

The falling away of orthodoxy became unavoidable when masses of people began to realize that life beyond the grave was no longer being guaranteed. If the churches, synagogues and mosques couldn't take care of that, they offered little but companionship before extinction. Consequently, those who had time to think beyond food and shelter began to take the drive toward immortality into their own hands. The Devil whispered again: "Ye shall be as gods. . . ."

The streets of civilization have since been turned into a proving ground for millions of do-it-yourself divinity programs. The simplest and most sophisticated play this game. What drives them is a generally unknowing but obsessive intent to pile up evidence showing that each one is worthy of eternal life. The process is carried forward, as everyone knows, by achieving reputation or status.

We can become gods. This is the underlying faith that drives megalomaniacal company presidents, a messianic poet, garrulous senators, salon hostesses, stand-up comedians—and, also in a smaller way, shoe clerks, those who make change in the subways, and every dry goods salesman and pastry cook, and their wives in the laundromat. Each feels the call, lest he be weeded out as unimportant, to prove himself at least as worthy as the next man—and in some competitive area or another, more distinguished. The law of survival demands that he stand out in *some* respect, if only for his skill at the pinball machine.

The unceasing quest for immortality is what makes us anxious. Atheists too, for reasons they find hard to explain, struggle to place their accomplishments on the record. The deeper the imprint the more pronounced the *being,* and the more secure the insurance coverage against annihilation. But we can never have too much immortality insurance. The imprint of the most honored man and woman can be erased by time, or by changing truths and ideals or beauty, or blurred in shifting memories. Yet it is also true that the neglected imprint can emerge later, as the archeologists of memory dig up old evidences of being. Here faith seems to be required: that a conscientious title search will uncover each bygone identity when the time of resurrection comes.

For this reason the strongest superstitions of our time are based on faith in measurement. Gifted and ordinary men alike have fallen back on a startling readiness to believe that measurements, records and statistics, as well as publicity listings, will somehow actually substantiate one's claim to survival. God may be dead, but Measurement is alive, calibrating our worthiness in all forms of competition.

Today, qualifications for divinity are manipulated and keep changing. What is *in* or *out* changes so rapidly with the fashion that for many the craft of keeping-up has become in itself the highest form of excellence. But perhaps the manipulators and followers of spiritual fashion have a motive: a fear that permanent excellence, if it exists, might disqualify them. Hence, they promote change itself as the quality the gods most love.

Still the competition goes on, bringing home the keenest anxiety. As Sir Thomas Browne lamented: "The number of those who pretend unto Salvation, and those infinite swarms who think to pass through the eye of this Needle, have much amazed me. That name and compellation of *little Flock*, doth not comfort, but deject, my devotion; especially [here again the prudent man makes a spiritual poor mouth so that the fates will not think him conceited] when I reflect upon my own unworthiness, wherein, according to my humble apprehension, I am below them all. . . ."

The doctor adds wistfully that far from aspiring to the first rank he will be glad enough to "be but the last man, and bring up the Rere in Heaven." Most of us would settle for that, provided we were assured of not being bumped from the rear rank at the last moment to make room for some latecoming celebrity. What we are asking for is permanent tenure, ownership of life. We want to be sure that we are at least eligible for the demigod society. The significant actions of a modern pagan are related in some manner to piling up supportive evidence, points, little passing triumphs that he uneasily hopes will add up to a reasonably impressive score—high enough to prevent his being mislaid in the last showdown.

The continuing effort to survive beyond death takes place on a number of levels. At the highest it produces devotion to causes, craftsmanship, beauty, efficiency and the ideal of service to others. But attempts to stand out from the neighbors may equally involve the use of picturesque and dirty language, possessing Acapulco Gold, being the first on your block to do anything, or exposing the pretensions of the one down the block who was just saying: "My daughter went to the Dalmatian Coast last year before the crowd got there. . . ."

Such boasting may be misinterpreted. It is not intended merely to show off to others. It is boasting for the record. The faith and superstition behind talk of this kind is that a record is being kept. In effect the individual gives testimony to his own or family excellence. By itself, the act of impressing others would be a waste of time. After all, they are going to die too. But much more important, they serve in our imagination as witnesses to the speaker's excellence. The testimony on the imagined record thereby becomes stronger.

But many, perhaps most, people still doubt the impressiveness of the deeds they can put on the record. As added insurance against the void, they try to associate with others who are accumulating immortality-credits. The idea of being seen in the right company goes back, for example, to early Roman times.

From Vergil's *Bucolia,* Eclogue IV:

Thine own Apollo now is king . . . Under thy govern-
ance any lingering traces of our guilt shall be wiped out,
and the earth shall be freed from its perpetual fear. He
shall have the gift of divine life, shall see heroes consort
with gods and shall himself be seen mingling with
them. . . .

"All beings," the Hindu saying goes, "try to capture
the beverage of immortality without which there is no
enjoyment, but only the gods can seize it. . . ." Here
are a few other paths men hope will lead to our sharing
this divine privilege.

Having Inside Knowledge. We know the experience of
bursting to tell a secret. Why should this be? What is
there about hidden information that moves us so? Being
in on a secret, possessing a corner of knowledge not avail-
able to outsiders, gives us a heady, pseudo-divine illusion
of power. The communication of such inside knowledge
—in its lowest form, gossip—becomes an act of low-grade
revelation.

If the information is to be kept confidential, the thrill
of witholding it, or sharing the news with a few chosen
others, can mount with something like sexual pleasure.
The statesman with his briefcase who descends from the
airline smiling: "No comment!" is for the moment a
small lord of creation. Such men have a noticeably special
smile, which is the secret smile.

Sharing a secret involves the strangely joyful act of
excluding others, mysteriously coupling separateness with
salvation. According to F. B. Jevons:

In ancient Greece one manifestation—and in the reli-
gious domain the first manifestation—of the individual's

consciousness of himself was the growth of "mysteries." Individuals voluntarily entered those associations . . . for the sake of individual purification and in the hope of personal immortality.

The same view is expressed by Jung and Kerenyi:

The celebrant of the mysteries saw and possibly experienced the supra-individual . . . the visionary knower [has] a special position with regard to being; happy he who has seen such things, says the poet, for things will be different [for him] after death than for the others.

Joy in secrecy, writes Robert M. Grant accounts for the powerful if self-limiting appeal of early Christian gnosticism:

The first impression we gain from the [apocryphal] Gospel of Thomas, and the impression the author intends us to gain, is that it is a collection of "secret words" which the risen Jesus spoke . . . They . . . contain a hidden sense. By finding it [the initiate] achieve knowledge, and by means of knowledge [the sharer] attains immortality. He will not taste death.

All initiation ceremonies involve the idea of an elite brotherhood or sisterhood with rites, rules, and mysteries not known to other mortals. The little boy's gang in the hidden tree house travels only a short way to the Elks, Lions, Moose, Shriners and other loyal orders with secret handshakes whose members run around at convention time with funny hats. Many of these groups are devoted to charity, a divine mode of action certainly beyond criticism. Still, in their exclusive and secret aspects, the adult fraternities represent touching attempts to rise above the common run of man and pretend to be privileged orders, at least while the members are in the club house. The disguised drive to immortality persists. Initiations into even the most trivial mysteries purport to open the door for the candidate and grant him an insight into some eternal truth which one day he will be able to flourish like a credit card.

The most exclusive branch of inside knowledge is the society of prophets. Evangelists of every description— economists, banker-speculators, public-opinion pollsters, high priests of journalism—all in their separate ways are bucking for immortality. In their grand or witty, modest or vainglorious styles, they aim to demonstrate before heaven, in the presence of thousands or millions of witnesses, that they *know what is going to happen*. An accurate prediction has the effect of placing one closer to the stars.

Being surprised is the prophets' mortal sin. Surprise means vulnerability, incalculable exposure and possible loss of being. All that prophets are really trying to do is to ward off their own individual deaths by knowing the future. This, we will see, is pure god-imitation. By embracing events with their supposed foreknowledge, they contain and sometimes create history. The prophet's hope is that this earthly god-act before enthusiastic audiences will attract the notice of talent scouts on high, so that when everybody stands exposed to judgment he above all others will be singled out for a place on Olympus.

I am speaking here of relatively high-level prophecy having to do with important affairs. On a distinctly lower plane we have the vulgar soothsayers whose names appear at the top of newspaper gossip columns. Even these were children once, and are children now, afraid of the black sack too, and with their limited means are only trying to be worthy of surviving in eternal light. They scramble for this privilege by consorting with successful people, knowing inside stories about them, and publicizing their gambols. Amid all this anxious striving it often seems, as Maxwell Anderson wrote, "that God's gone away," and left the celebrities, their chroniclers, and all the pundits and prophets, each whirling around alone in his own little god-act.

Yet there can be no point in shaking our heads over their antics. Most of us try to accomplish the same thing (to capture the gods' attention) on a smaller scale. What celebrities and their hangers-on want, we want. If we resent them it is only because they are performing before a greater number of witnesses.

The effortless way to divine status is to inherit it by *belonging to an aristocracy.* A degree of ancestral divinity has always been granted to the nobly born. The divine right of kings descends on those who can gracefully wear small crowns. Grace as defined by Herbert Spencer is the economy of movement. Effortlessness is economy of spirit as well as muscle. Ideally, aristocrats should never seem to try hard. "Look, no hands!" is a vain effort to attain the aristocratic state of being, since aristocrats would never bother to do it with no hands, or if they did, would certainly not call attention to the feat.

In pagan Rome, writes Franz Cumont, if a man "became a god after his death, it was sometimes because he had been one ever since his birth. For men were not all born equal; if each of them possessed the *psyche* which nourished and animated the body, yet all men did not equally receive the divine effluence. . . ." Some possessed it, and "from the moment of their appearance on the earth these men were really gods; their soul kept its higher nature in all its purity; it would indubitably [return] after death to its place of origin."

Divine aspirations may well account in large measure for bourgeois man's obsession with genealogy. This is not to overlook a natural interest in identifying the kind of ancestors who helped make us. But beyond that those who cherish family trees hope to prove, if possible, that they have great genes going for them, that "the stuff they are made of" will make itself felt on Judgment Day. Genealogical research is the pursuit of biological eminence. It is not surprising that some will fake and buy family trees in order to fool the imaginary record-keeper.

Purchasing eternal life has become increasingly common in our supposedly enlightened time. This is done, for example, by starting a foundation and giving it your name. If your son was killed in action during the war, name a parkway after him. Name a scholarship after him. In your mother's name, make available a free occupational therapy room for the poor and maimed of spirit. Put together a lot of little houses and build a town and give your name to it. Give your notebooks to a university library. Procure potentially divine companions for your dinner table. Become a collector of paintings, and name the collection after yourself, and donate it to a museum. Name a theater after yourself. Surround yourself with attractive and powerful witnesses to launch your solar boat when the time comes. Arrange things so that candles in church will burn for you after you have gone. In this way you will have done your best to remind the gods of your devotion to them and your worthiness to join their company.

Pursuing the importance of *belonging to a club* or *exclusive group*, the first club was Noah's Ark. The Noah's Ark Syndrome involves a compulsion to get aboard a platform, remaining high and dry and potentially immortal, in the company of other preferred souls, while the less privileged tread water as best they can.

Every social club is formed in order that its members can station themselves on high and safe ground, away from other mortals who are probably doomed. The joiner gains assurance with each new in-group that accepts him: from his standpoint, the more acceptable in the more places, the greater the likelihood through an expanding consensus that he will qualify for preference after death. Social-climbing is simply a noticeable, frequently lunging attempt to climb aboard an ark. When we drop names we are saying: I exist more; I am making a deeper impression on the cosmos because I know this famous person. When the ark sails I will be on it. Note also the curious pleasure some people take in snubbing others, an evidently gratifying exercise in discrimination. It arises in part from a genuine concern: our ark will sink with too many of these types aboard. I had better help get rid of them.

There must exist something like a Boyle's Law of Exclusiveness. It would state that after an optimum membership has been gathered together, the life-saving power of a club dwindles with the addition of newcomers. (A prominent man asked to join a club in Boston replied: "I would just as soon join the South Station.") The basis of all club life—excepting that of professional associations—is, of course, discriminatory. The very word "discrimination" now has both a good and evil edge to it. To discriminate is to separate what seems worthwhile from what seems not. You show good taste. But some people are the victims of others' good taste. Discrimination can then be damning. The uninvited or ignored guest has his being sharply reduced; before witnesses he is deemed unsuitable for the ark. It is all but mathematically certain that he will at least dream of striking back in some way, to restore himself to good standing in the gods' eyes. A simple mathematics of emotion demands this.

Being present at an important occasion also scores points for us, impressing our imaginary judges. I am thinking for instance of the Whitney Museum's official opening in New York. It had to be a rare and memorable party, since there can be only one opening of anything.

Attractive people in evening dresses and dinner jackets strolled among the paintings. They could be seen looking out of the strange little windows, and upward from the sunken courtyard, gazing at the crowds out on the sidewalk. They would appear on one floor, and then, the same couples, on another, looking out. Through a trapezoidal window the mayor could be seen gesturing at a painting, then he too turned and looked out. The crowd outside grew larger. People were standing on tiptoe, craning their necks and pointing at the windows.

The elite stood like punctuation marks behind the trapezoidal panes. Inside, the guests could be observed wandering about dreamily. As they turned from the windows their faces were not only attractive but had an extraordinarily peaceful look. Waiters ran among them with trays of champagne. The guests moved serenely, two by two. Time turned into bubbles, and inside a big one the ark floated gently toward morning.

Being recognized before many witnesses strengthens our claim to membership in the immortal company. This accounts in part for the unprecedented magic of live television. Watch any crowd scene when the electronic eye moves in. People begin jumping up and down and waving, and making faces at the camera. Primitive man is often afraid that a photograph will steal his soul. But modern pagan man believes that the camera will *confirm* his. The television eye confirms his existence to a far greater degree than, say, home movies because he feels assured of a million witnesses.

Belief in film as an actual reproduction of existence has become accepted in our time. We live on in microfilm. Our faith is that all the footage in the world will be stored somewhere, and that on Judgment Day the gods will review every reel. Living by this faith, the more ambitious among us, such as television personalities, program their Olympian aspirations. But the compulsion to become a demigod on film has its drawbacks. Such an exposed position can never be secure. One exists mainly in the form of a negative. The individual may be eternally reproduced, but only as a performer, an image, a shade. Will the judges be able to determine who *he* is? Might they permit his image to live on, but not himself? And how about recording stars—would it be possible to live on only as a voice? No, because immortality needs eyes.

Personal appearances in the flesh are essential here, but these too (because of the relatively small number of witnesses) must be recorded on film to achieve validity. Thus, the process of maintaining celebrity is one of endless confirmation. Whenever flashbulbs are present, the performer is simultaneously being exposed and confirmed, as in a religious ceremony. Confirmation and exposure are the same for them. Heaven's camera must remain fixed on their performance; otherwise the impression they make on the scene will fade. (There was the landing at Le Bourget, and forty years later the twelve-year-old with a model jet in his hand, asking: "Who's Lindbergh?")

Celebrity, according to writers ranging from Tolstoy to Stanley Elkin, causes public personalities of one magnitude or another to send forth a noticeable radiance. In *Anna Karenina*, a recently-promoted officer in Vronsky's regiment attends a party, giving off a "subdued glow" of success. Elkin's hero in *Boswell* sees Orson Welles in a bookstore and detects the same golden softening of the air around him.

Exposure to others' celebrity is considered by almost everyone to have a contagious magic. On a modest level, possession of a celebrity's autograph confers slightly deeper being on us. Better, we can improve our divine qualifications by being photographed, if possible, shaking hands with the champion, or at least standing near him, even as one member of a group. Notice that in such pictures the entourage seems to lean in toward the star, as if this photograph, the record of their closeness to eminence, were going to be preserved for all time.

Before Christmas a customer in Korvette's department store in New York waited in line to pay for a record album. A beautiful girl followed by several respectful men came out of the crowds carrying an album, and took her place in line next to him. In a moment he became aware that the scene before him had turned into a frieze of faces. He had an impression that he had turned to stone and that everybody was looking at him. But they were staring at the girl beside him whom he suddenly recognized as Sophia Loren. There was a flurry of embarrassment. She demurred a little before being escorted to the head of the line. What amazed the customer who had been standing next to her was the power of one woman virtually to stop all motion in the store. Wherever she moved publicly, there would be this same mural of awed faces, and it seemed to him that she was living at the very top of human capability.

Finally, those who have given up hope of qualifying for eternal life on their own still hope to pass through the turnstile as a *member of an honored unit* or as the result of *having been present at an historic event*. The second of these is well known as "the Blizzard of '88 mentality." The pagan motivation behind the garrulous recountings of old men, and all compulsive story-tellers, is that their presence on the scene of a disaster or spectacular event will glue them into one of the gods' scrapbooks if they repeat the tale often enough.

Commitment to unit-membership produces men who

love and need reunions. Many such gatherings are built around an artificial vagueness created by liquor. Through this haze a rainbow of immortality arches above the good-fellowship. There's a long long trail a-winding back through the Argonne Forest, to the Normandy beach head, the Wichita under fire, the team that beat Yale in the rain, got the other side's goat and painted it green, the wild blue yonder, short snorters, and also sandhogs who shook hands under the East River, and aging astronauts, actors' tales at the Lamb's Club, those who directed traffic in the New York power blackout, the Class of '39 with joyous, sagging faces truckin' on down to an old Count Basie rhythm.

Watching closely, visualize across much of the civilized world a Breughel-like scape of revelers singing now and then, clustered with their arms around each other's shoulders, celebrating the old memories that testify to their fitness for the beyond.

"I see no reason why my grocer should be immortal," said Ernest Renan. "Or why I should. But I do see a reason why great souls should not die when they depart the flesh."

But today grocers and real estate salesmen, and all of us, consider ourselves fully entitled (as, of course, did Renan) to extend our lifelines by every means possible. We go about this by showing off to the very gods we hope some day to destroy.

VII

SHOWING OFF BEFORE THE COMPUTER OF EXCELLENCE

God is not dead. He will turn up in some other form in the human psyche. This is a matter of placing the idea of Him somewhere else.

JUNG

. . . Pseudo-atheists, who believe that they do not believe in God, but who in actual fact unconsciously believe in Him. . . .

MARITAIN

Among the middle classes, God, supposedly dead, has reappeared in the form of a gigantic Computer of Excellence. He has an aura of technology, and has become allied with the ideal of scientific precision. Not that this computing function is new: the idea of a scroll or ledger kept by a celestial recording authority not only goes back to the beginning of history but, more than that, accounts for there being such a thing as history.

The Human Chronicle is written for the gods to review, so that they will appreciate the importance of our tribe. My individual history and yours will also be fed into the reviewing system. Our obituaries serve as résumés for eternity. Memorial services of one sort or another are finally nothing more than advertising campaigns designed to sell our virtues, to promote the immortality-potential of our departed bodies.

Middle-class people in particular have always competed for the gods' notice, but today, with religious authority on the wane, the competition has become frantic, in some arenas unbearably so. We have a merciless obsession with accomplishment. Millions are caught up in the neurotic new faith that a human being must succeed or die. For such individuals it is not enough to enjoy life, or simply to do a good job or be a good person. No, the main project, pushing all other concerns into the background, is to make a name that the gods will recognize.

Many spend practically all of their time doing this. Their remorseless self-promotion is sometimes inadequately described as "ego," which explains nothing. The only way to make sense out of the immortalists in the crowd (to a varying degree, nearly everyone) is to understand that they are trying to post scores on an imaginary record.

The succeed-or-die neurosis haunting middle-class American life afflicts people of all intelligences. For instance, those of us who stopped believing in God long ago will often be found trying harder than anyone else to impress the Computer of Excellence, not realizing that we are just as superstitious, and in our own way just as devout, as peasants kneeling all over the world. God has simply taken up a new position, and now manifests himself to the sophisticated as a testing machine. This unit has many faces; reversing an ancient process, God has split into little gods. He appears as a constellation of deities revealed especially to the civilized middle classes, and revered by them as guardians of immortality.

These deities are Standards to Be Met worshipped in the abstract, but with fervor. We petition them in the language of statistics. (To project qualifications for eternal life, we even appeal to and take comfort from the god of our own public opinion.) One shows off to the machine by displaying fame, wealth, a job with the power to hire and fire, suitable house and wife, handsome husband, enough children, mention in the newspapers or the company house organ, our face on television or close to the president in the company portrait; or by making something beautiful, damming a river, dominating a staff meeting, and so on.

The faith of this anxious, climbing mortal is that degrees of excellence are somehow calibrated in the stars. If we are persistent enough, our achievements will be xeroxed all over heaven. Our scores are being tabulated and processed by a master calculator. The gods, keepers of immortality, pass our data into this system. By some nameless procedure each of us will be tested out. Our reward, a passing grade, will be that of life beyond death; our punishment for failure, annihilation.

In 365 B.C. Herostratus burned down the temple of Artemis in Ephesus in order to make his name immortal. Recently an accused mass murderer in Arizona explained why he had gunned down a roomful of women: "I wanted to get known." Wading ashore on Leyte Island, General Douglas MacArthur called out for the gods to hear: "I have returned!"

All such showing off, whether glorious or degrading, arises from the conviction that if our deeds are printed boldly enough on the historical record, not merely the name but the person himself will be saved. As long as you have committed a memorable—even if also horrible—act, the gods will not let you sink into nothingness. At this extreme we have the hunt for glory. More commonly the trivial triumphs of modern status-seeking, little footsteps toward eternity, are directed toward the same end.

The unrelenting drive to be remembered grows from two assumptions which, primitive as they may seem, dictate life-programs all over the civilized world. First, again, that a cosmic apparatus for recording and evaluating events actually exists. Second, that most of us, including those who no longer believe in God, still inwardly anticipate the possibility of resurrection.

Why return every year to place flowers next to a cemetery stone? In part, to symbolize the possibility that the loved one will grow again. Even closer to our inward and often unknowing faith is the general abhorrence of being buried in an unmarked grave—the disaster of ending in Potter's Field. Also of anonymous or unattended death: leaving corpses unclaimed after the battle. "Pledged to recover the bodies of comrades who died in bitter fighting . . . two battalions of United States marines pushed forward slowly today against stubborn North Vietnamese resistance," Tom Buckley of *The New York Times* reported July 4, 1967, from Conthien, South Vietnam. " 'We don't leave our people,' said First Lieut. Jerry Howell of Alameda, Calif. 'I'm sure they'd do the same for me.' "

Unsentimentally, this seems beautifully human and brave but nonetheless ridiculous. Our comrade is dead. The soul, if he has one, has flown. The body is nothing now, not his or anyone's. Yet we recover it. We are painstakingly careful of the body as well as the reputations of the dead, providing them with resting places and a farewell notice. The soldier's name, at least, is preserved in granite on a war memorial slab near the center of his hometown. If he has been a drifter, coming from nowhere with no proper place to rest, or died namelessly "missing", it is still possible to be saved. In the eyes of God, the Unknown Soldier may be you.

Home in peace time, why not speak ill of the dead if they deserve it? Why do funeral orations and obituary notices almost never turn out to be unfavorable to the individual in the casket? We are kind to the recent dead because people are charged with testifying as witnesses to one another's fitness for resurrection. A Chicago ward boss said: "If you don't go to other people's funerals they won't go to yours."

The cultures that made us are filled with Judgment Day fantasies. In our supposedly enlightened times, millions program their lives as if they believe that resurrection teams are going to roam the earth someday. There will be Judgment Committees. When the investigators come around with our dossiers, each of us will be expected to give proof of our existence and net worth. Above all, we must be identifiable. In this fantasy, namelessness will be the unforgivable sin. For if the name has made no impression the computer in the sky may miss us, and we will be dead forever. No eternal flame burns for the unknown civilian. And so the desperate struggle to place ourselves on file. We make deals; families and friends help each other. You can see the competition everywhere around. Names of people who might otherwise be obscure given to streets, highways, American Legion posts, museum wings and scholarships are intended as guides for resurrection officials, the assessors of the spirit, who will come down to certify Who's Who.

Therefore, the middle classes of this time are not, in Leslie Fiedler's phrase, waiting for the end, but rather hustling for the end. They are preoccupied with keeping the deed and the attached name alive. The hope is to be able to rise up when the immortality census-takers pass by, and speak out confidently: "Wait! Don't you know who I am? Look at the record. . . ."

The fear of not being remembered pervades the race's literature and song. In psalms, fables, poems and ballads, life is described in terms of shifting substances: sand, chaff, straw, tumbleweed. Or no substance at all: blowing in the wind. We have the sands of time and the river of eternity. Keats's epitaph: "Here lies one whose name was writ in water," condenses the passion of all immortality-seekers.

The quest for everlasting life led to a touching faith in the power of the word to influence the grand computation. "In the beginning was the *logos.* . . ." "The moving finger writes. . . ." "It is written that. . . ." Written or spoken, the word has consistently been used to certify one's excellence before the imaginary judges.

Similarly, in China, we are told by Holmes Welch: "Words *were* power. For instance, when a man died, his coffin used to be decorated with the word '*Longevity.*' It was put there not to celebrate the ripe old age he had reached, for he may have died young, and not, as at a Western funeral, to emphasize the immortality of the soul. Its purpose was to assert the immortality of the body, to counteract the fact of death."

For the Egyptians, according to Seligmann, nothing could come into being before its name had been uttered. " 'The word,' the hieroglyphics tell us, 'creates all things: everything that we love and hate, the totality of being. Nothing *is* before it has been uttered in a clear voice.' "

Frazer says that in the mind of the Egyptians "the highest powers of all, the supernatural rulers of the world [were] obedient to mortal words. . . ." The Egyptian gods, while all-powerful, could be swayed by an artful presentation of a candidate's bid for immortality. Priests instructed the aspirant how to deceive the judges in the tribunal hall. Answers "uttered with the correct intonation and in the prescribed phraseology would pass for truth."

Our present-day approach to the Immortality Committee and its machine in the sky is not very different.

Ambitious pilgrims act on the assumption that the Computer of Excellence, while all-knowing, may not be entirely attentive, so that to a limited extent it can be influenced by publicity. Work well done may sometimes go unnoticed unless we call attention to it, and have witnesses to make sure that the credit is registered and assigned to where it belongs. Some of us imagine that the machine processes only images, and does not see below the surface into motivations, inner purity or evil, etc., caring only for the scores we ring up.

Everyone pretends to disapprove of the rat-race for fame, status and money, but most middle-class individuals still join in it. The usual hypocrisy prevails: success is described as the bitch-goddess; fame and status are supposed to turn to ashes. But does anyone ever really want to trade in his success for anonymity? Only if he has enjoyed it to the fullest, and registered his identity beyond all doubt with the celestial machine.

The drive for fame has one purpose: to achieve an imitation of divinity before witnesses. It is true that public eminence has been downgraded with a philosophical sigh by many celebrities, but this is likely to be an affectation, and misleading. It represents, first, mock humility to placate the forces that might take good fortune away. Second, it may serve to reduce the ambition of potential challengers. Third, the famous individual experiences a genuine confusion in that he has enjoyed the taste of divinity but not its substance. Though treated like a god at the moment, he is after all mortal, will grow older, may lose his charm and image. In these precarious circumstances his double identity shifts between emulation of a god and the imitation of a human being. This accounts for the fluky temperament of such people as actors who have had excessive renown thrust upon them too early and are not quite sure how a god ought to act.

Not surprisingly, success is disparaged by those who haven't been able to make it. They can quote Ecclesiastes to the effect that all is vanity and a striving after wind, or, say, Carl Sandburg, who reminded us that human endeavors of every kind end in the cool tombs. But such wisdom misses the point that through worldly striving our dream is to *avoid* ending up in the cool tombs —by registering excellence on the Calculator. Hence, given the superstition that drives us, the compulsion to hunt for fame or join the rat-race is not nearly so meaningless as wise men like to think.

Lorenz notes that "the process of so-called status-seeking . . . produces the bizarre excrescences in social norms and rites, which are so typical of intra-specific selection." But we really are different from birds and animals. Striving men and women aim to rise up out of the species, and not suffer the fate of other mortals, which is to die and usually to be forgotten.

Status—marked-down fame in a small environment— has something but by no means everything to do with surviving comfortably here and now. Beyond that the climbing man, great or trivial, plays to the computer in the sky. If he does not, it becomes difficult to explain the fierce envy of people supposedly concerned only with excellence directed at competitors in the same field. "Fretful of other men's virtues . . ." as John of the Cross said, "they depreciate them as much as they can, looking on them with an evil eye."

One rich man envies another; one talented man or woman with plenty of money maintains the bitterest rivalry with another; a famed inventor, philosopher, or ballerina permanently assured of material comfort and honor, may still pray for a rival's downfall or disgrace. This sort of envy has nothing to do with earthly well-being.

Envy means that he probably scores higher on the sky-chart than I do. He "amounts to" more. He has a better claim to eternal life. And if there is room in my field for just so many at the top, all those witnesses down here applauding him may influence the gods and jump his score on the machine, and if he is that good, then quite literally I am dead.

The most eminent creative fathers among us succumb to this mean superstition. Jung has written: "One might think that a man of genius could browse in the greatness of his own thoughts and dispense with the cheap applause of the mob he despises. But actually he falls a victim to the more mighty herd instinct; his searching, his findings, and his call are inexorably meant for the crowd and must be heard."

For the crowd? No, for the sky machine, with the crowd serving as a choir of angels, witnesses chorusing the great man's praise before the Resurrection Review Board. And who, by the way, could this man of genius be, the one Jung is talking about? Undoubtedly Freud, with a score on the Register of Being at that time higher than Jung's, therefore closer to the gods than Jung, and intolerably closer to immortality.

The hunt for status and glory, the struggle for heaven's recognition, will always be both exhilarating and wearying to the spirit—more than ever today with the competition no longer being regulated by orthdox referees. For this reason we have rampant paranoia, the suspicion that others are trying to cut us down in the arena with the gods looking on: a projection of our intent to reduce *them.*

We have also pressures toward conformity (no less prevalent today than before, even though they have been identified and ridiculed) in which the mediocre members of society do their best to prevent more creative ones from showing off to heaven. They aim to spread responsibility for all action, so that individual excellence will not be recognizable—because if it is, the mediocrities among us will be left for dead. For this reason the lumpen-bureaucrat must be devoted, in Heidegger's expression, to the "levelling down of all possibilities of being."

Envy and meanness overcome me when I suspect that a rival is pushing ahead and making a better impression on the Computer of Excellence than I—and in doing so, reducing my potential for immortality to the vanishing point. Such paranoia, which like all other manifestations of extreme suspicion comes from the fear of being reduced (ultimately the fear of death), is almost impossible to resist.

For example, I have general feelings of hostility toward stage and screen actors. This attitude may be paranoid and irrational, but it remains. With a few exceptions, I find these people bumptious and empty. This must be because I fear that—by means of enormous ego and false charm—they know how to make a deeper imprint on the Universal Registry than I can. The more prominent have universal faces and are treated as gods and goddesses in their own lifetimes, which, to the envious, is unbearable.

The knowledge that all this is nonsensical and silly; that there is, after all, no Judgment Machinery; that actors are themselves as a rule pathetically insecure, has nothing to do with the immortality-thrust of envy. That will not be reasoned away, and almost seems to have a life of its own inside one's being.

VIII

FOUR STYLES OF CONSCIOUSNESS IN THE FACE OF DEATH

It is very interesting to see how . . . in the overheated psychic striving of vain individuals, the striving for power assumes the expression of a desire for God-likeness. . .

ALFRED ADLER

Within the mass man feels no sense of responsibility, but also no fear.

JUNG

In the face of its thrownness Dasein flees to the relief which comes with the supposed freedom of the they-self . . . Fleeing in the face of uncanniness.

HEIDEGGER

Avalanche, take me with you in your slide!

BAUDELAIRE

In his disguised drive to become divine, the immortality-hunter searches unendingly for whatever means he can find to get around death. This involves manipulating his imagination to ignore nothingness or rise above it. If unable to do either, he protects himself by deliberately falling into a state of reduced or scattered being.

As death waits at the finish line, we carry on with what can be distinguished as four life-styles: 1) the way of *standing out* against the laws of creation and decay, imposing one's will on the world, dominating others or ascending over them, commanding life and someday death by talent, force, drive or magnetism; 2) the way of *retracting the self,* yielding up one's being to the management of others, or sharing it with others, settling for collective immortality; 3) the way of *deliberately dulling one's awareness of things,* drawing away from experience, seeking safety in the familiar, and 4) the way of trying to by-pass death through the *gentle diffusion* or *violent shattering of the self.*

Except in rare instances, these dispositions of consciousness do not exist purely and alone in one person. Contrary approaches to life move us, and sometimes we try to follow several at once. An outlook changes or dissolves into another. The one determined to stand out from everybody else and win the approval of imaginary gods may also, as a soldier, have known the strangely exhilarating experience of vanishing into a communion of marching men. The same consciousness may feel a marvelous alertness and a passing sense of being united with all creation—and not long afterward sink into a round of office work and watching television at night.

Granted that the states exist in us at different times, still, over the long term one of them tends to emerge and begin dominating our affairs. If the prevailing life-style meets with resistance and becomes too painful, we may shift to its opposite, or shuttle indecisively between the two.

Under death's gun, every consciousness, knowingly or not, decides whether to advance or retreat. Gradually a life-plan forms. At the beginning there will be a choice of two programs. The first is to stand out, reach, grasp and try to overpower our mortal condition; the second to shrink, yield, blend our transient awareness into a master plan (usually one we are unworthy to question), or to entrust our destiny to the life-plans of others. One impulse is to subdue the environment, the other to hide in it. One seeks immortality by dominance, the other by subservience. The first style pushes the individual toward achievements that show off his worthiness to be a god; the second seeks union and collective safety.

But the tendencies may intermingle, in that the impulse to dominate seems often to be collective, as with Storm Troopers, Red Guards, and in the late 1960s, on an international scale, the revolutionary students of the New Left; while apartness can appear to be meek, for example, in the person of a cloistered monk. This need not be contradictory; cloistered meekness may disguise an aggressive attempt to stand out from the rest of humanity in the eyes of God and thereby qualify for divine status, while the habit of joining crowds, even for the sake of violence, is still retractive and represents a willingness to settle for pin-point survival in a mass of selves.

Neither approach by itself can be labeled good or harmful. The one obsessed with standing out from the rest may be noble or harshly exploitive, or both; the need to blend in with others can derive from love or cowardice, affection for mankind or fear of competition.

In summary at the four corners of unitary being we have the god-imitator, chameleon, dud, and ecstatic. Confronting life and death, some attack the obstacle course alone; some prefer to keep their heads down, and go to the end *en masse;* many fold up their awareness, retreating into a pocket of dullness and repetition, while others dissolve the unit of their own resistance so that death can never find them, using such means as liquor, drugs, madness and multimedia bombardment.

We see god-imitators all around, and with God Himself nearly dead they are on the increase. The purpose of the god-imitator is to subdue his environment absolutely. He intends to win divinity in the world and take it with him after death, his method being that of remorselessly imposing his presence on everyone. All within his ken must eventually yield to him, in the presence of the astral machine. In effect, he declares, as one film and television star informed his business help, "I'm King Kong, and you've got to bow down to me." He will dominate either the animate or inanimate environment, and often both. He may concentrate on moving people around; controlling forces, (rivers, armies, electronics systems, disease and crime) or processes (the movement of money, trade, production, and all kinds of traffic) .

This kind of nature will plan and work ceaselessly to move you in order to get what it wants, which is the feeling of Divinity Now. The would-be god on earth never stops trying to incorporate the environment into himself. He simultaneously imitates and shows off to God. Overriding determination separates him from the rest of humanity. He views others through a one-way window. His project is to surround and contain their consciousness, and thereby to control life utterly so that it will not move unless he says so.

Most of the time the god-imitator is sealed off from other people by a vacuum of indifference. Occasionally he may cross this space and make a brief emotional connection, but the interlude seldom lasts long. He soon feels compelled to return to his program, which allows for only the briefest emotional commitment to beings he is primarily out to manage and maneuver. The self-made deity stands ready to subdue and exploit others, but goes about this in an oddly impersonal way, since for him they hardly exist except as the people of his dream. The experience of eternal separateness may be hard and lonely. Still, he can practically be guaranteed not to change, having decided long ago that it is better to survive alone than perish with the rest of the crowd.

The god-imitator puts space between himself and the rest of the world. Suspicious that the unexpected may bring death, he reduces the chance of surprise to a minimum, which means reducing the initiative of others to a minimum. Paranoia becomes his natural condition. Allen Ginsberg has said: "Because I am open, I am vulnerable; because I am open, I am free." The god-imitator can never afford this risk. He may make occasional sorties into comradeship, even joining in "Sweet Adeline" around the bar, but distrust of his companions will always return. Behind all smiles and bursts of temper, or the facade of steely resolve, he is determined to control them absolutely, and has a deathly fear that if he does not, others will contrive to dim his star, control and reduce him, and bring to nothing his superhuman intentions.

By turns a tyrant and benefactor, he keeps others off balance. This tactic need not be planned; more than likely it arises spontaneously from his conception of himself as being free from mortal restraints. The president of a railroad forces his associates to attend meetings, shivering at dawn, in an old circus tent. In another frame of mind, he will suddenly present a browbeaten underling with a new Lincoln Continental or a two-week vacation in Hawaii. A comedian humiliates his production assistant in front of a dozen observers, and then a day later gives him a huge gold watch.

Once in power, the most vulgar seem to have an instinct for indulging in such divine caprice. The god-imitator delights in making surprise announcements that confound reasonable predictions, since to be predictable is to be mortal. Charm and kindliness follow cruelty. Pain and happiness must come only through him.

Beyond the display of flightiness, he tries also through his random behavior to break down the transparent wall between himself and the inhabitants of his dream, and touch them. But brotherhood and subduing the next man cannot go together. The ambition to rise out of his species and attain a higher form of being—not only after death, like most people, but now, today—cuts him off, sometimes intolerably, and when this happens he lunges in the direction of humanity. For him, sudden gifts are the coin of brotherhood. They perform a dual service, at once binding and unsettling to the recipient, and at the same time allowing the imitation-deity an illusion of having reached someone.

The god-imitator frequently exhibits childlike qualities which, depending on his or her mood, may be endearing or impossible to bear. According to Adler (*Understanding Human Nature*), habits of conquest begin very early:

Children do not express their striving for power openly, but hide it under the guise of charity and tenderness, and carry out their work behind a veil. Modestly, they expect to escape disclosure in this way. Every natural . . . expression finally carries with it a hypocritical afterthought whose final purpose is the subjugation of the environment.

From this proceeds the drive to power:

It is the feeling of inferiority, inadequacy, insecurity, which determines the goal of the individual's existence.

The tendency to push into the limelight, to compel the attention of parents, makes itself felt in the first days of life. Here are found the first indications of the awakening desire for recognition developing itself under the concomitant influence of the sense of superiority, with its purpose the attainment of a goal in which the individual is seemingly superior to his environment.

Superior or inferior with respect to what? From its earliest moments the fledgling consciousness organizes itself for survival. Once precipitated into the light, the living unit determines unceasingly to keep going. It begins as if immortal and all-powerful, and at first encounters no recognizable threat to this state. After a while it comes up against other units, bigger and stronger, with different programs that necessarily thwart its own design. These emerging forces saying *No* and *Don't* and *I'll hurt you* seem to tower like giants menacing existence itself. Alarm signals begin to go off in the emotional stronghold of the little self. Now, if things go well, love comes to the rescue (fondling, reassurance from somebody, lullabies of approval). The baby soul discovers that the flat hand comes down only occasionally and can be avoided, and that the bigger, stronger shapes can be affectionate too, *if I do what they want.*

Thereafter, techniques of dealing with outside forces are refined. The self, gaining know-how, experiments with systems of challenge and appeasement and accommodates perhaps grudgingly to the notion of others' rights. Later, probabilities of the game are learned, and what chances there may be of safely violating or changing the rules. The occurrence of injustice is painfully absorbed by the innocent understanding, and soon the fledgling learns to operate in the world.

Evidently the child who has been loved early, in the right way at the right time, grows up learning to make room for another's desire. (At least he will not automatically suspect everyone of trying to reduce him.) But the consciousness that makes a lifetime project of overpowering others must be that of a damaged child. Deprived in some manner of early support, it is harried by the fear of being unworthy to survive. The individual proceeds with a fixed suspicion of danger. He must stand above all the rest, or they will reduce him again. No one can be trusted, least of all those supposed to love you. They will be the very ones, as before, to let you drop, or leave you alone in the dark.

No wonder that, later on when he grows up, childlike qualities—impetuousness, changeability and sudden cravings—possess this domineering bundle of fear. Early habits of watchfulness and going his own way sharpen his understanding of others' little fashion shows before God. We often find the perceptiveness of an aggressive child in entertainers, notably comedians.

The comedian forces laughter as the tragic impersonator forces tears. Both are god-imitators, with the clowns usually being more aggressive. The tragic hero or even non-hero has a nobility about him—if only of the frustrated sort—tending to project dignity which he can take into the streets when he leaves the theatre. The comedian forces a living by making a fool of himself or of others. He is the silly prince of sado-masochism whose dignity before God and men (worthiness to become immortal) seems always in question. In fact, he makes his mark by destroying dignity—his own or that of his foils.

Entertainers, especially comedians, employ deception and childlike foolery to command the attention of the gods as well as of men. They aim to prove before as many witnesses as possible that they can bring life down around everybody's heads by means of tears or laughter— a supremely godlike accomplishment.

The comedian seduces and deceives his audiences into

believing that he is life's buffoon. He and his fellow clowns and straight men are seemingly little more than butts of misfortune. The audience has the illusion of privilege; of sitting in judgment, reacting or not. But, inside the clown's frame of being, members of the audience have unknowingly been corraled into his act. They belong to it, and when they laugh, belong to him. They merely serve as witnesses, while he . . . As one comedian bellowed at Las Vegas: "I am your emperor!"

Privately the child strikes back. Comedians often exact frightful retribution for having to make fools of themselves in front of their inferiors. One entertainer capriciously left a fund raising reception in the middle of the hostess's speech thanking him for being present, saying loudly: "I don't want to listen to that old whore!" His publicity man made hurried apologies and ran after him. The press agent found his client enraged in the elevator: "You kept me waiting forty-five seconds—never do that again!" This man has also said: "I create the weather in any room. I can make it storm, or bright and sunny." He is hailed for loving children and making them laugh. Intimates know his foul mouth. He curses and blasphemes to demonstrate his freedom from elementary laws of courtesy, because these are for mortals.

The child courts kings and queens who hold him, the god-imitating fool, in affection and esteem. They have no idea that they are characters in his game, as he is in theirs. Finally, the court fool despises every prince. If he dared he would emulate the comic who years ago shouted across the Stork Club to a visiting nobleman: "Hey, Lord, come on over and meet the Ritz Brothers!" This is not merely *chutzpah* but the envious child's unwavering project to reduce all ranks, to cut down all supposed eminence to size, and ultimately destroy it by means of laughter.

The god-imitator characteristically forces people to do

things they don't want to do. This confirms his omnipotence. But cruelty by itself will not be the central act in his circus; it only serves the higher ambition. Sadism, sexual or otherwise, demonstrates absolute manipulative control over other bodies and souls. Pain is employed as a measurement of power. Sadism proves divine right. By breaking another's form against his will, one exists more, becomes more godlike. Cruelty is playing dolls with people. It also arises from the god-imitator's need to hold the environment in place. Cruelty comes from his wild fear of being nothing. If he did not feel his existence ringed with death, there would be no point in reducing others and making them cry out.

Always, he must keep order. The unexpected must never be allowed to arise and threaten, because then he might die. But cruelty also feeds on itself. The more order is kept, the more it must be kept. Demonstrations of power are redoubled, and still there can be no lasting satisfaction. He feels the spring of potential revolt among the injured and humilated coiling tighter. Rage comes, as Caligula felt it, rage over non-resistance. He grows older. Repetitions of dominance weary him, even as he grows more frantic in its exercise. Finally he is not a god no matter what symbolism he devises, and this turns into the dead end of sadism.

Nor can the god-imitator find much relief in love. Putting oneself in another's power invites too strong a possibility of disaster. Others with their own immortality programs will surely take advantage of the defenseless soul. Who then can be trusted with the god-imitator's affections? Only those, he subconsciously reasons, who are *forced* to love. If, after resisting domination, such conquests submit to his power and charm, they must mean it.

Now and then the man trying to be a god is shaken by passion. He feels, in the words of the Jefferson Airplane

song, as though he would "burst apart and start to cry."
But this is essentially narcissistic, a yearning for love
which—so long as he refuses to trust anyone—he will ex-
perience only fleetingly, though often inspiring it in
others.

Exploiting and subduing everyone within reach to its
grand design, the consciousness grasping for divinity on
earth rightly fears sabotage. Paranoia, which in the be-
ginning may be based on imaginary evidence, will sooner
or later have to deal with real plots and conspiracies. A
mathematics of betrayal eventually catches up with the
god-imitator.

Often children will be the first to resist him. A son can
strike back: deliberately become graceless and stupid,
turn hippie or heroin-peddler. The daughter runs away
with a motorcyclist or rock 'n roll singer. But setbacks of
this kind will not significantly damage his aspirations; after
all, many gods have had offspring who rebelled against
them.

Far more important, among those he has put in the
shade there will always be lurking the Judas, Cassius or
Iago resentful of his demigodly bravura. There is no
quicker way to become godlike on one's own account than
to strike down someone who has strutted before the
gods. The act of betrayal itself yields a passing illusion
of divinity. The betrayer, saboteur, assassin of another's
life-plan catches the pretender's crown as it falls off, and
the deed will be imprinted boldly for all time in the
Olympian Record.

God-imitation taken all the way tends almost in-
evitably to produce an ethic justifying murder. Sade de-
fends the act in these terms:

Death . . . is only a change of form, an imperceptible
transition from one existence to another, which is what

Pythagoras called metempsychosis . . . given the assurance that the only thing we are doing in allowing ourselves to destroy is to make a change in the form of things, but without extinguishing life, then it is beyond human power to prove that there is any crime in the so-called destruction of a creature, of any age, sex, or species you can imagine. . . .

Here wrapped in irony we have nothing but anguish and fury because of God's disappearance, coupled with a baleful determination to replace him. In the style of Leopold and Loeb, kill precisely because we have no way of avoiding death. Go with life's animal rules. What good is compassion, since we die? Lord it over this kingdom of cheated animals. Kill before death comes, get even with it, top death by inflicting it, doing unto others that which someday will be done unto you.

Luckily, few have the chance to play Caligula. Most would-be gods settle for the destruction for another's name or self-esteem. The god-imitator tries to reduce everyone around him, to put a stop to unauthorized movement of any kind. And since, as Faulkner said, life is motion, what the earthbound god really hopes to do is stop others from living without his permission.

The chameleon entrusts his consciousness to the management of others. He decided long ago that the larger shapes and forces were too formidable to take on alone. The struggle to impress the gods intimidated him.

This style of being pulls in its horns early, learns to follow the leader and aim toward collective immortality. Thereafter the chameleon gravitates to groups and crowds. This does not necessarily mean falling into a passive state. He simply lives in a more vivid and confident way and uses his talents more effectively as a member of the group. Resembling to some degree Riesman's "other-directed" man, he may, but also may not, be one of Eric Hoffer's true believers. To describe him as a conformist tells very little. We have to go beyond inner- and other-direction and true-believing. The business of identity is to seek life beyond death. The urge to conform may be understood as one more tactical employment of consciousness for this purpose. Seeking immortality in the mass, the poor conformist only does what he can with the impossible situation everybody faces.

The tendency is to avoid death by huddling together. Maritain calls it the thirst for communion. Communal experience serves another purpose besides the one of securing a man from loneliness. Blending in with the crowd, he escapes the judgment of the sky-calculator. His bid for life beyond death will not be reviewed alone, by itself, and found wanting. So long as it stays within the group, the vulnerable consciousness is safe. The ungifted individual keeps death away through anonymity. No harm will come to him while he stays with other souls at the political rally or prayer meeting, on the peace march, in the choir or lynch mob.

Group experience also creates an effect of suspended time. Crowds live in eternity. Passively this was true at the time of President Kennedy's violent death, and again with the assassinations of Martin Luther King, Jr. and Robert Kennedy. The massive loss, the simultaneous burst of grief shared by millions, caused the passing hours to hang as though suspended and to repeat themselves. Television became a communal ribbon of existence. We all turned into a crowd. There was a curious feeling of exaltation amid the horror; together, we were living more. The name of this feeling is immortality.

Time can be suspended by true-believing. Fiercely-held convictions, especially when shared within a group, take you out of yourself and put you on another time-track in which there is no aging and death—and in this sense faith in a cause helps keep you young. In the mass, such a state can be devotional or orgiastic; either way the ultimate goal is to pass safely through death's turnstile on the group ticket.

The mass-assault on immortality accounts for our latter-day worship of averages, which comfort the mediocre. Averages offer a shield against feelings of isolation and incompetence. (Only a genius or monster can be all alone on the Bell Graph.) They provide balm and absolution for the deficient. Averages serve, too, to perpetuate a commune of mediocrity and a state of mind, the conforming part of us, named by Heidegger the "theyself":

In this averageness with which it prescribes what can and may be ventured, it keeps watch over everything exceptional that thrusts itself to the fore. Every kind of priority gets noiselessly suppressed. Overnight everything that is primordial gets glossed over as something that has long been well known. Everything gained by struggle becomes just something to be manipulated. . . .

When hundreds fall into my category I feel forgiven. The life beyond death that I may not be able to earn (not scoring impressively enough on the machine) could be within reach after all. I and my mediocre friends must simply make sure to devise rules that will prevent dangerously talented people from showing off too effectively. Thus, hoping to save themselves from oblivion, the ungifted invariably try to pass off averageness as a form of excellence.

Most cowardly in the face of death are the duds of humanity who commit suicide on the installment plan, deliberately dulling consciousness and sinking into a round of repetition. Conquer oblivion by anesthesia. To avoid anxiety, shut out both life and death.

In this slow suicide of non-being—as distinct from an attempt really to kill oneself—the despairing soul never hits bottom but floats in apathy, partly submerged, as if waterlogged. Such incomplete suicide offers no chance for renewal. The simulation of death and rebirth has not been carried all the way. An actual suicide attempt will be likely to envision resurrection or some kind of living on; the slow drift into non-being is part of a refusal to go down to the depths from which rebirth would be possible.

We have a voluntary reduction of being without hope of renewal, a dwindling to death of the spirit before the body. The dud burrows into administrative structures or household affairs. He or she anesthetizes thoughts of death and meaninglessness by establishing for self and family, if there is one, a round of doing almost exactly the same things over and over again. The defense against nothingness: die before you die. Triumph will be the attainment of torpor; the unknowing hope that by remaining in this half-life without curiosity or verve, "sans everything," one will slip unnoticed into whatever form of survival the authorities may provide.

Hiding from death, a growing number of disenchanted people are seeking to relax and dissolve into the Great Oneness of Being. This is often called ecstasy. In the United States it has developed into a new ideal of pop-immortality managed in a variety of ways, all resolving down to the deliberate diffusion of consciousness. The burden of self grows too heavy. The pursuit of eternal life to be gained by means of worldly accomplishment seems to lead down the corridors of an endless rat maze. The gods have evaporated leaving only an unattended labyrinth; death may be waiting around the corner. Though jostled by others, the traveler feels unbearably exposed and all by himself. He comes to a decision that the fight for individual survival is hopeless, and that the only way to be saved is quickly to unload one's egocentric nature.

An Arab saying has it that when I am present, death is not; when death is present, I am not. Living by this, to get away from the descending fist I will make sure not to be around when death visits. Not, anyhow, as a frightened unit of resistance. Instead I will have gone out of myself. I will live in a timeless present, blended into the life around me. Past and future will not bother me; oblivion will never be able to single out my unit of consciousness. The fixed self is a dying unit having a sure prognosis of decay and sorrow. By embracing the Primordial Oneness I escape death before it can hit me. How can that shadowy menace keep an appointment in Samara with a man whose consciousness has already been dissolved?

Drifting idly on Walden Pond, Thoreau said, "I cease to live and begin to be." Alone in nature, the self breaks away from the rat maze and finds its way back to Eden. There are varied means of transportation. Sports such as skiing and auto-racing break through to the illusion of immortality by means of speed. Skating, sailing, riding the surf, skin- and sky-diving take us "out of ourselves" so that we become temporarily death-free. We escape death by dancing, moving into a new kind of time based on variations of our heart beat. Bongos drum identity out of our heads. In a discotheque, the careworn self is smashed by echoing guitars and electronic shrieking, and its fragments are scattered even more finely by showering and splitting light effects. The same result will be produced by massed violins and miasmic drunkenness. The narcotic drift will take you to spaces beyond time and death, as will an orgy or a church organ.

All these can produce a deliberate stupefying of the intellect, especially of one's analytical powers, Analysis itself is imagined as useless to the point of being evil.

The act of separating things into categories becomes anti-life. The fact that this process has been responsible for the development, say, of smallpox vaccine and penicillin is viewed as utterly unimportant.

Periodic scrambling of one's reason is useful—perhaps even necessary—to enjoy the years. But for many scrambling has become no longer a form of relief, or a vacation, but the basic and most satisfying state of consciousness. Intellect has failed to deliver us from death. Worse, by stripping away illusions, the inductive pursuit of knowledge has made our forthcoming oblivion more disturbing than ever and the meaninglessness of existence more vividly clear. Therefore, the emotional reaction has been, if this is all the intellect can do, abandon it. Shrinking from nothingness the voyager falls back into the eternal *now*, which is reversion to the state of the baby animal.

"Only the feeble," said Unamuno, "resign themselves to final death and substitute some other desire for the longing for personal immortality."

But there remains this compromise: shutting out past and future and living in a timeless present—and also, for example, "returning to the All," the stream of energy, the river of cells, etc. from which each of us came. The transcendentalists, those who have fled the fearful self, can see themselves surviving in a stage hovering somewhere between life and death. A fantasy of Thoreau's unintentionally illuminates their cosmic narcissism:

I used to see a large box by the railroad, six feet long by three feet wide, in which the laborers locked up their tools at night; and it suggested to me that every man who was hard pushed might get such a one for a dollar, and having bored a few auger holes in it, to admit the air at least, get into it when it rained and at night, and hook down the lid, and so, have freedom in his love, and in his soul be free. . . .

This vision of immortality offers us death with eyes. (No one imagines "All-ness" without seeing.) We picture ourselves bedded down somewhere, safe, breathing and watching. It is a child's vision of lying very still under the covers, peeping out through little, starry holes in our blanket of being. Peering from the holes in his black box, Thoreau could feel himself absorbed into the divine intelligence. He experienced "freedom in his love" inside a coffin with holes bored in it.

Death and immortality merge in the transcendental imagination, which arranges a compromise. We have no fixed form but live on in a sort of colloidal suspension, peeking out at eternity—like a chemical solution with a drop of spirit added.

IX

EMOTIONAL
MATHEMATICS

. . . hence this tremendous struggle to singularize ourselves, to survive in some way in the memory of others and of posterity. It is this struggle, a thousand times more terrible than the struggle for life, that gives its tone, colour, and character to our society. . . .

UNAMUNO

e have tried to impose any number of ethical systems on our competitive struggle to win personal immortality. All of them have been designed to prevent us from destroying one another in the fight. We are asked to do unto others as we would have them do unto us; act as if our maxim, thought, deed were to become universal; be honest, pay up on time, refrain from assaulting the weak, and so on.

These are good ideas, and now and then they help restrain the more barbarous individuals among us. Responding even a little bit, the stupid and brutish have been kept in line far longer than the race had any reason to expect. But the old precepts have shown a tendency to buckle. After all, why love my neighbor when he pushes ahead of me? Why render full value, if I can gain more by cheating? Why respect the rights of the next man if he stands in my way? How can honesty be the best policy, when I look around and see exploiters prospering everywhere? Only two must never cheat: my surgeon and my airline pilot. For the rest, when it comes to laying down the law, *who says so?*

Unfortunately, no ethical system amounts to anything unless it can promise some kind of immortality as a reward for good conduct. If both hustler and virtuous man end up in the same dark alley, what can my teacher say to me? Yet despite the collapse of orthodox assurances we are not completely lawless. Though we injure our neighbors, we also help one another. Considering the meaningless fix mankind finds itself in, we treat each other surprisingly well. True, among civilized people of the West there have been signs of a vast nervous breakdown gathering momentum. Looking back over its shoulder, pursued by the fear of death, paranoia runs ahead of the culture, racing in circles. Look around for trust and love, and sometimes they appear to be in hiding. Even so, the world garrison fights on. A structure of order and discipline remains. Large numbers have deserted to drugs and madness. Behind our lines all sorts of violence, as well as casual insults to human dignity, have become commonplace. But they are not yet the rule. The main body of an amazingly resilient human decency has not broken ranks. We hang on, with each survivor clinging to the possibility that he and perhaps even you will somehow be rescued.

What can the moral force be, the one still holding the community together in the face of nothingness? Our strength seems to come from a natural ethic built into the struggle to live forever. This ethic develops from a sort of Emotional Mathematics, or a Mathematics of Being.

Being translates here as immortality-potential, the impression made on the gods, one's score registered on the imaginary Calculator of Excellence. The more definitely you exist now, the greater your chances of qualifying for the hereafter. Turning this around, the meaner and more ordinary your life, the closer to death, and the more aesthetically appropriate that you should dwindle into nothingness. Life's key struggle then becomes that involving the Enhancement vs the Reduction of Being, with Enhancement adding luster to your immortality-claim and Reduction lowering you toward the pit of non-existence. All other conflicts arrange themselves around this one; which is to say that all human interplay arises from our attempts to force eternity, to gain the illusion of some sort of everlasting life.

Everyone carries around with him an existential credit balance. This is his net worth as a person and candidate for divinity; the supply of funded being, the reserve of dignity he can bring to bear in pushing his claim to immortality. The value of your net worth and mine continually fluctuates. We must at all times seek to maintain and strengthen our being, keep our self-esteem and the respect of others. Brotherhood is experienced as an Equation of Worthiness. You have to qualify for it, remembering that the state of grace must also be a state of attractiveness and that all emotional relationships are governed not only by a moral mathematics, based on respect, but to a large degree by aesthetic considerations: whether the individual acquits himself pleasingly before gods and men.

Hence, the foremost imperative of the Immortalist Ethic (the one really lived by all tribe members, beyond creed and culture) is to remain strong and stay attractive. This means at the same time protecting and pleasing oneself and impressing others. When this is done, you will be in a state of grace because the imaginary gods love you. The first imperative, to protect and please yourself, remains more important; the second, gaining the favorable opinion of others (witnesses to your excellence), helps reinforce your claim. But the strong-minded do not absolutely need the testimony of their fellow men. For example, a filthy, ragged monk may seem unattractive to you and me, but to himself (and therefore to the gods) he is delightful. Similarly, we may consider a hunger striker not much more than a starving fool, but to himself he shines with probity.

Most people lack the fortitude to try for eternal life completely on their own. They need recognition, friendliness and good opinion. The ethic they commonly live by rests on a balance of respect between oneself and others. The practical ideal is to build up our own bargaining power—and within reason, allow other men to do the same. In the language of earlier times, the race's commandment might be: "Thou shalt not wantonly reduce another's self-respect and humiliate him in the eyes of the gods." Though competitors, we are brothers and sisters too, fighting the universal death sentence, in need of witnesses, and longing now and then to huddle together. We hope to make a better score than the next man. Sometimes, filled with vicious death thoughts, we may try to bait and humiliate him. There are destructive ones among us too—individuals for whom common decency is meaningless. Yet most of the species knows how to be gentle.

Beyond any natural forbearance, we still fear in our bones the ancient Law of Talion, imagining that forces of symmetrical retribution actually exist and wield power over events. We look for both human and cosmic retaliation. If I reduce my neighbor and wantonly defile his good name, he will—in accordance with the emotional

mathematics involved—have to get back at me, and if
he can't, fate will arrange for me to make a suitable pay-
ment. The Symmetry of Existence will take care of this.

The act of breaking another person's form must be
counted a deadly sin, second only to that of permitting
our own form to be broken. (Loss or failure by itself will
not destroy identity but humiliation does.) Everybody
recognizes a humiliated man, but what exactly is so
shameful about this condition? Why should humiliation
be such a disaster? The disgraced man suffers a cata-
strophic loss of immortality-potential. He turns out not
to be the person he implied he was. At the wrong time,
courage fled; he trembled and backed down. Unless he can
somehow redress the balance of dignity, he no longer
exists except as an impostor—or, perhaps tolerated as an
apology in the shape of a man. The machine in the sky
can be imagined ejecting his identity card and shredding
it.

The mathematics of immortality counts cruelty and
cowardice as the extreme transgressions against being.
Yet cruelty, though tending toward god-imitation, may
also be employed defensively to shore up self-esteem. In
particular, it strikes back against the outlandish and
alien. Cruelty can arise from the aesthetic outrage we
sometimes feel in the presence of strange individuals who
seem to be making out all right, and who give the im-
pression, even while minding their own business, of un-
derstanding something about life that we don't.

Have they found some secret passage to eternal life?
It can't be. If those weird individuals with beards and
funny hats are acceptable, then what about my claim to
superiority? Can someone like that be my equal in God's
eyes? Does he, that one, dare hope to live forever too—
and perhaps crowd me out? I don't like it. All I know is,
if he's right I'm wrong. So different and funny-looking. I
think he's trying to fool the gods with his sly ways. Let's

show him up. He's not very strong. For a start, see what
he'll do when I poke him.

From this beginning it becomes easy to move into
monstrousness. The tendency is to despise the victim
all the more angrily as his suffering increases. Since
amateur sadists consider helplessness a perversion and
fair game, the most horrible acts may follow. Weakness
offends the persecutor in a strangely moral way. (He may
be a temporary sadist made unexpectedly cruel by the
other's humiliation.) An *aesthetic of cruelty* possesses the
tormentor, convincing him that graceless forms are fit
only to be broken. In these circumstances he is driven, if
only symbolically, to kill in order to become divine.

Cowardice turns into a little death, a crumbling of
form. The coward abandons his will, style and dignity;
rushing too soon into the lifeboat ahead of the women
and children and blots his family shield forever. Having
sold out for transient salvation, the poor man inspires
no sympathy, only contempt. The surrender of self under
pressure is supremely unaesthetic.

Of course, nearly everyone has been a coward at one
time or another. We have been through the loss of grace
and temporary abandonment of the person we thought
we were. Here a great deal depends upon the way we
have come on. For instance, James Joyce in Paris was not
a coward when, threatened by a fist, he hid behind the
big writer, saying: "Deal with him, Mr. Hemingway!",
since Joyce had never defined his manhood in terms of
fistfighting. But, in accordance with the mathematics of
behavior, we all understand that had Hemingway de-
clined to stand up, he would have received a craven rating
in his own conscience and in the minds of witnesses.

Courage holds being together, and makes you feel im-
mortal. The experience of having been brave rewards us
with a marvelous serenity. While it lasts we enjoy an
Olympian feeling of elevation, and walk around free of
time and fear. The Christian ideal of turning the other

cheek has never really caught on, and survives only by be-
ing ignored. Christianity—a beautiful religion, but also
the one most useful to hypocrites—tries for the impossi-
ble, pretending not to recognize the healing power of
retaliation. In cold fact, as everyone must know, the
power to retaliate is indispensable to emotional health.
Forgiving the offender will never be good enough, since
reduced people lack the power to forgive. Only when the
disgraced or insulted man has won back his self-respect
can there be talk of reconciliation.

An insult offers a sudden and intolerable threat to my
net worth. The next man seeks to force-feed a little
death into me and knock down my credit rating. Seizing
hold of my dignity, he anticipates brandishing it to
heaven like a scalp. By insulting me and getting away
with it, he boosts his standing on the immortality chart
while I sink correspondingly. Perhaps more than anyone,
sophisticated hoodlums know how to crush the decent
citizen's self-respect. First, do it before his dear ones
while, say, they are out for a family stroll. Surround and
terrify them; force the honest burgher to beg for his life
and lick the gang boots. This amounts to stealing what
he thought was his immortal soul. Then they vanish,
leaving the victim tormented forever by the agonizing
memory. The mathematics of self-respect will leave him
no escape.

The need for an insulted man to square accounts (the
language of dignity is oddly financial) seems to be uni-
versally recognized. He will never be able to get out of
the box of humiliation until he hits back in some way, or
does something heroic. Acts of contrition will not ex-
piate the sin of accepting an insult; only retaliation can.

A family entertainer once insisted that a bass-player in
his supporting orchestra sing for the radio listeners. The
man had not sung in years and answered emotionally that

he didn't want to. But the boss wouldn't leave it alone. The man would have to sing, and the confrontation grew tense. The band leader interceded: they would arrange a song for tomorrow's program. The man would be forced to perform, even though listeners along the network had heard him say that he could not. And this is the way a collision was avoided: the music started up, and the musician came in with a series of rhythmic howls. Everybody was laughing. He had performed but not exactly sung, and his boss let it go. In a test of pride, both sides perfectly understood the credit balance. The bass-player saved his dignity, the big shot his authority, and they both emerged from the confrontation with their net worth intact.

Lately our show-business culture has developed an antidote to humiliation: adroitly-managed publicity. An imprint of any kind, favorable or not, stamps our imperishable being on the nature of things. "I don't care what they say about me, so long as they mention my name." In the fevered, often upside-down world of stage and café, even a collapse of dignity can be made to pay off. Imagine that you are a popular singer and an actor publicly makes off with your wife, ordering you to leave the premises, and you have conducted yourself in a generally pusillanimous fashion. Yet the affair can be so managed that your cowardice appears glamorous. Even with horns on, you are declared bigger than ever. The gods take new notice of you. Audiences responding to publicity agree, and your price and rating go up.

Ethical imperatives growing out of the drive to live forever dictate our most commonplace rules of behavior. For instance, they produce the mathematical values of gratitude and modesty.

The Sin of Ingratitude would seem to be relatively trivial, but in our time it has become serious. By thanking you, I place your goodness on the record. I testify to your generosity, sacrifice, nobility and excellence. Failure to thank someone often upsets him terribly. This anxiety arises from the suspicion, gone into earlier, that members of the celestial review board who will judge our credentials for immortality are not always attentive. They may forget to monitor the machine. The lazy attendant-god may refuse to note down our claim unless (by thanking) it has been registered on our behalf by somebody else.

Also, in the absence of orthodoxy, credit-stealing is on the increase. Our competitors find no trouble in actually coming to believe that credit stolen from us belongs to them. The jury of gods may be omniscient, but we also darkly fear their susceptibility to being swayed, charmed and deceived. Again, the only answer is to pile up the right kind of evidence in our imaginary dossier. Of all testimony, thanking is the best. Beyond this, gratitude connects two individuals in at least a fleeting moment of brotherhood.

The virtue of modesty came into being as a tactical measure. We hoped that it would help ingratiate us with the gods. Through a mildly self-deprecating demeanor, we avoid symmetrical retribution for *hubris.* Remaining modest also helps us get along with the competition. Those who boast and preen before the gods are resented because they tend to distract attention from us. A braggart almost surely will be disliked; he makes other people nervous, and they long for his downfall. When he finds himself in trouble someday, witnesses will not step forward. In contrast, the modest man or woman not only devises magic against the gods' annoyance but sees to it that emotional retribution from the neighbors will be far less likely.

Martin Buber said that "The lie is the specific evil which man has introduced into nature." Why evil necessarily? Lying helps us to deal with an unsatisfactory reality. Its purpose is to improve somebody's chances of surviving.

There are falsehoods of love: to save others from suffering, conceal the hiding place of a comrade, or (as when we pretend not to know where the Christmas presents are) to give greater pleasure an hour from now. Every surprise party is based on a lie. (The astounded guest of honor becomes an instant god.) But Buber refers to a more sinister twisting of the truth, the kind employed, say, to get ahead by destroying the colleague who suspects nothing. Or mean lies: trying to shift responsibility, bearing false witness, falsely taking credit.

The ungodly, according to the Old Testament, "are not so." This is precisely what the liar fears: that unless he changes reality he will be nothing. Reflecting on it, the lie is an amazing device. To think that members of our race should actually go to so much trouble as to invent what does not exist. Consider the provocation, the enormous anxiety weighing on our species for thousands of years, that could produce such an extraordinary breakthrough as the decision to reject one reality and substitute another. Of course it was the same dimly realized obsession that created our myths and poetry. There can be no reason for lying except to escape death, and if there were no death people would not bother to lie.

The liar misshapes reality in order to make himself less vulnerable and more godlike. Grand, vicious or trivial, the lie is meant to increase his being, if need be at the expense of others. He may be dangerous or pathetic, arrogant or frightened. Whatever his game, he is willing to take a chance on deceiving the gods. The would-be enchanter declares in effect: "If the truth prevails, I'll die."

We deeply resent liars because they introduce a wild variable into the conventional mathemathics of immortality. The rogue soul upsets us by toying with truth. Yet no one shows more resentment and outrage than men caught lying. How to explain their furious cries of innocence? You see this act over and over again. A murderer who must know what he has done carries on with outbursts of indignation like the victim of a conspiracy. If somehow acquitted, he weeps not only for joy but as though he really were guiltless.

Malefactors trapped absolutely and beyond doubt swear that they are being smeared and picked on. The official who took a bribe and has the money in a Swiss bank account sobs at the injustices of the indictment against him.

All such frauds are playing to the gallery and the archives. A man may not mind admitting confidentially that he has always been a cynical opportunist, but he cannot stand having it on the record that he *is* a fraud, and particularly objects to witnesses saying so.

"You're a liar!" has always been a fighting insult, whereas, say, "That's not true!" is far less serious. In fact, the dialogue usually builds like this: "That's not true!"— "Are you calling me a liar?" One contradicts a dubious statement, whatever it was, but the second calls to account the whole person. To have told a lie is one thing. To be judged a liar is to have your existence contradicted, which means that your immortality-card will no longer be valid.

When my credibility is gone, I am gone. The gods and the sky-calculator will no longer tally the evidence of my net worth because I am, my very existence is, a lie. Such a disastrous loss of identity must be intolerable. That is why guilty men weep, shout and proclaim their innocence in court and before television cameras: again to fool the gods in their own heads and deceive the Big Machine.

Even a successful fraud comes across as strangely pitiful. Every professional hates phonies. They clutter up the way to achievement. Pretending to talent, they try to attach themselves to their betters. Nothing comes easier than to despise them. Yet for all their meanness of spirit, they belong to a sad order of being. The poor cousins, liar and phony, decided at some point that to qualify for life beyond the grave they must cheat, that otherwise their bids would not be good enough. Distrusting themselves, they employ guile on others. But like Peter Schlemiel, the liar and phony have no shadow. This means being nowhere. They exist outside of the equation of brotherhood. The relief of loving comes hard for them, and the curse of triviality follows them everywhere.

X

LOVE AND EVIL

Love consists in the constant beaming forth of a favorable atmosphere . . . the love of a man for a woman is like an attempt at transmigration, at going beyond ourselves, it inspires migratory tendencies in us.

ORTEGA Y GASSET

The problem of evil is the problem of liberty . . . The dwelling place of freedom is the abyss of darkness and nothingness, and yet apart from freedom everything is without meaning. It is the source of evil as well as good. Thus the fact of evil does not imply that all is meaningless; on the contrary. it actually establishes the existence of meaning. Freedom . . . is prior to the world and has its origin in the primal void. God is all-powerful in relation to being but not in relation to nothingness and to freedom, and that is why evil exists . . .

BERDYAEV

These are the species' two extreme reactions to mortality. Both love and evil seek eternal life, one reaching out with the idea of sharing the prize, the other grasping for it.

Falling in love, we share consciousness with someone

in an eternity which unfortunately fades away. But during this period we discover how we would feel if we were gods beyond time. Most people will agree there can be no more blissful sensation—excepting, perhaps, that of glory: the same thing but felt and shared en masse, with oneself standing in briefly for God, or with our legion suddenly become heavenly.

Love for a friend has nothing to do with this, or familial devotion, or even the joy experienced on first seeing our newborn infant (small deposit on immortality, but uncollectable, only for the race's benefit). The love projected here involves mingling with another person outside of time. This enhancement of being, as Ortega calls it, "the beaming forth of a favorable atmosphere," in which we feel haloed and far more than human, has been captured by Tolstoy in *Anna Karenina*:

All that night and morning Levin lived perfectly unconsciously, and felt lifted out of the condition of material life. He had eaten nothing for a whole day; he had not slept for two nights, had spent several hours undressed in the frozen air, and felt not simply fresher and stronger than ever, but felt utterly independent of his body; he moved without muscular effort, and felt as if he could do anything. He was convinced he could fly upwards or lift the corner of the house, if need be. He spent the remainder of the time in the street, incessantly looking at his watch and gazing about him.

And what he saw then he never saw again after. The children especially going to school, the bluish doves flying down from the roofs to the pavement and the little loaves covered with flour, thrust out by an unseen hand, touched him. Those loaves, those doves, and those two boys were not earthly creatures. It all happened at the same time: a boy ran towards a dove and glanced smiling at Levin; the dove, with a whir of her wings, darted away, flashing in the sun, amid grains of snow that quivered in the air, while from a little window there came a smell of fresh-baked bread, and the loaves were put out.

All of this together was so extraordinarily nice that Levin laughed and cried with delight.

Alan Watts says that love is grounded in "freedom from self and time." As Ortega has pointed out, we wish immortality for the loved one; we want to share divinity with the other. According to Watts: "The general idea of Tantric maithuna, as of its Taoist counterpart, is that sexual love may be transformed into a type of worship in which the partners are, for each other, incarnations of the divine."

Jung reflects that complete sexual harmony "is extolled as a great happiness ('one heart and one soul'), and with reason, because the return to the original condition of unconscious unity is like a return to childhood. . . . Even more it is like a return into the mother's womb —into the teeming depths of a still unconscious fertility. It is indeed a true and undeniable experience of divinity, the power of which blots out and consumes everything individual. . . ." This last ecstacy appears to be moving toward death. It seems that whenever we write about love, death inevitably comes in through the back door. Why must the two so frequently be considered together?

In *Love in the Western World,* Denis De Rougemont painstakingly develops the thesis that romantic love seeks its own non-fulfillment; that it carries forward our secret longing for death, has nothing to do with marriage, and in fact remains at all times in active opposition to it. But De Rougemont's analysis of the Tristan and Isolde legend (which he believes to be the source of Western romantic love) is flawed by his assumption that union in eternity must be identical with a death wish. He correctly reminds us that ". . . a myth arises whenever it becomes dangerous or impossible to speak plainly about certain social or religious matters. . . ." Then he makes the leap: "Myth is needed to express the dark and unmentionable fact that passion is linked with death, and involves the destruction of anyone yielding himself up to it with all his strength."

But why should a desire for death be so dark and fearful a crime? My death offends no one in authority. If I want to pay my dues in this way, who cares? And what can there be to fear? How can I be punished for my death drive? By being killed?

The passionate transports of Western love certainly conceal a forbidden desire, but De Rougemont has uncovered the wrong secret. What we want is to be transported, to cross over, from the human condition into a divine state. We may aspire to lose consciousness now, but only so that we will awake on the other side. The real nature of our longing is brought out by D. H. Lawrence in *Women in Love,* in this exchange between Birkin and Ursula:

"Death is all right—nothing better!"
"Yet you don't want to die," she challenged him.
He was silent for a time. Then he said, in a voice that was frightening to her in its change: "I should like to be through with it—I should like to be through with the death process."
"And aren't you?" asked Ursula nervously. . .
. . . he said slowly, as if afraid: "There is life which belongs to death, and there is life which isn't death. One is tired of the life that belongs to death—our kind of life. But whether it is finished, God knows. I want love that is like sleep, like being born again, vulnerable as a baby that just comes into the world."

Once more we have testimony that what De Rougemont terms "the active passion for darkness" does not intend to rest in the dark, but to break through the darkness into a realm of eternal light; that we don't want to die, but desperately, more than anything else, to live, to be reassembled on the other side of time.

De Rougemont finds that rapture "is now no more than a sensation, and it leads nowhere." He considers this sort of thing being in love with love, ultimately to embrace death. But somehow being in love, at least during the hours of delight, does not feel that way. The ecstacy of Levin—stopping time and observing the doves flashing in the sun, the grains of snow, and the smell of fresh bread—can hardly be dismissed as a mere cover-up for a death wish. The forbidden passion stirring love's delirium is not for death but for eternal life.

Passion takes us out of time. In its thrall we have the illusion of becoming more alive by means of induced suffering. Since its referent is immortal being, this kind of suffering is filled with sensations of uneasy pleasure. Pain in love keeps us young, and keeps the affair young, since pain holds back the passage of time.

Difficulties, misunderstandings and forced separations postpone the threatened deadliness inherent in familiarity. Completion brings the lovers down to earth, and is therefore to be feared. The moment complacency sets in, housekeeping emotions will soon take over. This seems a dismal encore to ecstacy, and the lovers can't bear the thought of it. Here pain comes to the rescue. Passion keeps the simulation of eternity alive by artificially prolonging the period of caring, with quarrels and reconciliations, or intrusions of a hostile family, providing timely injections of useful suffering.

During times of social upheaval, in wars and revolutions, when the stability of love is threatened at every moment, uncertainty (which suspends time) thrusts in on the lovers from outside. The resulting tension is sweet. The feeling of immortality comes over us during the London blitz, the New York City blackout and the black revolution. We seldom quarrel, but take love when we can. The police may break in. The ship will sail, and the furlough soon expire. ". . . Darling, it's late; the curtain descends, everything ends too soon. . . . " Thus, we have a paradox. The imminence of death projects us into simulated eternity—but the fear of aging and death is no longer with us. Emergencies free us from real time. The hands of the clock move faster, yet time is suspended, because only a bomb, not the clock, can make us die. We will go, if we go, all at once. But inevitability no longer haunts us. Under the gun we are gods, and marvelous lovers.

In summary, Tristan's deliberate placing of obstructions in the path of love should be understood not as a subconscious effort to fail or die, but rather as an attempt to hold back time, string out the divine experience and preserve it from housekeeping-love that must soon follow if things go well. Romantic love does its best to put off our coming back from eternity into real time. The rule of love seems to be that first we are divine together, but then, with familiarity, we must be human together.

This emotional law, that the sensation of divinity must fade away, is accepted by mature people. The immature will not reconcile themselves to giving up the divine experience. They persist in trying to bring it back. Therefore, it is commonly observed that immature natures, especially lovers, make fools of themselves over and over again. Since maturity involves the acceptance of death, they refuse to grow up. This refusal invites not only suffering but possible disaster in many forms: failure; sexual misery; neurotic ill-health; a terrible feeling of apartness, of being no one, nothing and nowhere in the general scheme of things; being unable to finish anything, and finding oneself generally incompatible with "life as it is." But if these self-imposed retributions can be risked and conquered, or at least lived with, the uncompromising child-voyager remains open to visions that do not come to his mature neighbors, with their wise, nodding resignation to nothingness.

What the immature retain is an insistence on their right to immortality, and a child's-eye-view of what might be. This gives them the strength to love again, try again, and dare foolish new things. They can say proudly: "When I became a man, I *held on* to childish things." Death will eventually be overcome by the foolish persistence of such losers.

The immature never stop trying to escape time. This makes them difficult lovers, since they find it hard to bear love's aging and coming back down to day-by-day familiarity—job, kitchen, children, bills. To bring back the feeling of immortality, they artificially create pain and mystery. This is done to screw up tensions which will then be happily resolved in bursts of forgiveness, a form of simulated rebirth.

The need to feel love again in a divine way, like gods, accounts for the dramatic content of bourgeois infidelity. Apart from its immediately seductive pleasures, the most commonplace affair—such as that of a businessman with his secretary—recaptures feelings of glory. To the rest of the world such a liaison may appear tawdry or ridiculous, but to the lovers the promise of fresh revelations has been restored. If only for a little while, life seems to begin again. The dear or dreary familiar round is by-passed. The lovers step off the moving sidewalk that carries everyone else toward death.

Among the envious, lovers are laughed at. But the laughter is uneasy—because they know something. Holding eternity in an hour, they escape for a while, beyond time and death. That is why the envious throw old shoes at them and fasten tin cans to the honeymoon car, and, whooping and hollering, shivaree the enchanted couple if their hideout can be found.

Evil is nothing but the destructive things people do because they are going to die. In the struggle to impress the gods and the astral machine, it uses more force than necessary to put down competition—breaking others' form rather than simply trying to outdo the next person. Evil sets out to deceive, manipulate, but above all to break down our neighbor and reinforce our claim to immortality at his expense.

Moralists generally presume that cruelty belongs to evil. If so, we have another paradox: that sometimes love and evil combine in cruel games in order to keep feeling alive. To this end, love and evil meet in pain. But such maneuvering always turns out to be an inefficient not to say agonizing means of going after eternal life: one which does not truly resist death, but in a sick and unconvinced way plays with it.

The sources of what we call evil are paranoia, god-imitation, boredom, and rage at nothingness. Another source might be the Eichmann-like inertia of neglecting to feel. The greatest of these is paranoia. As everyone knows, this exacerbated form of suspicion senses a conspiracy lurking everywhere to reduce the individual, and —in his own mind, as well as in the eyes of others—make him fit for death. Yet have we not every reason to imagine that there *could* be such a plot? After all, nature itself has been organized to do away with us. Given the imaginary gods and the competition to survive on Judgment Day, nearly everyone becomes a rival for a place in eternity and may indeed be plotting (even if unconsciously) to reduce our score in heaven in comparison with his own.

The god-imitator, we know, resists death by commanding his environment and reducing other people so that they will bow down to him. Boredom is the languid perception of death and meaninglessness. (The only reason for cynicism, and for deriding others' commitments and small pleasures, is the presence of death.) Boredom licenses horror, if possible in an intriguing form, in order to relieve unendurable monotony. The fourth kind of evil is cold rage at being surrounded by death, with no God to save or even condemn the victim. Feeling this, Caligula seeks by monstrous acts to summon up meaning, and to make the Almighty reveal Himself in the form of retribution.

Evil is not Dracula prowling through the opera house searching for his next victim. (Dracula though is precisely *un*dead, seeking life blood in order to live on.) Rather, it should be understood as merely one more attempt to get around death. But it goes too far; the evil impulse shows itself actually willing to destroy surrounding life in its avidity for survival. On an every-day level, it does its best to knock down others' confidence and effectiveness, reduce their ability to feel their own being and project it exuberantly, and works diligently to prevent you from loving or trusting yourself.

Defining this supposedly mysterious force has been an obsession endlessly fascinating to philosophers. Buber calls evil "the grasping, seizing, devouring, compelling, seducing, exploiting, humiliating, torturing, and destroying of what offers itself. . . ."

"Evil," says Berdyaev, "is non-being, and has its roots in non-existence." Also: "Evil passions of whatever kind destroy themselves in the end and involve death both for men and for the world."

Unamuno sees the origin of evil as "the inertia of matter . . . sloth." He adds that "sloth is the mother of all vices, not forgetting that the supreme sloth is that of not longing madly for immortality." (Jung, too, finds idleness to be the curse of mankind.)

Schelling marks evil as a return to pure power. The same position has been taken by Lord Acton in his axiom that power tends to corrupt, with absolute power corrupting absolutely. This, we have seen, must be the almost necessary result of successful god-imitation. The illusion of divinity tips over into psychosis when it continues without hindrance over too long a period, because the god-on-earth knows that in spite of all homage death waits for him.

Berdyaev and Buber agree that the seductive power of evil lies in deception: secret plans to reduce another's being. Buber distinguishes between sinners and the wicked. The first are fallible but human. Defining the second, he quotes the psalmist: ". . . the wicked are far from Thee," and adds that "the wicked have in the end a direct experience of their own non-being."

This seems probably not true, in that psychopaths (our term for the wicked) may be separated from others, and from love, but even so may plunge into life and experience *being* more profoundly than a meek, inhibited clerk who never did anybody any harm. It would be foolishly complacent to suppose that evildoers have a smaller sense of being than good people, for Evil Lives, and often fully.

Philosophers generally describe evil as a separating force, and it would be consoling to believe this. But how then can we account for the lusty and vicious brotherhoods of evil such as Storm Troopers and Hell's Angels who joyously share the pleasures of stomping and degrading inoffensive people, and join in beer-swilling celebrations of the fear they inspire? Here we have the loneliness of paranoia healed by group cruelty, and the gang members hug and kiss each other.

Evil, according to Webster's Collegiate Dictionary, has the effect of "producing or threatening sorrow." But so, sometimes, does love. Perhaps the polar confrontation of being does not pit love against evil but trust vs paranoia. We may recognize paranoia as the opposite of love since, in the end, it mortally fears sharing. Paranoia can never end well. The inability to trust (being reflexively afraid that, given a chance, others will bring you closer to death) amounts to the same thing as fear of love (unwillingness to open up and share consciousness with another, leaving oneself vulnerable to a death thrust).

Can love conquer paranoia? That is, can it overcome the suspicion, grounded in childhood, of others as potential death-bringers? Never completely. Once implanted, the habit of suspicion never dies. But it can be controlled and temporarily dispelled, perhaps teased, so that now and then the damaged self will open up a little and let love in.

A certain amount of paranoia must come naturally to intelligent men, because there is death. Small systems of suspicion may be observed at work in almost everyone. *Not* to be paranoid in the presence of a cosmic plan to kill every last one of us would be extremely difficult. To help alleviate this illness of civilization, we must first of all love little children and hold them tenderly, so that they will not fear darkness, random punishment and being left alone. But to children of kindness as well as the others, death will sooner or later reveal itself, bringing with it the natural fears and suspicions that all members of the human family, excepting saints and clods, must feel.

"Only by mastering unmitigated evil does existence attain to transfiguration," writes Martin Buber. ". . . Men's task, therefore, is not to extirpate the evil urge, but to reunite it with the good."

Love is often mistakenly counted on to accomplish this. Paul Tillich among countless others has declared love to be stronger than death. In *The New Being*, he puts the idea like this: "Every death means parting, separation, isolation, opposition and not participating . . . love overcomes separation and creates participation in which there is more than that which the individuals involved can bring to it. . . ."

A nice rationalization, and unfortunately nothing more. The sad truth is that at the present time death continues to be stronger than anything, as the philosopher himself has found out.

The best way to overcome evil is relentlessly to expose its sources. Prayer may accomplish a little: ". . . deliver us from evil." But like love its effects wear off quickly, at least for most people. The practical way to deliver ourselves from evil is to know that we must deliver ourselves from death. Until the day of freedom from death arrives, we must understand, point out ceaselessly, and pass along the word, even to the brutes, that when they are doing what we call evil, the real action is that of trying to become divine in a rude way, escaping death by injuring the being of others. Evil, we must make clear to ourselves, is brought on by showing off to or imitating imaginary gods, or by flying into a rage or descending to slothful cruelty because they don't exist.

Once it is generally recognized that death is the real enemy, not our neighbors; that there are no gods in the reviewing stand to be impressed by our deeds or the achievements of others, then we may learn to forgo the destructive competition for the approval of nonexistent judges. When that time comes, Evil with a big E, as we know it now, will begin to wither away.

XI

SHARED CONSCIOUSNESS

Therefore Aristotle and the followers of Averroes believed that there was in the Universe a single nous *or intelligence, that insofar as we were intelligent, we were all one single intelligence.*

ORTEGA Y GASSET

Each consciousness seeks to be itself and to be all other consciousnesses without ceasing to be itself: it seeks to be God.

UNAMUNO

dvancing toward divinity, men and women suffer the curse of loneliness. The more advanced and aware of our unaccountably brief time on earth, the more vulnerable we become to feelings of isolation and midnight attacks of despair.

As Jung has said: "Higher consciousness . . . is the equivalent of being all alone in the world." Ortega expresses the idea more emotionally: ". . . we find that we are alone in the universe, that each 'I' is in its very essence solitude, fundamental solitude." "[Consciousness] shuts me up within myself, makes of me at once a prison and a prisoner. I am perpetually arrested within myself. I am a Universe, but at the same time I am one—alone. The element of which I am made, the thread of which I am woven, is solitude."

Not that we need these eminent men to tell us how it feels to glimpse oblivion. The "nameless dread" that visits so many older people in the middle of the night can perfectly well be given a name. It is simply the fear of death wearing its blank mask.

Wise men reprove us: "The only ones who fear death are those who are afraid to live." But this is just talk, a sophisticated way of appeasing the imaginary gods, the hope being that through apparent acceptance of death we will gain exemption from it. The truth is that unknowingly we fight death all the time, and that, in Unamuno's words, "you, I, and Spinoza wish never to die and that this longing of ours never to die is our actual essence." We are like the Russian peasant in the fable; old, exhausted, groaning, as he hauls a bundle of faggots through the forest. He falters and collapses whipped by the icy winds, calling out: "Oh Death, come to me now!" And Death appears, asking: "Did you call?" The old man starts up. "Yes, yes, please. . . could you help me on with my bundle."

A very few individuals, most having a remarkable capacity for self-deception, manage not to fear the end. The rest who claim that they are not afraid are either lying or keeping so busy that, blocked by bustling trivialities, thoughts of death rarely penetrate their reveries. But fear waits behind the door nevertheless. And the day they peer out and discover nothingness, the result can be catastrophic.

For most people of even minimum sensitivity, the awareness of each man's and each woman's final loneliness is unbearable. Alan Watts has noted that humanity's so-called bestial acts are not in the least animal-like but a protest against isolation.

Evidently—again, rare exceptions must be admitted—the human spirit can not bear to be alone for very long. It must reach out and, by one means or another, share consciousness with others. This is to say that without God (as opposed to the old gods lingering in our heads) and the promise of an afterlife, the separated consciousness feels hopelessly lost, a speck in the cosmos. It gravitates toward clusters of being—other people. The tendency to gather or huddle together may be explained in many ways, but however you interpret it, units of humanity seem predisposed to share a state of mind. Or, some believe, to assemble into a single consciousness. Whether this may represent a return to an original massive intelligence, Aristotle's *nous;* whether such a cosmic awareness actually contains all our little intelligences, seems beside the point. Much more important, even if cosmic being is nothing but a bubble inside our heads, men appear determined to create it. If we have not evolved from it, we may be self-consciously evolving toward such a group soul.

Whether it exists or we simply long for it, universal being manifests itself to anyone on a psychedelic trip, or during hallucinatory passages of the psyche in periods of fasting or sleeplessness. Journeys of this kind will take you "back into" an undifferentiated state of being (or forward into it). The climactic visions project a single throbbing awareness. We are released from individual dying, and seem "through with the death process," as D. H. Lawrence had Birkin say.

The question is, at what price? Will the fear of death, without God to sustain us, lower the individual soul's bargaining power and cause men to settle for the communal vision? The master, Buber, told Allen Ginsberg

that visions were not important. But today the chemi-
cally-assisted vision provides cut-rate shared conscious-
ness and feelings of immortality for the faint-hearted.
Timothy Leary said to the youth of the world, a battle
for the control of consciousness is on. One's identity
comes under assault from every direction. Technologies
understood only by the specialists move in to save men—
and at the same time make them feel terribly weak and
small. Death remains, huge. The temptation is to break
and run; run to the vision, run to the communal soul.
Seek brotherhood, even at the cost of intelligence. Melt
into the common perception, and downgrade the pursuit
of knowledge in order to justify your abandonment of it.

Until recently civilized men and women were able to
strike a balance between sharing consciousness and assert-
ing themselves; that is, between experiencing feelings of
immortality en masse and striking out for it on one's
own. These alternating tendencies, kept in line by vari-
ous orthodoxies, enabled the species to work fairly well
with death, and produced in synthesis what we know as
progress (defined by Frederik Pohl, for one, as the in-
crease in the number of options each of us has available
and, from the immortalist point of view, as advances to-
ward solving the mystery of death in one area or another).

A compromise between sharing and asserting was
managed by *words.* Educated men and women devoted
themselves endlessly to communicating. On the every-
day level this was done the clumsy way, through speech.
Semanticists enjoy insisting that people seldom communi-
cate exactly what they mean, but these students of meaning
miss the point. When it comes to sharing consciousness,
words are as crude as stone axes. Verbal explanations may
well not bring us closer together. They are intended pri-
marily to get across to you what I mean, which is some-
thing quite different from our sharing a moment. They
serve as a medium of exchange, not sharing. Whoever

speaks, asserts himself. Words used precisely and deliberately to explain something become tools of aggression against nature—they take apart the environment so that we can compare (though not necessarily share) experience in order to get on top of it.

Disdain for words arises from fear of them, and fear of words comes from the fear of death, because words define our precarious condition. We may also say that to abandon words as a respected medium of exchange would mean to abandon our revolution against the gods and against death.

When death seems to be winning, and masses of advanced people—who once depended on words—begin to feel lost and frightened, then sharing consciousness offers itself once again as the best means to mimic immortality. In these circumstances, words that expound and explain the nature of things come into disfavor. If honest, they lead to death; if dishonest, they merely lay one more fraud on us. And at this point, if it is to work, the fraudulent promise that death can be evaded must be mystical and beyond speech.

Hence, it has become fashionable today to put down words as an inferior medium of exchange. A new generation actively despises printed messages, particularly as they are used in conveying the slow freight of laborious explanation. Among many young people, language at the same time evades and reaches beyond the explicit. It is best listened to in chants and songs. It is used tonally, employed as rhythm, deliberately empties words of content, such as "like" and "man," dropping them in for cadence or no reason.

Expression of the imprecise, such as "your thing," aims positively not to break apart reality. It refuses denotive speech but seeks rather to combine words into a general impression which is not to be nailed down. "What exactly do you mean?" would be considered hopelessly unanswerable, since exactness implies that the scene can be

broken into segments. Analysis of any sort leads to lone-
liness and death. Reaching for an eternal present, one
does not examine things critically, but enjoys each part
of life as it comes along.

Hence, according to this view, the value of language
has diminished. Words that explain and analyze only
offer futile resistance to death, the hard way. Sometimes,
used drearily, they take all life out of the present, con-
stitute a hopeless drag, and themselves smell of death.
Through insistence on definition and the segmentation
of knowledge, words set mankind against nature and,
more grievously, lessen the possibilities of enjoying na-
ture and the pleasures of today.

In contrast, music helps create shared consciousness, as
does silence. Bringing home what Bertrand Russell calls
"the experience of sudden wisdom" and "sudden beauty
in the midst of strife," silent communication makes life
feel as though it were lasting forever. In love the deep-
est moments come when people don't say anything. As
time holds, our understanding seems to have no limits.
In this state, Levin and Kitty in *Anna Karenina* (the
incident was taken from Tolstoy's own experience) each
divine the meaning of a long string of initials written
down by the other. "W, y, t, m, i, c, n, b, d, t, m, n, o, t" is
understood at once: "When you told me it could never
be, did that mean never, or then?" and "i, y, c, f, a, f, w, h"
as "if you could forget and forgive what happened. . . ."

Many go about saving their souls by sharing in the
massive consciousness of one crowd or another. In a crowd,
time stops. Among scores or thousands of other identi-
ties, we break free. The longing for communion within
the crowd-soul is not necessarily disgraceful; all it means
is that one more person has given up in the face of
death and announced his willingness to settle for nirvana
with eyes.

Group activities entered into emotionally take us out

of time and recapture feelings of immortality. Regardless
of their moral content and social desirability, they are
born out of the same need: to free the formerly unat-
tached soul from loneliness and the fear of death. Thus,
choral groups, lynch mobs, cheering sections and pilgrims
shuffling to Mecca are all made up of people striving for
the same thing: escape into a communal consciousness.

A dispatch from Peiping printed in the *New York
Times* (2/1/67) quotes *Hsinhua,* the national press
agency of China: "The broad masses of revolutionary
workers, cadres, students and intellectuals are united with
the masses of lower and lower-middle peasants to unleash
the storm of seizure of power."

The rhetoric here summons up an ecstacy that happens
to spring from political slogans but might just as well
rise out of a Chinese Mardi Gras or Feast of San Gennaro.
The scene could as well be transported to the Pasadena
Rose Bowl on New Year's Day (in fact the card manipu-
lations of Maoist cadres on national holidays resemble
those of the USC rooting section) ; the Chinese howl of
hatred and admonishing of revisionist professors by put-
ting their heads in toilet bowls seems not too different
from the Nazi brownshirt howl, or the howl of a Djakarta
mob at high noon.

All mass-action, for good or ill, gives members of the
crowd an illusion of being immortal and vaguely godlike.
Mass prayers, pep meetings, rallies of every description,
community sings, riots, peace marches, and motorcycle
runs lend divinity to the unprotected soul, lift it out of
time, and for as long as their spell holds, remove dread.

The devout Chinese Communist running around and
waving his little red book of Mao's aphorisms, may ap-
pear psychotic to me. Yet he is less conscious of death
than I am, closer to "the All," much farther from death
and less afraid of it, safer, and secure from cosmic anxiety.
He may be better off as the member of what I imagine to

be a psychotic commune than I am with my lonely and fearful sanity.

Today, all kinds of group activists spill into the street. They are all over, shouting, waving signs and flags. Elsewhere, indoors, other groups huddle together in corporate citadels. Groups lie down in Greenwich Village crash pads, burst into the offices of college presidents; they lie down at submarine bases, at the entrance to the draft board; in front of induction centers; they protest racial evil, rent control, and school busing. This sort of thing is all to the good, the best way for citizens to express themselves, get action, stop the war, end racial complacency. Even so, beyond good and evil, such communalism in our time has become a refuge from death, and to some extent a refuge from oneself. Perhaps a majority of the board of directors (all of us) reviewing the course of our species' evolution has decided that the time has come to turn ourselves into the Group God.

Supposing Jung to be on the right track, we could, for example, have evolved from the primeval Collective Unconscious to multiple precipitations of Individuated Awareness. Then—since death is unbearable for individuals to contemplate once mythic self-deceptions are stripped away—we may be about to move on toward Shared Consciousness which evades time and the fear of oblivion.

If so, from the immortalist point of view, the evolutionary process would be taking a wrong turn. We would be dishonoring our species. We must never forget that we are cosmic revolutionaries, not stooges conscripted to advance a natural order that kills everybody. Have we evolved this far only to drift off into a communal pipe dream at the last moment before the end of time and the end of death?

Yet the proliferating group-mindedness taking shape around us can hardly be dismissed as "bad." Shared Consciousness is a state, fallen into with another person or in a crowd, that imitates immortality. It produces the most blissful sensations we know. It reduces anxiety and loneliness, and blurs the separation between "I and Thou." Shared Consciousness provides us with regular vacations from aging time, and invites us to simulations of divine and immortal being.

Moving in and out of this state nourishes the soul. But to stay in it, stay and hide from death in the group, take too many trips out of time by whatever means, melt into the communal intelligence, represents an evasion of responsibility to ourselves and our children.

Mastering the tools that will destroy death takes hard work, planning, studying, all of which a person must do by himself and not in a group, and not necessarily with pleasure. Faith in such activity must survive recurring attacks of doubt and depression. The work will have to be accomplished in the face of annihilation, but still it is the proper destiny of our race to carry it forward.

Humanity has two ways to avoid suicide. One is to wrap itself in a massive dream, fall into various kinds of group consciousness, turning away from death and pretending it isn't there. Or it will face up to a meaningless universe, put up with doubt and unbelief a little while longer, and attack the problem of aging with the same enthusiasm and singleness of purpose we showed in liberating atomic energy and sending rockets to the moon.

PART III

XII

THE END OF
PHILOSOPHY

*Where is the philosopher who would not willingly deceive
mankind for his own glory?*

J. J. Rousseau

*As we well know, the imbecility of "profound" philosophers is
so immense that it is exceeded only by the infinite mercy of
God.*

Giovanni Papini

Until now the assignment of philosophy has
been to devise reasonable explanations for
our being caught in this mortal trap, and ac-
curately to describe the trap. Some of its
speculations start from a theological base; others proceed
mathematically. There have been philosophers—Spinoza,
for example—who combine these two approaches. A more
recent school of thought has been devoted exclusively to
semantic studies of the way in which we think. We may be
thankful for all of these efforts. Brave and disciplined in-

telligences from Pythagoras to Wittgenstein have taught
us how to reason and to inquire with some success into
the nature of the universe. Others have done their best to
make sense out of man's fate. Fabulous minds (Aquinas)
have demonstrated logically that God is everywhere, is
good, and death in this world good enough for us. Other
serene persons (Buber) have shown the way to direct and
vivid experience of the divine. All respect and honor to
these instructors. We would probably have been lost with-
out them, and still running around, intellectually speaking,
with spears and slingshots.

But the immortalist position is that all philosophical sys-
tems relating to ethical conduct in the shadow of mortality,
insofar as they teach us sportingly to accept extinction,
are a waste of time. In the face of death, such wisdom is
a waste of time. The philosophy that accepts death must
itself be considered dead, its questions meaningless, its
consolations worn out. (If the philosophy does not
bother with life and death, confining itself, say, to our
semantic confusions in approaching knowledge, then it
must be judged profound but trivial, which is to say pro-
foundly unimportant.)

"The true votary of philosophy is likely to be misun-
derstood by other men," according to Plato. "They do
not perceive that he is always pursuing death and dying;
and if this be so. . . he has had the desire of death all his
life long. . . . "

Does such a pursuit of death account in part for the ex-
traordinarily emotional hostility aroused among philoso-
phers and theologians by the efforts of men and women to
control their environment without God's help? The strug-
gle to evade annihilation is viewed not merely with dis-
approval but anger. Something happens to the most serene
sages when they suspect men of trying to usurp the powers
of divinity. Their warnings were noted by Unamuno:
"They also call this pride—'stinking pride,' Leopardi

called it—and they ask us who we are, vile earthworms, to pretend to immortality; in virtue of what? Wherefore? By what right . . . ?"

The wisdom of philosophers may nearly always be found trying to blanket our program to conquer death. Even so liberal a teacher as Reinhold Niebuhr gently stifles our desire. From *The Nature and Destiny of Man,* with a few added interpolations and italics:

The ambition of man to be something is always partly prompted by the fear of meaninglessness . . . which threatens him by reason of the contingent character of his existence [THAT IS, DEATH]. His creativity is therefore always *corrupted* by some effort to overcome contingency [TO BECOME IMMORTAL] by raising precisely what is contingent to absolute and unlimited dimensions [ASPIRING TO DIVINITY]. This effort is always *destructive.* Yet obviously the destructive aspect of anxiety is so intimately involved in the creative aspect that there is no possibility of making a simple separation between them. The two are inextricably bound together by reason of man being anxious both to realize his unlimited possibilities [TO STEAL IMMORTALITY FROM THE GODS] and to overcome and to hide the dependent and contingent character of his existence [TO RESIST AND DENY DEATH].

Niebuhr detects the nature of our underground and disguised drive to become gods. Yet he feels impelled to resist it. The effort is "always destructive." Man's creative powers are "corrupted" by his dangerous desire. Why corrupted? According to Webster's Collegiate Dictionary, this means "changed from a state of uprightness, correctness, truth, etc. to a bad state; depraved." In other words, each man's struggle not to die amounts to a form of depravity—an obviously nonsensical proposition. To resist nothingness seems a reasonable enough project for the individual members of our species. Ought we rather to embrace the void? If the effort to "overcome contingency" is judged as corrupt, then the race itself must be corrupt. And if this is so, corruption—a rotten form of life, but at least intelligent life in the universe—must be a good thing.

Still, eminent men throw their weight against our thesis. Stern fathers admonish us. Simply posting a few of their names should be enough to dissuade the foolhardy from persisting in this unnatural immortality project. What an intimidating billboard! Against such authority, we have only one weapon: to italicize the warnings. At random:

Pascal: "Nothing is more *dastardly* than to act with bravado before God."

Buber: "The *lust* of the human race to whittle away the secret of death. . . " and "By glorifying himself as his own creator, he commits the *lie against being.*"

Niebuhr: ". . . man's *wilful* refusal to acknowledge the finite and determinate character of his existence," and ". . . the *primal sin* of self-love."

Alan Watts: ". . . the Christian consciousness cannot understand Lucifer's mistake because it is making the same mistake itself. It thinks that it is self-conscious, and that it can commit the *evil* of self-love."

Maritain: "Great spiritual errors . . . seek the deification of man, by man's own energies and by the *mere* development of the powers in his nature."

Berdyaev: "*Pride* is the temptation of a higher order of spirit which seeks to put itself in the place of God."

St. Augustine: "What could begin this *evil will* but *pride* that is the beginning of all sin. And what is pride but a *perverse desire* of height . . ."

Jung (even the master): ". . . a *foolish* clutching at consciousness on the part of mortal man . . ." and ". . . inflation and man's hybris between them have elected to make the ego in all its *ridiculous paltriness,* lord of the universe."

Norman O. Brown: " 'I shall not altogether die'—the hope of the man who has *not lived,* whose life has been spent conquering death. . . ."

Hegel (quoted by Brown): "Without death individuals are reduced to the status of *mere* modes of one infinite. 'One has individuality precisely because one dies.' "

Lord Keynes (quoted by Brown) : "The 'purposive' man is always trying to secure a *spurious* and *delusive* immortality for his acts by pushing his interest in them forward into time."

Denis De Rougemont: "A man wishes to be his own God. Passion brands the heart the moment the cold-blooded serpent—the *complete cynic*—has whispered his eternally unfulfilled promise: *'Eritis sicut dei!'* "

The foregoing simply demonstrates that brilliant men are as capable of humbug as anyone else, and probably more prone to self-deception. You don't develop into a philosopher without entertaining godlike visions of yourself in the first place. Standing apart from humanity, you are forever lecturing your fellow men and women, writing one book after another, familiarly interpreting the cosmos as though the gods had taken you on a personal tour behind the divine curtain. Is this not an act of amazing presumption: to expect an audience to gather around you, and to suppose that its members will not only stop and listen but sometimes actually pay to hear or read what you think?

How strange for such an individual to denounce self-love! Can he seriously deplore the sin of pride? Keynes, for instance, must be joking when he denigrates the purposive man. You will not write exhaustive treatises on defict financing that change systems of economic planning around the world without having been a little bit purposeful or, more likely, obsessed by your mission on earth.

Alan Watts and Norman O. Brown write passionately, with intimidating erudition, about the unimportance of erudition. Supremely self-conscious and egocentric men advance themselves, their systems and anti-systems, never stop talking, all the while insisting that the mind should be retracted, the intellect forsaken, and that everyone should instead worship the sensuous present. Man's self-love is denounced, his arrogance scorned and pitied, when it should be perfectly evident by now that self-hatred has been his most damaging vice, and helplessness rather than pride the curse of humanity.

Of all the false consolations for dying that philosophy has given us, one of the more dishonest is that, as individuals, we don't really exist anyway. This may be filed under what Alan Watts and numerous thinkers before him put down as "the illusion of identity." The sense of self is described as a kind of illness. Individual consciousness must heal over, like any other wound. As Buber summarizes our condition: "Individuality. . . . revels in its special being . . . the fiction of its special being which it has made up for itself."

It may be tempting to argue back: "If I am illusion, from whose point of view?" etc. But this simply leads into a semantic mine field. Better to attack *ad hominem* by pointing out that no philosopher who ever lived has had the slightest doubt about the preeminence of his own identity. The emperor may have no clothes, but he does have a powerful feeling of self-importance—and if you don't believe it start disagreeing with him, or suggest that he write his books anonymously. A creative individual such as Alan Watts loved to teach. It was practically impossible to imagine him not teaching. Self-evidently Watts, the one lecturing around the country—as Unamuno puts it, the "flesh and bone" Watts—did not consider himself the "transient stream of atoms" he wrote about. On the contrary, he had a bold, quite unabashed conception of his own presence in the universe. And so do all philosophers who amount to anything.

The holiest of theologians may also leap from his platform of serenity to quarrel over his relative nearness to the truth. Niebuhr cites the controversy between Karl Barth and Emil Brunner. Barth's answer, he says, was "informed by a peculiar quality of personal arrogance and disrespect for the opponent." Then, eighteen pages later, Niebuhr himself joins in:

Theologies, such as that of Barth, which threaten to destroy all relative moral judgments by their exclusive emphasis upon the ultimate religious fact of the sinfulness of all men, are rightly suspected of imperilling relative moral achievements of history.

This sort of exchange ought not to be in the least surprising when we remind ourselves that the preachers of humility and other virtues are themselves only trying to score with imaginary authorities, just as we are. Philosophers and theologians compete before the Calculator of Excellence; they also imitate God and interpret His Will as though they were old friends of the Almighty. The philosopher and preacher sell their papers, each working his side of the street like everybody else, hawking his excellence on street corners so that death will pass him by. If the profound and sometimes reverend newsboy were not primarily concerned with imprinting his identity on the Great Scroll in the Sky, he would smile with gentle understanding at his opponents' mistakes. But he is driven by the same obsession that afflicts most of us: "If my opponent is right, I may be wrong. If I am wrong, my rating will be dimmed, and I will die," and so he attacks the rival master savagely.

"Death is part of life." So runs another familiar philosophical consolation. Decomposition of the body, according to Watts, is "essential to life." The conversion of a human being into a lump can be "understood as the instrument of eternal renewal. It is not only the transformation of life into food; it is also the wiping away of memory. . . . " Or as Tillich phrases the same idea: death and life "belong to each other. At the moment of our birth we begin to die, and we continue to do so daily. Growth is death. . . ." So, coolly and complacently, our forthcoming annihilation is made to seem reasonable. Shakespeare died and became food; so did Einstein. Why not you? Why do the members of our species stubbornly refuse to acknowledge that they belong to the worms?

The truth is, of course, that death should no more be considered an acceptable part of life than smallpox or polio, both of which we have managed to bring under control without denouncing ourselves as presumptuous. Dr. Salk and Dr. Sabin have not been hunted down as devils for putting a halt to the crippling of children; they were not called proud or foolish for trying. But death kills forever. Why should the hope of overcoming that be thought in any way unnatural? The argument that because everybody has always dissolved painfully back into the earth, that this is exactly what *ought* to happen, and that we are somehow out of line in trying to prevent it, makes no sense at all. Hitler, the black plague, floods and hurricanes have also been "part of life." But since they are an undesirable part, we resist them, or at least build our defenses as best we can.

In his beautifully tortured prose, Heidegger describes death as "the ownmost, non-relational possibility [that] is *not to be outstripped.*" For the reason that, so far as he knew, nothing could be done to get around death, he counseled us courageously to make clear to ourselves that we really are going to die. By this act "one is liberated from one's lostness." Unreserved acceptance of the void "shatters all one's tenaciousness"—that is, loosens the knot of self which fears the end.

This is manly advice reminiscent of Sade's earlier counsel: ". . . leave your prejudices, be a man, be human, fearless and without expectation, leave your gods and your religions; they are only good for putting swords in men's hands."

In Sade's time, a realistic man could only be "without expectation" of survival. Looking death in the face, he himself converted despair into monstrousness. But he did not deal in guilt. Two centuries apart, Heidegger and Sade confronted the end without succumbing or persuading us to succumb to the worship of finger-shaking gods. Neither tried to placate the sky-calculator at our expense.

This can never be said for the preachers against pride, especially those exponents of Christian philosophy, which Ortega y Gasset once described as the "sad and useless chain which Christianity drags behind it." What has possessed these men, the sowers of guilt? Nothing but the drive that pushes nearly all of us. The difference is that master thinkers feel it even more powerfully, the determination to rise out of the species and join the gods on Olympus.

We come back to the curiously harsh responses to the undisguised assertion of this desire. Seldom in philosophical discourse will you encounter any attempt at a kindly understanding of hubris. Assuming that our pride ought to be seen as monstrous, idiotic, etc., why do sages become so furious about this rather than straighten us out with a calm reproof? Why thunder at mankind's presumption in an almost panicky way? People do not become so wrought-up unless they feel threatened. One explanation for anger may be that Prometheus and Icarus arouse false hope in the thinking master, and he knows bitterly that they represent only dreams. Since he cannot bear having his hopes dashed, he rails at the dreamer.

But this is not enough to account for the anger. More

important, philosophers, and especially theologians, imagine themselves to be overseers of mankind. Theoretically they are supposed to mediate lovingly between the gods and men, but too many, particularly in the Christian camp, carry a big whip which they flourish at us whenever the peasants seem to be getting out of line. These stewards of heaven have the self-appointed mission of putting down our resistance to death, and seeing to it that men meekly accept the blow from the divine meat axe. In churches, temples and forest clearings, mounted on rostrums of every kind, sages and medicine men appease the celestial establishment.

Such Wise. Persons—in their superstitious hearts—have their own game going, and grow furious and afraid when they are crossed. The game is to climb to immortality on our backs. Beneath the veneer of wisdom they are as superstitious as the wildest Papuan, lost children too, on the same darkling plain as we are, just as bewildered and afraid to die, but more corrupt in that to advance their own disguised claims to divine status they are willing to sell us out; to win their imaginary masters' approval by stifling our revolutionary longings. The wise man today who counsels us to go quietly, accepting death, shows himself to be a traitor to his kind. To win the indulgence of the gods and thereby separate himself from the rest of his doomed tribe, he undertakes to tout the shabby deal called death as he might promote underwater acreage in the Florida tidelands.

For centuries we have been carefully, fearfully, but also determinedly, preparing a strike against death. The philosophical overseer has chosen his role: to serve the Force That Might Be There. He serves as strike-breaker and Judas Goat to the human spirit. Inveighing against pride and presumption, selling death, he registers on the Master's cosmic machine how much he has done to keep men modestly in line. Righteously he cools down the crowd's hope of overcoming death. In doing so he signals his worthiness to be tapped for the Heavenly Fraternity, and we become victims in our bones and very reflexes of the overseer's own neurotic drive to qualify for paradise.

As the sage grows older, his convictions about the pathetic inadequacies and monstrous pretensions of the ego grow stronger. He decries bold new attempts to penetrate old mysteries that he could not solve. This is done mostly to discourage younger challengers to his eminence, whose investigations might tend to reduce the importance of his own earlier perceptions. As he approaches the finish line he becomes more and more jealous of his reputation, and more dependent on the gods' good opinion of him. At this stage, just before his powers fail, he becomes overbearingly wise. The foolishness and vanity of human striving seem very clear to the one who himself can no longer strive.

But if in the face of death all philosophical systems (insofar as they are preoccupied with the proper conduct and the end of man) must now be considered a waste of time, who will take charge of the mysteries? Who will inquire into the Highest Good, and help guide us during the period when, in the future which may not be remote, we are in the process of closing out death amid riotous clamorings and clashes over medical priorities? And if we break through to divinity, who will help us readjust to the problems involved in indefinite living?

There are probably two highest goods: suicide and survival. Suicide, seeking instant rebirth, solves all problems. Survival remains, since even if it may not be the highest good it gives us time to work out answers to what *is*.

If we have outgrown such philosophical speculation, what can replace it? After all, life must have some frame of thought. To a degree, philosophers and theologians are already being replaced by chemicals such as LSD, with revelation substituting for wisdom. The insights of Zen help many to see around corners, confronting life open-eyed at every moment. Today art also has taken over a share of philosophy's traditional role. And in the process of dealing with our mortal situation art has begun to destroy itself.

XIII

THE END OF ART

... man is, for the tragic poets, born with a flaw that prevents his attaining the happiness he wants, a flaw to the sensitive Greek as the flaw of original sin to the sensitive Christian. This flaw is hubris, *still best translated as pride, which is also the great Christian sin.*

The parallel with the Judeo-Christian moral tradition can be carried further. Greek hubris *is the overweening individual's rebellion against the ordering of the universe; Adam's sin, which is ours, is also rebellion, disobedience. ...*

CRANE BRINTON

From the beginning—insofar as it deals with matters of life and death—Western art has waged an incomplete rebellion against the gods and their plans for us. It has partly resisted, partly accepted the human situation, conducting an intermittently effective underground resistance movement against our senseless fate. Yet art remains an unreliable vehicle for revolution. It expresses the race's passion, our love and fear of life.

Unfortunately, it seldom speaks out against the system which calls for our extinction. It wails and moans, sometimes laughs, invents geometrical excuses, and all too often celebrates death as a sad necessity, permitting it grandeur.

The practical effort to conquer death and the gods who decree it for us has been carried forward by means generally identified as Western. Dreams and fantasies of an afterlife, return to life, eternal life, all kinds of rebirth hopes, occur around the world. But the obsession—the idea of actually doing something about death—grows primarily out of our Mediterranean origins. It has found expression above ground (though with carefully limited aims, proceeding one step at a time) in the scientific method. Meanwhile, as we have advanced slowly and haltingly toward immortality, Western art has played a dual role: that of inspiring our fight against the mortal condition thrust upon us and at the same time of reconciling us to the divine plan, natural order, etc. so that the race will not kill itself en route.

Through the years, then, the role of art in the covert war against death has been curiously exasperating. At one and the same time it incites our protest and then sedates it with beauty or riddles it with laughter. It embellishes our sorrows or, in its comic mood distracts us from what Bertrand Russell calls "the terror of cosmic loneliness" by making rebellion against this condition seem ridiculous.

Hence, though we use art to project our disguised intention to become immortal, its revolutionary ardor is suspect. Lenin was neither childish nor robot-like in refusing to listen to the Beethoven *Appassionata*; he understood that art can dissipate rebellious fervor. Harmony, or pleasing dissonance, softens indignation. The resulting emotional purge can drain off revolutionary energy. With the best of intentions, the artist may enchant us out of our anger. This becomes all the more likely if his art inspires compassion for humanity's lot. From the revolutionary standpoint, an agitprop specialist who merely stirs up our emotions without satisfying them, leaving his hearers hungry and savage, may turn out to be considerably more effective.

Norman Brown returns us to the Freudian view that "art has the function of making public the contents of the unconscious," and that it "liberates repressed instincts." But it may also weaken them. A desire lived out in sublimated form can become harmless. Our indignation may then "suffer out" its energies in the artistic experience.

The Western concept glamorized as tragedy has been one of the most pernicious notions ever to occur to mankind. Tragedy perpetuates the superstitious conviction that hubris must be punished with symmetrical appropriateness in accordance with divine mathematics. The species punishes itself by means of triumphantly masochistic rituals. All over the Western world curtains go up on the contrived downfall of our desire. The tragic flaw (obsession gone wrong) duly leads to disaster. Retribution is followed by applause; we approve the symbolic reenactment of our failed rebellion. The old superstition has momentarily been appeased, and our hearts are at rest. Thus, witnessing again our stand-in's fate, we resolve not to challenge the gods and, smugly in the audience, congratulate ourselves for never having tried to do so. Yet the timidly concealed message peeps out: we really want to try.

Comedy, too, appeases the fates. Ambition and pride slip on banana peels. Affectation, said Fielding, is the source of the true ridiculous. Comedy or tragedy, whichever happens to be on the bill, lets steam out of our revolutionary program. Through Job, Faust or Simon Magus, we describe ourselves as tragic figures or clowns, but, the management promises, losers either way.

Tragedy as an art form institutionalizes acceptance of life's unfair conditions and also institutionalizes guilt—in fact, makes it possible for guilt itself to become an entrapping art form. But of course it need not be. In his last novel, *Island,* Aldous Huxley shows how familiar guilt structures can be knocked apart like children's blocks in a playroom. The scene takes place in the utopian community of Pala:

"Oedipus?" Mary Sarojini repeated. "But that's the name of a marionette show. . . . Would you like to see it? It's nice."

"Nice?" he repeated. "Nice? Even when the old lady turns out to be his mother and hangs herself? Even when Oedipus puts out his eyes?"

"But he doesn't put out his eyes," said Mary Sarojini. "He does where *I* hail from."

"Not here. He only says he's going to put out his eyes, and she only tries to hang herself. They're talked out of it . . . the boy and girl from Pala tell them not to be silly. After all, it was an accident. He didn't know the old man was his father. And anyhow the old man began it, hit him over the head, and that made Oedipus lose his temper . . . And when they made him a king, he had to marry the old queen. She really was his mother; but neither of them knew it. And of course all they had to do when they did find out was just to stop being married. . . . "

Artists were considered by Plato to be mere imitators of truth, understanding only the appearance of things. Most art was barred from his republic: "Only hymns in honor of the gods and the eulogies of great men and noble actions are to be admitted into the perfect state." Plato was immoderately hostile to poets, painters and actors. ". . . we ought on no account to admit that branch of poetry which is imitative. . . such poetry must unhesitatingly be refused admittance." The tragedian amounts to no more than an imitation "third in descent from the sovereign and from truth . . . all writers of poetry, beginning with Homer, copy unsubstantial images of every subject about which they write, including virtue, and do not grasp the truth. . . . "

This sort of attack on poets and painters, and on art in general, could only have been made by an artist himself playing king of the hill. Only a poet would bother to attack others' poetry with such vehemence. Plato, god of his own republic, barred other poets from the ideal state for the usual reason that he wanted no rivals for his place in eternity. This is hardly exceptional. Most artists wish their close rivals no good luck, and would not suffer if the competitive talents dried up or better yet, somehow vanished from the memory of man.

Of all immortality-hunters, artists may be the most ruthless and persistent. They not only compete in the everyday world, showing off to their fellows and posturing before the gods, but from time to time, just like the One God, they issue worlds of their own, fashioned by themselves, for the entire cosmos to admire. The artist aims not only to be immortal by registering his creations with the Computer of Excellence but to make sure that his productions will astonish audiences through eternity. To be sure, these works are extensions of himself and also serve as evidence of his superiority, kept alive before (he hopes) a multitude of witnesses. Beyond this, they are creations arising from, given birth by, his unequaled, never to be imitated, identity.

He correctly perceives that there are many other acts, each launched by individuals with the same pretensions to being already divine. The competitors in his field float their own balloons of creation. In this great assemblage of balloons, the air being thick with them, there is always the chance that his may be lost. This fear causes him to explode as many competing balloons as he can or, failing that, tactfully to let the air out of them so that they will live on as smaller, low-flying and less noticeable creations. The important thing to remember is that all artists, if they could manage it, would try to bring off the impossible feat of wrapping their balloons around the entire globe, so that their dream and the world would become identical, with themselves as lord of it all—which, quite obviously, was Plato's design in *The Republic*.

This may be seen as a child's vision. Norman Brown has it that "the consolations of art are childish, and they reinforce mankind's willful refusal to put away childish things." Childhood can be understood as "the ideal kingdom of pleasure which art knows how to recover." This also is the kingdom of timelessness.

Art, even though it takes us out of our time and puts us in another, can never be independent of urgency. A painting is an island surrounded by aging time; music takes flight from it; the novel and drama in their different ways play against time, racing the clock, shuffling time around, moving in and out of successive frames—trying always in Heidegger's term to *outstrip* the fatal end, rise above it, forget it or bow down "tragically" to it.

Although they may belong to our tribe, the creators of all this have something else going: we are their characters. The goal of the artist has always been to join the divine company. He will use any materials he can, including you, to build his immortality credits. He will put you in one of his scenes just as he would a rock or a tree. Further if need be he will distort you, even, say, make a pinpoint in the canvas and declare it to be you. For this reason the artist tends to inspire nervousness in others. Even when treated with contempt, he will be up against nervous contempt. Until recent years large elements of the bourgeoisie tended to resist art. It gave them an uneasy feeling to suspect even faintly that there might be ways of making an impression on the sky-calculator that they didn't know about.

Odd and mystical persons with incomprehensible arrogance pretend to be in on some secret that baffles the materialist. He may scorn or pity the artist and deride his impractical mode of being, but still the odd man bothers him. (Today reasonably successful artists make more money than middle-level business people, a circumstance which has led to a greater rapport between the two groups.)

The artist still risks his identity and self-respect to an extent undreamed of by the man of business. He must always live with the fearful possibility that his work is no good, his daring departure from the safe world a bore to everyone else. And if he lacks talent, no one will care one way or another what revolutionary notions he may entertain. Even after he attains some success, he can go dry and lose his talent. Or he may be taken up and dropped, as tastes change. He remains exposed and on the firing line. When things go wrong the outcome becomes doubly unbearable. He fails twice—in his own mind dwindling alarmingly before the gods, and also in the public mind. The sensitive failed artist runs the risk of dying twice, spiritually and materially, which is why, as Eric Hoffer has shown in *The True Believer*, frustrated individuals of this kind have turned into the most dangerous people on earth: Hitler, Goebbels, Mussolini, etc.

Art can no longer deal satisfactorily with death, and therefore has set out to destroy itself. This means that in decades to come it will gradually cease to be a medium separate from everyday life. Changes in the character of art will take place unevenly and raggedly, with spectacular remissions here and there, comebacks of grand traditions, and so forth. But as we move toward the end of the century the blending of art and mechanics, art and the banal, beatification of the banal, and the uplifting and perhaps glorification of the commonplace, will be part of the race's drive toward eternal life.

The creative leaders of the modern pop movement were among the first to perceive this. John Cage in music or whatever he does; Merce Cunningham in the dance; Robert Rauschenberg in painting and dancing; Andy Warhol in films; William Burroughs (though hardly pop) in prose, randomly cut up or otherwise; and Marshall McLuhan in his deliberately absurdist approach to media, all show the way, or new ways, in which art has begun to approach life and death.

Until now art attempted to rise above death, make excuses for it, courageously to oppose meaninglessness, avowing man's worth ("Hurrah for Karamazov!") or lamenting his end ("Sans teeth, sans eyes, sans taste, sans everything") by means of edited fantasy. With all its superstitious readiness to appease the gods, art has vigorously asserted our primacy in the general scheme of things by insisting on the values of form against chaos. Or this was true until the last decade. Now everything has been changed around. One of many artists can say, apparently with no fear of contradiction: "There is no such thing as form and content; only the experience of the moment."

The enlarging role of today's anti-art has become that of helping us to hide from death. It denies fixed form. All the arts have been influenced by strong tendencies to present life unedited, to draw the audience into the experience so that what happens will be indistinguishable from the way life might actually be at that moment—as opposed to safely observing a fixed representation of life through the prisms and formal structures of somebody else's imagination. The purpose here is to shut out the acute awareness of death—which can no longer be excused or rationalized—by obliterating linear time. The immediate enemy is time passing. Through the talents of our anti-artists we seek to bury individual consciousness as deeply as possible in one sensation after another. Or paradoxically to save ourselves by boredom. When life unreels, let it run as it does in an Andy Warhol film. Console ourselves with the aggressively languid celebration of banality. Let there be no structure, no plan of action, and no explanation for what happens: art no longer explains since life itself is inexplicable.

This type of realism in the face of death was described by Brian O'Doherty in a *Newsweek* essay (1/4/65) as "the comedy of acceptance." In his views "The new move toward acceptance, whether pop acceptance of mass culture, or op [optical] acceptance of physiological sensitivity, is therefore in a large part a movement toward security. At the end of this road, of course, stands the ultimate security—dehumanization." He quotes Andy Warhol: " 'I think everybody should be like everybody. I think everybody should be a machine,' " and a young art critic: " 'Sensitivity is a bore.' "

As O'Doherty points out, the pop movement involves "a whole new strategy to evade extinction." Another such strategy in this period involved the formation of creative Group Souls among younger people. Spiritual collectives such as The Living Theatre of Julian Beck and Judith Malina and the informal family known briefly in the East Village section of New York as the Group Image (two examples out of many), sleeping, singing and playing together, provided a refuge for the previously isolated, frightened identity. Today, of course, in the late 1970s we have religious collectives, some tattered and impoverished, others enormous enterprises such as the Reverend Moon's, that of the Hare Krishna people, and so on, embracing the lost among us in spiritual artworks.

"The Group Image," according to an article in the *Village Voice* [by the late Don McNeill (5/4/67)], "defies labels. It's a tribe. It's a multi-media orchestra. It's an open-ended group with a penchant for anonymity. . . . " In performing, which is really not the word for it, " 'We don't warm up. We don't tune up. We don't do anything like that. It's just sort of a mass sound that starts to happen.' " At one of these more or less impromptu events, the audience came up on stage with the Group members. "The stage was a tangled mass of bodies and the dance floor was practically empty. Then the Group Image, audience and all, seemed to slide off the stage and onto the floor, and the stage was barren. You couldn't tell the Group Image from the audience. 'We wanted to destroy the stage,' one of the Group Image said. Their ambition is to destroy stages everywhere and turn people onto themselves. They want to bring audience involvement to the final phase where the distinction between entertainment and audience dissolves, where the audience, in fact, entertains itself."

The Group Image at that time, and many similar performing groups since, joined in the increasingly common collective embrace of the moment. Members of such units in their carefully unorganized productions no longer have to strive by means of art to cross a bridge to eternity. In Norman Brown's phrase, the participant "is no longer an artist, he has become art." Ideally artists and audiences wrap the environment around themselves, intermingle and evade time and death by escaping into what Norman Mailer has called the "enormous present."

Today art tends less and less to be exclusive. The entire culture has been invited into it. Electronics and engineering contribute to kinetic and luminous sculpture. We have "the poetry of technology." McLuhan informs us that the environment itself has become our story—and now artists, engineers and businessmen, bankers, stock brokers, the lot, many smoking marijuana and listening to the same guitars, have found a common playground.

This escape into a mind-blowing, continuously exploding *Now* moves from one environmental form to another at a frantic pace. Thus, as long ago as August 1967, the critic and reporter John Gruen felt impelled to ask in *Vogue:* "Why is it that such people as Marshall McLuhan, Andy Warhol or Allen Ginsberg are already beginning to suggest an aura of the passé and déjà vu?" His answer: "It's because something else is brewing. . . ." Some time ago "The New Bohemia began to merge the arts, creating Intermedia, Happenings, Lightworks, Combines, and Environments, and went further still by merging all the merged arts with electronics, engineering—to bring about a dazzling, if often erratic and inconclusive, display of bravura and daring—all of it designed to discombobulate and jar the senses."

In this way, Intermedia served a purpose similar to that, in its beginnings, of the period's therapeutic rioting and massive, shouting invasions of college administrative offices. Sporadic liberation from time (and the horrible Viet Nam war taking place in it, and prospects of the draft) was achieved by calculated confusion. Sensory bombardment then, and now still, had and has the effect of making us forget meaninglessness and our mortality, and—for too many—the passing of swift, unsatisfactory years by loud and dazzling interference with word-thoughts. According to the multimedia poet and mixing specialist Gerd Stern: "Here, we create an overload situation where you can't bring in all of your critical baggage. The techniques block out the analytical and judgmental faculties. . . ."

The arts of fragmentation have as their mission to break the fearful self apart, and to provide ersatz death and rebirth simulations. In order to stay young forever, the wandering psyche embraces electronic Buddhism. The pandemonium of sensory circuses drives out the feeling of identity. In this environment the lost self finds protective non-existence, since if it does not really exist it can not be killed. Within this framework the artists and technologists administer their kinetic environments to the superstitious folk of our time in the manner of boomalaying witch doctors driving out evil spirits—this spirit, the self, being called evil because it dies.

Among large numbers of people, mostly young, art and life-style have turned into the same thing. While for many the prevailing life-style involves a collective flight from death, this need not be. Nor need the remedy for death be the deliberate stupefaction of the intellect or the denial of scientific exploration.

A more virile alternative was projected a dozen years ago by Norman Mailer in his essay, "The White Negro." The American existentialist, the hipster, described by Mailer, "knows that if our collective condition is to live with instant death by atomic war, relatively quick death by the state as *l'univers concentrationnaire,* or with a slow death by conformity with every creative and rebellious instinct stifled . . . if the faith of twentieth century man is to live with death from adolescence to premature senescence, why then the only life-giving answer is to accept the terms of death, to live with death as immediate danger, to divorce oneself from society, to exist without roots, to set out on that uncharted journey into the rebellious imperatives of the self. . . ."

The existentialist, psychopath, saint, bullfighter and lover "remain in life only by engaging death." Such an art or life-style "often takes disproportionate courage. So it is no accident that the source of Hip is the Negro. . . . Any Negro who wishes to live must live with danger from his first day, and no experience can ever be casual to him. . . ."

Mailer's view of life as performance at all times in the presence of death, with every man and woman as a performer, brings life and art together in a fiercely demanding play. It requires, as does Heidegger's approach, that close to death as we are, we still perform—not to appease imaginary gods or to score on an imaginary astral machine, but simply to *be*.

The code of North American *machismo* has its limitations. For one thing, there appears to be little room for mercy in it. Second, the commandment to perform well and be with it at all times seems to exclude the functional collapse of the ego, the occasionally useful sensation of being lost and in tears, of breaking apart—in short, means of simulated death and rebirth. As Norman Brown stresses in another context, "Dionysian experience can only be bought at the price of ego-dissolution." For Mailer's hipster this would seem to be virtually impossible—and according to his code, weak and therefore immoral—to achieve except through violence. Thirdly, and far more important, the existential style of which Mailer speaks, while in many ways admirable, can and ought to have an end beyond performance itself. Doing tricks in the presence of death is not enough. We can direct our *machismo* toward a more ambitious end: to see to it that death will no longer be our audience; to storm over the footlights and try to destroy this unwanted presence that makes us dance.

True, the life-style or art simply of being your own man, your own woman, living in the constant awareness of challenge and possible danger, is a beautiful style. As Mailer has said, black people, especially in the United States, have become the models for it. Claude Brown writes in *Esquire*: "Soul is bein' true to yourself, to what is *you*. Now, hold on: soul is . . . that . . . uninhibited . . . no, *extremely* uninhibited self . . . expression that goes into practically every Negro endeavor. That's soul. And there's swagger in it, man. It's exhibitionism, and it's effortless. Effortless. You don't need to put it on; it just comes out."

Soul emerged as the answer to oppression. But when the day-to-day emergency ends, will it be useful in countering the cosmic oppression, which is death? We will see whether the art and life form of soul will be able to survive once black identity triumphantly comes on, when black retribution has been visited on the oppressors, and all that has been gone through.

The immortalist view is that the art of living freely and bravely in an ever-changing now need not exclude the systematic hunting down, cornering and destruction of death. We can live a "perpetual, uncalculated life in the present" without hiding in the present. We need not pay the price of letting death have its way by ruling out work, discipline and planning.

Enjoyment of the present and at the same time carrying on, without cynicism or discouragement, our Permanent Revolution against Death can be managed if we learn properly to maneuver our various time-experiences to allow both for random exuberance and for order. This means living, as many of us do now, in more than one zone of experience, each governed by different sorts of time. The technique will be to avoid remaining in any single zone of action for too long. Instead, renew ourselves by moving easily, without stress or confusion, from one theater of experience to another. The ideal (until death is conquered) : escape the fear of nothingness by living multiple lives in one. To an extent, many people are already doing this.

XIV

TIME AND GAMES

. . . In existential time, which is akin to eternity, there is no distinction between the future and the past, between the end and the beginning. In it the eternal accomplishment of the mystery of the spirit takes place. Time is not the image of eternity, time is eternity which has collapsed into ruin.

BERDYAEV

The game is simply the totality of the rules which describe it.

JOHN VON NEUMANN AND
OSKAR MORGENSTERN

We grow older, toward death, in the day-by-day linear passage of the hours. This "real" time in which we live in a mortal and limited way offers no discharge from the war. It remains our life-long combat zone, and like soldiers, if we are to keep our sanity, we must be rotated out of it every once in a while.

Hence, men and women are always trying to get out of

real time, to shift their activities into parallel ribbons and blocks of time. Millions take refuge in the divine world of games, because the management and manipulation of time, especially in game form, helps us to feel young.

Still new and fascinating to humanity, television—as Marshall McLuhan forecast—will soon connect the people of the global village in a single network of energy. Millions now turn on together and are present at the same event, and as we watch it on the screen this event passes through all of us. Television unreels a communal ribbon of experience, providing each member of the audience with a parallel life track which travels alongside his own. We have in effect another life, the television existence. Sometimes it moves beside us on a second level. On other occasions, the television tape and our own unreeling life become as one, when, say, we join the march honoring the memory of Martin Luther King, Jr. while sitting in an armchair.

During periods of emergency, sudden moves for war or peace, at election time or during a riot, I have had the feeling, without television, of being walled off, having no window on events. In this frame of mind, lacking TV, I feel out of touch with humanity. The trouble is, were I to step out of doors and actually try to see with my own eyes what was going on I could at best be in only one place; whereas television seems to put me in the center of the world and bring the entire mix of that day's history for me to watch with my feet up on a stool. Perhaps this massive and also passive sharing of the experience that comes out of the tube represents for millions the beginning in rudimentary form of an electronically-born communal consciousness.

Television—though the medium itself may be riddled by false time values—releases me from my own lonely time. It carries me instantly to other worlds and zones of being where death is not real. In the side-by-side worlds

of my living room and the passing television scene (with
TV Guide to help) we look out passively on eternal
games. The family sits with gods and goddesses on late-
night shows listening to them talk, watching them grow
angry and argue and laugh together. Or staying with a
late movie, I may go to the refrigerator for a beer, the
cowboy in the frontier town is also having a beer, and
then the commercial comes on showing the fellows at
the tavern hoisting their beers, and I join them and the
cowboy too.

As life and television blend into a single ribbon of ex-
perience, it becomes increasingly difficult to say which
track is more real. Because having hung in front of the
screen for too many days and nights, incorporating TV
into me and transferring the sensitive part of my being
into it, *I* may gradually have turned unreal—and in this
way the shadow of a man attends flesh and blood events
passing before him in color.

Obviously, if the lives we lead all day long did not age
and trouble us, or if we were not bored by them, people
would not bury themselves in television. Our aim seems to
be to escape the human condition by living in multiple
time zones.

Television is only one of many sanctuaries. Acutely
aware that everyone's journey leads to a bottomless pit,
the anxious soul, we know, tries to reach a state of im-
mortality now. The generations manage this differently.
The middle-aged do it with martinis, or find safety is-
lands in the living deaths of roulette, bingo, bridge and
canasta. Many younger people escape from linear time
(meaningless progression to death) by means of mari-
juana. This does not stun the senses but sharpens them
as we drift free. Psychedelic flights, as we have seen, carry
us out farther on journeys in which we can die without
dying and feel born again. Such travels take us to unex-
plored areas where, as Timothy Leary has said, "The uni-

verse within our skulls is infinitely more than the flimsy game-world which our words and minds create."

More acceptably, skiing, driving fast, racing of all kinds, also remove time from us. On another level the hours can be splintered by the rhythmic fall of pins in the bowling alley. One more zone of suspended time is that filled by the voice of the radio disk jockey. His delivery, so rapid as to be incomprehensible (to adults), condenses standard speech in order to annihilate the intervals between rock 'n roll numbers. The final explosion of pop-time takes place in the discotheque. Here crashing chords, acoustical bombs bursting in air, lightworks and intermingled films, knock out all doubt and fear until morning.

Games—that is, formal sports and pastimes—may be the best simulators of eternal life that humanity has at its disposal. They take place in their own special time, and no other, on the playground of immortality. It is true that games begin, mature and end like a person's life. (An endless game would have no point.) The contests, especially within the framework of league play, should be understood as successive existences, little forms of reincarnation in which we participate directly while playing, or vicariously as spectators.

Sport is death-free play, and games shut out death. We have the commonly-recognized but still quite amazing circumstance that for masses of people around the world the outcome of football, baseball, soccer, basketball and boxing matches can sometimes be far more important than actual wars and revolutions. In wartime Europe, American soldiers returning from the front with their heads bandaged would yell at reporters: "How're the Dodgers doing?" For them, a World Series contested by older men and draft-rejects had more emotional impact than the World War.

Why does a grown-up alumnus moan and carry on when the old team loses? Why has it become necessary for moats to be dug around Latin American football fields to save referees from being torn apart? Ask again why national shame and mourning must be involved when, say, Brazil's cup team loses to Hungary? And furthermore not only the uneducated succumb to this madness. Oxford dons can be depressed by bad news from the cricket pitch.

With a few exceptions, the theater offers nothing like this, since any play created from a script must be a fixed contest. Author, director, and actors all know how it is going to come out. But you never know how a game will end. During the action, unexpected heroes and goats emerge. The underdog rises up and outplays the favorite. The momentum shifts. Pandemonium. But the team of desire strikes back, and the moral advantage shifts its way. Then—a sudden break, arrival of the counter-hero "changes the complexion of the game." What now? Will he? Triumph, exhaustion, despair. Wait until next time. The theater can seldom match this; the only dramatic equivalent would be an entirely improvised play in which the characters themselves would not know from moment to moment how the action was going to end.

The madness of spectators and the dedication of the players can best be understood if such games are viewed as man-made immortality rites. They take place in time zones relating only to the particular sport. The coaches and players becomes masters of time. In football, for instance, we become connoisseurs of managed time. At the close of the first half, or near game's end, we "eat up" and "kill" the clock, "control the clock," or "let the clock run." Or we take time out, and make it do special tricks.

The stadium turns into a pit of the gods in which heroes fight to become divine. And trailing behind them come the legions—all of us, fans and spectators—who derive our being, our excellence, and our own worthiness to be converted into gods from the performance of our heroic representatives.

By itself one game or another may be only incidentally enjoyable, and only a few are likely to be crucial. Far more significant, and what builds up the hysteria attending public games, will be the long-term standing of the clubs and of individual players. Immortal possibilities are recorded in the form of statistics and of league standings. These form the steps in the ladders of excellence leading to heaven. As part of our split-level experience of sport—compounded by television's split screens and its instant replays, stopping time and immortalizing chosen moments, running them over and over again—we experience the game statistically as we watch the action.

In ice hockey we simultaneously appreciate not only the goal but the assist, the number of goals the left-winger now has for the season, how many pucks have gone by the goal tender this year, which teams have scored most against him, and so on. In basketball we have the same, minus the goal tender and with the addition of rebounds and frequent foul shots. American football and baseball give the impression that the athletes are playing on a field of statistics rather than dirt and grass. Every play is immediately incorporated into an endless network of achievement. A football game provides the spectators with no more than eleven or twelve minutes of actual playing time, when something is happening on the field. Most of the game is spent unpiling, trotting back to the huddle, and planning the next attack. In other words, what we pay to witness, for the most part, is periods of tension building to the next action. During this interval everybody thinks about strategy, tactics, past performance, probabilities—in this way nothing but somehow everything is happening, furiously, as if the statistics themselves were contending furiously above the battlefield while the players rested.

Ridiculous as they may seem at times, these elaborate sets of supporting figures endow the game with meaning by relating it to the entire sporting universe. For immortality-hunters, statistics make imprints on the stars. They make it possible for players, experts and fans to live in a beautifully-enclosed artificial cosmos, in a death-free time of man's own making. All mysteries vanish. We have no need to ask the "meaning" of professional football. It means what it *is*.

The management of games provides us a clue to the satisfying management of immortality. We will see that in the Utopia Beyond Time, our present game structures can serve as models for the structures of the successive lives that each man and woman will someday live out in eternity. Or, expressed in a formula:

$$\frac{\text{GAMES}}{\text{IN THIS LIFE}} = \frac{\text{SUCCESSIVE LIVES}}{\text{IN ETERNITY}}$$

This means that in eternity historical time would be replaced by a variety of game times. Put another way, if each of us had the power to live indefinitely, such a state would require simulations of clock time, just as artificial gravity must be provided for the colonizers of space. A certain emotional gravity will have to be offered restless natures newly freed from death. Only then can all human activities be enjoyed as games. And they will be taken seriously, with emotional commitments, as millions of us now take football.

XV

THE GREAT DEFIANCE

. . . the great defiance which turns us again and again into the enemies of God and of our fellow men, even of our own selves. This defiance in us all is the sin, the lord and master we serve, for whom and by whom we are paid in return with death. This is the only reward this lord and master can offer; it is the only one we deserve. . . .

KARL BARTH

In his inspirational sermon to the prisoners of Zurich, Karl Barth precisely defines the human situation. He describes death as the great "no" to mankind, and as "the shadow that hangs over our human life and accompanies all its movement." What he denounces as the great defiance of this condition is nothing other than man's drive to live forever in the flesh.

The formidable evangelist goes on in great, rolling phrases, first to frighten the prisoners with the specter of advancing death, and secondly, at the last moment, to extend hope of salvation: "Jesus volunteered in our behalf to pocket the wages of sin. The wages of *our* sin were paid on Easter morning." The preacher affirms to his audience that "the free gift of God is eternal life." This comes as the "joyous outcome of the Easter story." It is no such thing, of course—the theologian himself has just died, and so will the convicts. We have once again the beautifully articulated, ancient cowardly counsel: accept, accept; kneel to the gods, only they can decree eternal life for us. (And furthermore if you don't kneel, your sin may rub off on me.)

Barth could not be much more eloquent, and the listener finds it exciting and pleasing to let himself be carried along on these superstitious flights, but only for a while. Sooner or later we come back down, unsaved, with brute death still there. Then, for some, a new and not particularly consoling revelation may be at hand: that phantasmic gods will not help us, nor "natural order" (which, since it kills us, is precisely what must be violated), and that the old crime of hubris—with all its attendant psychological dangers for self-punishing man—committed systematically, in the open, has become our only chance of achieving salvation. Therefore we will appropriate Barth's term, but celebrate the Great Defiance rather than damn it.

Needed, for one thing, is a bold new attitude. We must stop apologizing to the cosmos and affirm who we are. Having invented the gods, we can turn into them. Death no longer fits into our plans. Conceivably suitable for animals and plants, meaningless extinction becomes improper when inflicted on a species possessing ability to reflect and care about meaning. Five thousand years ago the evolution of human intelligence made death, as applied to our side, inappropriate and obsolescent. Today, with advance elements of humanity no longer able to tolerate eventual non-being, either death must soon become obsolete or *we* will.

Alan Watts has said that "the normal state of consciousness in our culture is both the context and the

breeding ground of mental disease." From the immortal-
ist standpoint, it would be amazing if this were not true.
Individually we find ourselves, in Ortega's image, in the
position of being brought asleep into a crowded theater,
and suddenly wakened there, to perform as best we can.

We awaken, as Heidegger says, "thrown" onto this
whirling, wobbling stage to take part in a senseless drama
that always comes to the same end. Nature generates the
actor, tells him a little about life and death, and then
whimsically kills him. In Pascal's succinct review: "The
last act is tragic, however happy all the rest of the play
is; at the last a little earth is thrown upon our head, and
that is the end for ever."

With darkness closing in, Tolstoy's Ivan Ilyitch cries
out to the silence around him: "I shall not be, but what
will be? There will be nothing. Then, where shall I be
when I am no more? Will that be death? No, I will not
have it!" And: "Would it might come very soon! What
very soon? Death, blackness? No, no. Anything rather
than death!" Near the end: "He wept over his helpless-
ness, over his terrible loneliness, over the cruelty of men,
over the cruelty of God, over the absence of God."

Only the hypocritical, it would seem, could conceive of
this torment endured by dying people as being anything
less than a cosmic outrage. "He can run, but he can't
hide." This has now become the position of transitional
man; our position as pre-immortalists. We live and work
in a mad factory operated by an Unknown Employer. All
we know is that monstrous conditions prevail. Every now
and then, for no apparent reason, someone on the assem-
bly line is crushed out by an overhanging machine. We
weep over the vanished one, who is then carted off to
some oven or dumping ground, and the work goes on. No
wonder we see humanity everywhere, by one means or
another, going on strike against these conditions.

Unfortunately, the strike tends to be conducted passively or self-destructively (for example, drinking too much), or in stupid and uncoordinated fashion. Struggling against death, we wreak violence on one another. Humanity has gone wrong here: we forget that we are brothers and sisters in the same trap.

How much better to unite our energies in the fight against extinction, instead of in opposition to one another. First, we have to organize against the gods of our own superstition, against the imaginary machine in the sky which we have always supposed to be measuring our efforts. We must understand that all ambition of the driven and anxiously competitive sort is founded on superstition—the idea that the gods or the sky-calculator will judge our score and accordingly approve or deny our bids for immortality. It may seem ridiculous to insist on it, but we must each clearly understand, particularly when self-esteem trembles, that there *is* no recording angel, no recording apparatus, to measure our bids for membership in the Olympian Society; that failure will *not* cause us to be blackballed in heaven as it does on earth; that we are all in this together, with neither competition nor competitive scores counting for anything except on earth. Knowing this, we can much more easily work together in a practical way, taking part in the laboratory revolution against death, or backing it with interest and support as best we can. Symbolically, it is time to parade and picket together. Our signs held aloft in defiance of Natural Law and all the non-existent lords of destiny should proclaim but one message: DON'T ACCEPT THIS DEAL!

Imagine being the only person on earth who is going to die, while all others around you live on. You vanish into the black void; they wake up every morning and walk in the sun. How unfair, if not excruciating—and, so far as we know, this will be precisely the fate of each one of us. Why Should Not Old Men Be Mad? Yeats asked—and indeed, in our circumstances why not all of us? Humanity may congratulate itself for not having long since gone out of its head. Still, the sages chide us. Our justified neurosis is called wrong-headed, as though recoiling from oblivion were completely uncalled for.

Barth quotes Luther's rendition of the ninetieth Psalm: "Teach us to remember that we must die, that we may become wise." And expanding this message to the poor prisoners of Zurich, the evangelist cries out: " '*Teach* us!' Give us, grant us, create within us the readiness and the ability to remember that we must die! You, O Lord God, must teach us to number our days, like a teacher teaches the alphabet and the two-plus-two to a little child who cannot know these things by himself. . . . "

Greater men give us the same song. Jacques Maritain: " . . . The man who knows that 'after all, death is only an episode' is ready to give himself with humility." An episode! When I read in the paper "Banker Dies After Long Illness" . . . How do I react? Probably I think of it as a 'deplorable episode', and no more—but only because I do not make his disgracefully agonizing "long illness" real enough in my imagination. No, even after the pain, for both Maritain and me, there will be no mere "episode" but a permanent blackout. When the world and I vanish from one another, the world ends too!

Voices preaching false consolation will not help us, no matter how skillfully and soothingly they arrange nothingness. Alan Watts' for one:

. . . death seems simply to be a return to that unknown inwardness out of which we were born. This is not to say that death, biologically speaking, is reversed birth. It is rather that the truly inward source of one's life was never born, but has always remained inside, somewhat as the life remains in the tree, though the fruits may come and go. Outwardly, I am one apple among many. Inwardly, I am the tree.

This may be appraised as fine writing, and even a valid perception of our place in nature (so far), but it serves also to pretty up and glamorize death, and therefore, in the context of humanity's long battle, to weaken and tranquilize our rebellion.

In his essay *The Ideology of Death* Herbert Marcuse disposes of all such complacency:

The exhortation to make death "one's own" is hardly more than a premature reconciliation with unmastered natural forces. A brute biological fact, permeated with pain, horror and despair, is transformed into an existential privilege. From the beginning to the end, philosophy has exhibited this strange masochism—and sadism, for the exaltation of one's own death involves the exaltation of the death of others . . .

In Arizona, I have seen an elderly Princeton man nearly terminal with cancer groveling in a faith-healer's tent, with sawdust all over him, begging for the charlatan's hand to be placed on his brow. And when the healer decided that day to bless all the sufferers at once instead of one by one, there being too many, the man from Nassau who had actually thrown money after him, began bellowing in agony: "No, no! On *me!*" until the hand of the sawdust master was laid on him.

Then there is John the delivery man with one lung already cut out wandering near the corner watching the people go by. His neck has withered to a stalk. His eyes are huge, shining with terror. Too bad he doesn't understand that his forthcoming annihilation is "part of life."

"The Babe died a beautiful death," a priest reported years ago when Babe Ruth died. "It's a privilege to die of cancer," said a New Bedford, Mass. priest, because he had time to prepare himself for grace. I saw one of the prettiest girls alive carried away within weeks by a wild mole, and her roommate said: "If Helen dies, I'll never go to church again."

Beauty and heroism should not blind us to the great Abuse, as Camus once described it. What in the world is there to worship or accept in a system that makes cancer, among other ills and misfortunes, part of life? I wish I could blind my intelligence, retaining the gift of clever dialogue, and turn into one of those fashionably intellectual Roman Catholics or High Episcopalians, filled with hip and haughty simulation of belief in a conservative mystery. Or even bury myself in the Buddhist's vivid present. But I know, and so do they all at two o'clock in the morning, that these formulas and pathways serve finally as systematized evasions of the void. (I anticipate my own probable death-bed cowardice, and even a possible conversion to some sort of faith, but until that time comes I will be straight.)

The immortalist argument holds this ground and will not step back from it: that death from deterioration of the body is an outrage and should be unceremoniously treated as such. "Do not go gentle into that good night" does not apply here. Rather aim not to go at all; mobilize the scientists, spend the money, and hunt death down like an outlaw. Go with Yeats, who confronted "that discourtesy of death." Or Ernest Renan:

I find death loathful, hateful, and senseless when it extends its coldly blind hand toward virtue and genius. A voice tells us unceasingly [that] "truth and goodness are the aims of your life; sacrifice everything else to these goals"; but when we arrive toward the end of our journey where we should have found our reward . . . this philosophy, which promised us the secret of death, excuses itself with an embarrassed stammer.

Railing against the end, of course, serves no purpose. Herbert Marcuse comes in with the clue we need, a beautiful imperative: Have "the good conscience to be a coward." Be afraid, but not passively so, not shivering, "accepting", and hiding. Also go beyond the bravado of Hemingway's and Mailer's grace-under-pressure style. Rather sweat out this fear in attacking action directed against its source, the very way in which the life process works—and change that.

Centuries ago Marcus Aurelius placed us in the situation that, unhappily, still defines who and what we are:

Of human life the time is a point, and the substance is in a flux, and the perception dull, and the composition of the whole body subject to putrefaction, and the soul a whirl, and fortune hard to define, and fame a thing devoid of judgment. And, to say all in a word, everything which belongs to the body is a stream, and what belongs to the soul is a dream and vapour, and life is a warfare and a stranger's sojourn, and after-fame is oblivion. . . .

Faced with this dubious scene, the man of today does his best to escape feelings of helplessness, lunging about, variously envisioning himself, in the words of one psychiatrist, as "a piece of shit, a wolf, a chicken, or a whirlwind." Or, he might have added, a saint. This goal has become increasingly popular, and the concept of sainthood hopelessly vulgarized to include the holiness of misanthropy and violence. The late comedian Lenny Bruce has been called a secular saint. Sartre has made Jean Genet a saint, and we have also Che Guevara, Allen Ginsberg, and others. Since the qualifications for holy orders have been eased, a new order of saintliness may be suggested here—to which, with courage, we may all aspire.

Our source, if not our conclusion, is Roman Catholic. Jacques Maritain had said it: "What takes place in the soul of a saint at the crucial moment when he makes his first irrevocable decision . . . I would say a simple refusal—not a movement or revolt which is temporary, or of despair, which is passive—rather a simple refusal, a total, stable, supremely active refusal to accept things as they are." This involves " . . . the inner act of rupture, of break concerned with an existential fact: things as they are are not tolerable, positively, definitely not tolerable."

Of course, Maritain's saint has a goal very different—at least on the surface—from that of the immortalist. As the philosopher expresses it:

Evil—I mean the power of sin, and the universal suffering it entails, the rot of nothingness that gnaws everywhere —evil is such that the only thing at hand which can remedy it, and which inebriates the saint with freedom and exaltation and love, is to give up everything, the sweetness of the world, and what is good, and what is better, and what is pleasurable and permissible, in order to be free with God; it is to be totally stripped and to give himself totally in order to lay hold of the power of the Cross; it is to die for those he loves. . . ."

Maritain starts out on the right path. Sainthood does indeed begin with the inspired and inspiring "simple refusal" of the current human condition, for the simplest of reasons: "things as they are are not tolerable." What is intolerable? "The rot of nothingness that gnaws everywhere." At this point, once more, we come up against the centuries-old Christian confusion: failure to identify "evil" as a state of mind and action arising initially from the fear of death. The saint is rebelling against death. The rot he finds unacceptable is the neurosis of the race around him, the sickliness of all the half-rebels taking refuge in symbols and superstition. He correctly observes that the struggle for immortality and the competition between man and man for eternal life is cruel and undignified, and that it smells both of vanity and fear. Therefore, he abandons the competition, the scramble for divinity. He abandons all "side" and self-promotion. Content to "be totally stripped and to give himself totally," that saint of which Maritain speaks comes to understand —through an agonized reversal, in a paroxysm of simulated rebirth—that one remedy for the fear of death is to embrace death. Through the simple refusal of fear, he frees himself to love God and others. Now a paradox: freed to love human creatures as they are, to go with life as it is, he comes around to defending the human condition he once rebelled against, and we have one more tamed revolutionary.

All saints must be better and more profound than the rest of us. And almost by definition it is graceless to criticize them, but the the unfortunate truth must be insisted on: Christian saints, valorous in spirit though they may be, undertake to cover over and justify the pointless sufferings of mankind, and—in all nobility—to pacify and head off humanity's revolution against death, of which (unconsciously) they were once leaders.

From the immortalist point of view, whoever teaches us to accept or, worse, embrace death in this world cannot be the last word in saints. A new kind of sainthood calls to us. We begin, like all past saints, with the "simple refusal." What must the new saint refuse? First, the acceptability of aging and death. Second, we who aspire to the new order of saintliness will rigorously refuse our own superstitions. We will simply not permit them to take hold in our psyches. We will, above all, resign from the competition for the gods' favor, knowing that this rat-race takes place under the auspices of fear, the fear of extinction—which, the saint recognizes is what impels us to confront one another in destructive games.

We will abstain from cruelty, recognizing its source as despair over death and meaninglessness. Out of this very despair, we will do what we can to build a new brotherhood; unflinchingly acknowledge our vulnerability to death. The new saint will then pledge not to injure others in the old scramble for preeminence but join with others in the race's no longer disguised hunt for immortality.

The new saint will not seek to die for those he loves but to live fully and exuberantly for himself and them. He will never forget that he is a rebel. He will understand that sheer performance, style and grace under pressure is no longer enough unless placed in the service of a remorseless and unsentimental drive against mortality itself.

XVI

THE FUTURE OF
UNNATURAL MAN

Modern man, however, must build his own personal world, after making himself lord and master of his own life and death . . .

LUDWIG BINSWANGER

The being that exists is man. Man alone exists. Rocks are, but they do not exist. Trees are, but they do not exist. Horses are, but they do not exist. Angels are, but they do not exist. God is, but he does not exist.

HEIDEGGER

Nature is not holy; it is not sacred. Certainly it preceded and formed us. It can never rightfully be ours to abuse. It is not for us to slaughter and abuse, and we must stop this or die. Yet in the end, only we are holy and sacred, because conscious. So long as we remember: our pleasure and fulfillment depend on moving with the natural energy that flows through us and all things—and also on controlling and redirecting that stream of energy whenever it (floods, fires, plague) threatens our well-being. We are that part of nature capable of re-ordering all the rest and turning inside out the very processes that brought us into being.

Prevalent for some time has been the intellectually chic view that man himself—particularly insofar as his consciousness has become highly developed—can best be understood as a disease, and all his activities as a sort of cosmic excrescence. The metaphor of Human Life as Defect appeals to great minds and small. It was a theme of Thomas Mann's in *The Magic Mountain*. We have from Jung: ". . . life itself is a disease with a very bad prognosis; it lingers on for years, only to end with death . . . normality is a general constitutional defect . . . man is an animal with a fatally overgrown brain. . . . " Jacques Choron takes note of Schopenhauer's conception that individuality in itself is a "wrong" because "at bottom every individual is really only a special error, a false step, something that had better not be. We are at bottom something that ought not to be; therefore we cease to be." Similarly Ludwig Klages decided that consciousness is the enemy of life and will destroy it, while Edgar Daqué concluded that man is a freak, "a sick primate." For Norman Brown "all organic life is then sick. . . . Our sickness is part of some universal sickness in nature." Buber calls birth "catastrophic separation." We have ". . . stepped out of the glowing darkness of chaos into the cool light of creation." This is bad, Alan Watts believes: "The opposition of human order to material chaos is false." Again bright men join in foisting on us this curiously seductive self-contempt. What strange being is this which enjoys describing itself as a disease, mistake, freak and defect of nature?

Another form of self-contempt has emerged in recent years. Thousands of readers enjoy descriptions of themselves—in books such as *The Naked Ape, The Territorial Imperative,* and *On Aggression*—in which men are depicted as being little different from animals. The essential corruption of our species has been dramatized in still another way in William Golding's *Lord of the Flies*. Here children on an island demonstrate mankind's basic cruelty. For some reason, the insistence on our fundamental brutishness comforts many people, perhaps because it seems to remove responsibility from them when they act in an inhuman fashion.

Consider the metaphor that humanity and life itself must be sick, and that consciousness has made our kind ill. True, life on the planet may now kill itself, and if this should happen, human consciousness will indeed be the agent of death. Even without war, the stupid disposition of radioactive wastes, pesticides and detergents; contamination by smog, willful overpopulation or massive worldwide psychosis, can bring us down fairly soon. In such an event, any sterile survivors wandering about will have the gloomy satisfaction of pointing out that humanity was sick, that thoughts of death drove the species crazy, and so it killed itself, possibly deserving to die. The murderer of life on earth could properly be identified as Unnatural Man.

Still, we may take heart. Our doom is not dictated, since we have choice. And if we do not have choice, then disaster was fated from the beginning, and who can be blamed? Alan Watts reminds us of Goethe's observation: "The most unnatural also is nature. . . . Even in resisting her laws one obeys them; and one works with her even in desiring to work against her."

Now we find ourselves in a tricky game. Suppose Nature on this planet has always "intended"; that is, has always been programmed to kill itself. Bewilderingly, wheels within wheels turn in opposite directions. If the long-range natural intent has been to foul and ultimately destroy the earth, then our detergents, smog and atomic bombs have all, according to plan, gone into the service of a suicidal Mother Nature, and our corruption of the environment by synthetic materials may be seen as part of the game. But if the natural intent of life is to continue without end—though species and individuals within the process flourish, evolve and die in their turn—then we, our revolutionary kind, may be a wild element in the cosmos, in that the overriding (if until lately disguised) drive for personal immortality has intruded to change all the rules.

Whatever the original program may have been, a new game evidently began as soon as human consciousness freed itself from what Bertrand Russell has called "the blind empire of matter." The race has now become deeply engaged in the risky and supremely fascinating game of Tampering With All Things; a game that, given consciousness, had to be played. There can be no point in complaining about this or trying to back out. Rather we must play well and win: the survival of all consciousness depends on the outcome. (Anyhow, it is not our fault that we are conscious. And, looking at the larger wheel, nature, by choosing to bring us forth, started a risky game with *her*self.)

There can be no question that Unnatural Man displays some appalling symptoms of hostility toward himself and his own environment. Among the worst of these may be his tendencies to foul the waters, air and earth, and to insult the beauty of the world with trash of every description, billboards and abandoned automobiles. When Timothy Leary said: "My cells hate metal," he was striking back, as so many younger people have in the last few years, against the desecration of flesh and earth by alloys originally intended to resist deterioration.

Perhaps we litter the world like a camp site partly out of a despairing and angry feeling that the earth is not our own. Each of us has only a short-term lease on life. Possibly if the litterer felt that the earth really belonged to him (believed in some sort of resurrection or return) he would not sack and insult the landscape. Separated from nature and assaulting the earth in destructive and unbecoming fashion, millions may be judged sick, with un-belief their illness. The immortalist conviction is that only belief in rebirth or the actual achievement of eternal life can restore the humanity of these separated people. Such as Billy Graham hear a call to give repeated injec-tions of faith to an unbelieving citizenry. But shots of this kind lose their potency after a while. We find our-selves unfortunately on the verge of concluding that the race has entered a period of dangerous emotional illness which only the renewed and believed-in promise of im-mortality can heal.

But what may meaningfully be defined as "sick" or viewed as "unnatural?" Bertrand Russell answers: "We are ourselves the ultimate and irrefutable arbiters of value, and in the world of value Nature is only a part. Thus in this world we are greater than Nature . . . It is we who create value and our desires which confer value. In this realm we are kings, and we debase our kingship if we bow down to nature."

The sickness of any living unit relates to the disorder-ing and breaking of its form. A "sick"—ripening before rotting—cheese would help keep well a man who might otherwise starve. One form's sickness or death contrib-utes to another form's survival. Thus, an illness becomes sick when treated with penicillin. We speak of a sick plant, tree or forest afflicted with blight, but never, after spraying, of a "sick blight." Hence, sickness and health must be seen as value judgments applied to stages of a form's bloom and decay—with the choice of one term or the other depending on whether we like that particular form and want it to live. A field of poppies will not be considered overgrown with weeds, because the blooms strike us as beautiful. The concept of a "cure," then, re-mains wholly relative. The curing of any illness involves destruction of that illness' own form. A lawn is "cured" of weeds or crab grass; if the flowers unexpectedly die, a garden is never said to have been "cured" of roses. Life kills life. As Dr. Alex Comfort (famed as an authority on aging long before delivering to us *The Joy of Sex*) has observed, cancer cells may be "subversive," bent on preserving themselves and escaping the general debilitation of the sinking body.

Now, looking again at Unnatural Man, should he be viewed as healing agent or disease in the planetary order of things? To the gods looking down, if there were any, he might by now appear as a blight as well as potential threat, and they would then be wise to weed him out.

Must death, we may ask once more, be "natural" for men? Only if they permit it. In the days of "either-or," we could assert belligerently that either we are free of nature and different from the rest, or we are following nature. If free, we are not bound by the "natural" dictates that control other forms. If we follow, then nature must have included our rebellion in her plans. Or if she did not, then she can hardly be all-powerful, and made a mistake, in which case we need not bow down and worship her, nor embrace death as being a necessary end for our privileged species.

But why impose either-or strictures on the Wheel of Being? Say perhaps—to set up the verbal ground rules for the struggle against death—that we are simultaneously both following and reordering the life process. We may properly imagine ourselves to be the climactic end product of consciousness, our species designed by nature (but also supremely self-designated) to carry out an evolutionary decision. This decision has called for nature to turn on itself, countermand its own laws and produce immortal beings. Infected by the human virus, it releases its higher intelligences from the birth-death cycle.

Biophysics Professor Robert L. Sinsheimer of the California Institute of Technology has pointed out that living organisms today have had the benefit of billions of years of selective molecular evolution. "Soon," he has said, "we shall have that cumulative ingenuity at our fingertips, as well as in our fingertips, and with it not only the power to alter the natural world but also the power to alter ourselves. . . . " We, the divine part, ascend over the whole, envelop the whole, turn the tennis ball inside out. The animate and fully conscious envelops and controls the inanimate. We—the form of life that reflects and questions itself—enclose, rule over, shape, invade, order, give meaning to and push around not only other life forms but all the rocks and dust whirling in space, residues of the very energy of which we are composed.

"The saving thought is that it is man who has these vistas," Dr. George Wald, Professor of Biology at Harvard recently observed. "Without our like, the universe might be, but not be known. Our grace is in knowing." Neither light years nor microscopic infinity need frighten us. Quintillions of molecular forms, a drifting assemblage of rocks—what is so impressive about the sheer multiplicity of things? There may be as many cells in my little finger as there are stars in the Milky Way. It doesn't matter. We are the cosmic virus. Galactic convulsions may some day be wrought by this tiny speck of the whole. Endless systems of rocks, a universal scrap heap, can become our building stones to be glued together and used as a base for satellite worlds whenever we need them. We will learn to manipulate the planet's own magnetic field. We will throw aloft shields of particles against cosmic rays. We will learn to forecast space cataclysms and guard against nova explosions that took place millions of years ago. One day we will discover how to navigate our globe like a new Noah's Ark, and steer the planet's course between flames and black cold; package ourselves if need be into electronic impulses and shoot for distant galaxies out of harm's way.

A single problem faces us: to preserve our forms from aging and deterioration; to escape this parabolic arch of existence that ends in pain, dissolution and ashes.

We are here, in Heidegger's term, "thrown." Consciousness always was and will be, or else it began with us. Either way, we are simply and foremost—and only this matters—agents of consciousness. Our goal must be to see that everyone alive will be able to preserve his being from death by deterioration (not likely at the moment surely, except conceivably by deep-freezing, but not forever impossible). Therefore we must set out to control, insofar as we can, all parts of the environment capable of destroying the human body.

Far from being a cause for despair, the Absurd is our ally. Possibilities of accidental death hold no terror. Such catastrophes "will happen", we have always understood. The Absurd spices our days, providing relief from the relentless probabilities that lead us down the road to extinction. Infinity too can be accepted as a friend. It offers a never-ending feast of mysteries, and all the time in the world to solve them.

The elastic earth thrusts up human forms which in due time fall back into it. Must we condemn as "unnatural" any attempt to resist this process? Let it be so, and let us be. The Unnatural Man acts from faith that his differentiated consciousness and capacity for reflection exempts him from the rules governing other forms of life. (He knows, for instance, that the Golden Rule is precisely "unnatural," yet often tries to live by it.)

No force but that of his own superstition, or hostility to himself, can defeat the Unnatural Man—unless the entire universe blows up, in which case we can forget the whole business. If no other Intelligence exists, we are king. Assuming a Divine Intelligence, so much the better. We are part of it. Our imagination must deliberately have been put on the track of doubting and opposing life-unto-death. If other sentient beings derived from a Primal Intelligence "know all about us," still better; we have potential allies and brothers.

Scorning those who "glut themselves on *chansons realistes*," Sartre has said: "Man is what he wills himself to be after his thrust toward existence. Man is nothing else but what he makes of himself."

And Jung: "The cleft which Christianity has torn between nature and spirit enabled the human mind to think not only beyond but even against nature, and thereby proves its—I might say—divine freedom."

PART IV

XVII

STATE OF THE
BIOMEDICAL ARTS

I believe we can be masters of our fate.

DR. GLENN T. SEABORG

I am a great believer in the idea of whatever man can imagine,
man can do.

MICHAEL E. DEBAKEY, M.D.

We are being carried in the direction of im-
mortality and the divine state on a river of
assembled information and discovery. The
trickle started in Babylon and Egypt . . .
nothing to disturb the gods. In the fourth millennium
B.C. cumulative records appear in the valleys of Mesopo-
tamia . . . cuneiform inscription, wedge writing, water
and sun clocks . . . because of the Nile floods, annual re-
measurement of the fields of Egypt, and geometry begins
. . . in the valley of the Euphrates, disemboweling of
animals for food and studying their entrails for divina-

tion eventually informs Sir William Osler and Dr. Christian Barnard.

Currents of speculation run together, and are confirmed. They begin to move more swiftly and turbulently. Now the gods of our invention grow dimly aware of the direction in which this life force is moving. Alarmed, they intervene. The flow is dammed by repression, confined in backwaters of superstition and ignorance. Sometimes it is forced underground. But soon, within a thousand years, the stream has been unified in a single method. It can no longer be contained.

Now it has all burst above ground. An enormous river of input rolls over us. Everyone knows the truism that most people who have ever worked in science are alive today. Growing numbers of them are issuing creative research papers of every description, so that we have a flood of information beyond our capacity to absorb. In practical terms, this means that specialists in a given discipline must carry on their own work; then after hours find time to track down and review numberless projects of others— an exhausting professional effort. How many engineers and scientists have wished that the river could temporarily be shut off, so that we might take time to pool our knowledge, put it in order, see what we have, and determine in what direction future study ought to be oriented. But often the professional will not be able to manage such a review. Desperately we command computers:

COMPUTER MAY EASE OVERFLOW
OF PHYSICS DATA FOR STUDENTS
The New York Times 1/28/68

The American Institute of Physics announced yesterday the start of a million-dollar project to explore ways to overcome the growing traffic jam in physics information . . .

It has become increasingly difficult for a physicist work-
ing in an area that overlaps a number of these fields to
keep informed of developments that bear on his research.
To do so means reading more literature than is feasible.

One idea being discussed as perhaps the ultimate solu-
tion is the creation of a computerized system that pro-
vides each scientist only with information bearing di-
rectly on his work. In subscribing to this service he would,
by filling out forms, "tell" the computer what lines of re-
search concerned him.

In the pursuit of immortality now beginning to sur-
face, the biomedical arts may be found in similar con-
fusion. Hence, in this and other master disciplines, the
computer has evolved into today's most conspicuous ren-
aissance man. A dilemma confronts the writer: how to
ground the immortalist thesis on hard biomedical evi-
dence, and at the same time make allowances for this
evidence becoming obsolete overnight.

Developments reinforcing the central argument are
cast up day after day. When the times comes to draw on
this carefully assembled material—the daring specula-
tions that, almost unthinkably, a heart may be trans-
planted, or that DNA will "someday" be synthesized—
three-quarters of it may have turned into old news.

THE BRAVE NEW WORLD OF GENETIC CONTROL
New York Post 4/20/68 by Bill Burrus

Home-grown hearts, limbs and livers to replace old ones.
. . . New teeth, hair and eyes. . . . An endless supply
of new brain cells to wipe out senility. . . 'vegetable'
breeding of 1,000,000 human beings from body cells, so
that all are identical twins to the donor. . .

. . . a group of eminent scientists told a New York audi-
ence recently that the era of genetic control is near, that

the evolution of a super-race is not too far from our grasp. . .

This conference on "The Far Reach of Science" sponsored by *Life* Magazine was moderated by Dr. Lee Dubridge, president of the California Institute of Technology (and once appointed scientific advisor to Richard Nixon). Robert Sinsheimer told the audience, mostly business executives: "Modern Biology is now poised to provide a new and profound approach to the understanding of the nature of man . . . with that understanding will come wholly new powers to alter man's very being. . . ."

Many of these new powers will derive from a single achievement: artificial reproduction of the deoxyribonucleic acid molecule; the DNA whose coiled threads control not only all of us but all of life. At last the species has performed the feat of reproducing its own substance. Or, in terms of our theme, the pretender to the throne of the gods has moved toward genetic control over his own future divinity.

The reproduction of DNA was a collaborative effort at Cal Tech and Stanford. "We had made then in a test tube the DNA which could serve as the progenitor of an indefinitely long chain of progeny virus from this day on throughout time," Dr. Sinsheimer explained at the *Life* conference in New York. "The big significance is that the infectivity of the copy proves the accuracy of the whole process, and that this process is open-ended. In principle it can be applied to any DNA from a virus or bacteria, an amoeba, or a mouse, or a man."

The audience also heard this from California Institute of Technology biologist Dr. James Bonner: "There is nothing to prevent you from taking two body cells from (a) donor and growing identical twins having the same genetic constitution of the donor . . . there is nothing to prevent you from making a thousand.

"There is nothing in principle to prevent us from doing

that same thing ultimately in man himself, and growing any number of genetically identical people from individuals who have what we assess as highly desirable genetic characteristics.

"In the future, we should be able to take a single cell and reset the genetic program to any desired point to make that cell or group of cells turn into, say, a new organ, a replacement organ, or a new liver. Or say you go to a doctor and he says: 'Well, I think your heart isn't so good now, maybe we had better start growing you a new one, and in two or three years it will be grown and we can plumb it in.' "

"The genetic age is unlikely to announce itself with a bang," a biologist has said. "Practiced in private and in secret on individual genes of individual persons, it will slip imperceptibly into our lives."

Imperceptibly, too, we are changing the terms of the human contract. Men are not sitting still for death any more, and the river that will take us out of time flows faster than we know. Through transplants alone, the immortality-hunter is learning how to replace his energies. With the ability to insert new organs into a sick or aging body, he finds at least a portion of youth again. The heart he receives may come from an animal or human cadaver; may be flesh or plastic. Or, some years from now, with genetically-ordered cells that can be grown *in vitro* into his specific replacement organs, the equivalent of his own younger cells, may be grafted into him with no fear of tissue-rejection. New heart, kidney, lungs and pancreas—these must almost necessarily add up to a newer man with a fresh expectation of years.

But organ replacement may be a crude and clumsy way to the prolongation of life. There are many others. For example, Dr. Holgar Hydén of the University of Goteborg in Sweden has injected DNA from the brains of young laboratory animals into the brains of aging animals, apparently stimulating protein production in the brain cells. He believes that research may evolve a technique of increasing an aging human brain's activity in this manner. With Dr. Bonner's forecast in mind, it is certainly conceivable that such a transfer of youth could be accomplished periodically by injections of one's own DNA newly-grown in a test-tube.

But "latest developments" of this sort must be seen as relatively unimportant to the immortalist argument. What matters is the accelerating swiftness of medical discovery.

Moving toward the end of time, the river of research overwhelms and renders obsolete each individual discovery along the way. Granting humanity's inevitable passage, the obsolescence of this or that laboratory breakthrough could not matter less.

The attack on death has not been organized properly, for the simple reason that we have not dared announce it as an over-all objective. Still unconsciously afraid of antagonizing the gods (in this regard, the medical profession being as superstitious as the rest of us), we cannot bear to "speak the word," let the hubris out, that we have a secret intent to do away with death entirely. Having no word, we have no program.

Fiefdoms of one specialty or another attempt to control the allocation of expenditures in their fields of study. Unfortunately, this will always be in part a political allocation. Since everybody wants to score and show off to the gods, in biomedical research as in any other line of work, every association of specialists naturally tries to obtain all the funds possible to advance research in its particular area.

Are not all medical specialists tacitly joined in the fight against death? May this not be assumed? The immortalist reply is that it most certainly can not be assumed. Rather, the modestly hidden intent is in danger of being buried under our river of papers. We appear to be lost and intimidated in the torrent of our own data. Everybody pursues little, special goals. Vague forecasts abound. (Scientists of the Rand Corporation have predicted a fifty-year increase in our life-expectancy in fifty years.) But from day to day researchers tend to work along established lines, take refuge in narrow professionalism, and never forget to contribute to the pension plan.

Lacking here is any sense of a grand mission such as those that animated the Manhattan Project or the National Space Program. Capturing atomic energy and reaching for the moon: you know what you are after. With the problem of meaningless annihilation having become so urgent in our time, threatening world-wide violence and madness, the simple pronouncement of a final War Against Death would give the biomedical arts the frame of dedication they need.

On a working level, we require a Central Planning Authority to carry through the climactic assault on death. It would first of all put a stop to the inefficient duplication of research. The commission would organize study teams as a general staff deploys an expeditionary force. In particular, it is to be hoped, an "Immortality Commission" of this nature would recommend wide-ranging research expenditures to be spent on the study of the aging process itself—about which little is known, and an area of exploration to which relatively few medical research dollars have been allocated. For the study of aging, conducted independently of the study of specific diseases, may lead more quickly to death's secret place.

The War Against Death will be an enormously complex undertaking. Even a glimpse into our own cells reveals a wilderness to be conquered. For one thing, we seem to be up against an evolutionary plan which calls for the individual to grow, procreate and die so that the species can go on. This appears to be our assignment, and nothing else. Hence, in determining to live on, we are resisting a program laid out for us and probably for all metazoan creatures. Yet we need not be intimidated. As will be seen, the master plan is not impenetrable. Death can be held off; we can look forward to renewed leases on life.

But what about the transitional generations who still must die—can any hope at all be offered to them? I am speaking of a practical hope, not the promises of salvation held out by half-mad evangelists or cool, pin-striped preachers at Madison Square Garden.

XVIII

THE CRYONICS UNDERGROUND

So we don't have long to wait before we shall know how to freeze the human organism without injuring it. When that happens, we shall have to replace cemeteries by dormitories, so that each of us may have the chance for immortality that the present state of knowledge seems to promise.

PROFESSOR JEAN ROSTAND

This is not a hobby or conversation piece: it is the principal activity of this phase of our lives; it is the struggle for survival. Drive a used car if the cost of a new one interferes. Divorce your wife if she will not cooperate; Save your money; get another job and save more money. Sometimes a fool will blunder through, but don't count on it. The universe has no malice, but neither has it mercy, and a miss is as good as a mile.

ROBERT C. W. ETTINGER

A L'ABJECTE ET REPUGNANTE INHUMATION
A LA TERRIFIANTE ET DANTESQUE INCINERATION
JE PREFERE LA PURE ET INALTERABLE CONGELA-
TION

DR. GUILLAUME ROY
L'Association Cryonics Française

... U nderground societies are being set up all over the United States to propagate and facilitate this new form of dying to live again," wrote correspondent Jean Campbell in the *London Evening Standard*, September 6, 1967. "I have just visited my local chapter, situated in a large, dark Victorian house, deep in Brooklyn. The atmosphere was not clinical. Three young men and a girl sat in an office piled with papers.

"The group turned out not to be doctors, but a lawyer, an industrial designer, and a trade writer. I felt, curiously enough, as if I were among a bunch of anarchists."

Not anarchists but certainly revolutionaries, the plotters visited by Miss Campbell belong to the Cryonics Society of New York Inc. Six cryonics groups in the United States and one in France have this mission: to encourage and promote freezing of the newly-dead rather than burying or incinerating them, in order that these individuals (still regarded as such) may be revived at some time in the future when technological means have been developed.

In theory, the promised resurrection from cold storage will take place when 1) damage done to cells and tissues while the suspended body is being frozen—unavoidable at present—can be repaired by methods as yet unknown 2) techniques of thawing have been developed, to prevent injury to cells in the re-warming process 3) remedies for the terminal illness or combination of deteriorative effects that ended the patient's life have been found, and ideally 4) ways to arrest, stabilize, and eventually reverse the aging process are uncovered by future research.

In Greek, *kryos* means icy cold. *Cryobiology* has to do with the relatively new science that studies and utilizes the effects of low temperatures on living material. Specialists may belong to the Society for Cryobiology which publishes the journal, *Cryobiology*.

Cryogenics refers to the branch of physics dealing with

low temperatures. *Cryonics* is something else: the term coined by Karl Werner, a young designer of underwater structures and a "Freeze-Wait-Reanimate" pioneer, to denote the preservation of the human body by freezing or supercooling to prevent the finality of death. The name was first given to the Cryonics Society of New York. Today, according to Robert Ettinger, the prophet and leader of the freezing movement: "We use 'cryonics' as a blanket, to cover all the disciplines and programs centered on human cold storage."

Ettinger, a physicist whose book, *The Prospect of Immortality,* inspired what may now without irony be called the cryonics faith, has regarded cryobiology as a "starveling discipline," and said he was told by an officer of the national society that only a half-dozen men in the country, and a dozen in the world, were engaged in it full time.

Some cryobiologists are skeptical about his cause. One scientist has this to say: ". . . the 'cryonics' societies around the country are often rather shady organizations whose partial purpose is to get money to freeze people before the technics are really worked out. They do often have available a certain amount of information, obtained through publications of more legitimate societies, but it's often blown up to be more than it is. Local physicians, who are not always so bright, are sometimes sucked into these societies to give them . . . the appearance of scientific approval."

But such a judgment fails to take into account the obsessive and emotional determination to hold off death that drives the cryonics people. Several cryobiologists have contributed to the literature of the movement. They appear to share the central faith that death is evil, and that by freezing our remains we may have some chance of saving ourselves.

Most faiths, orthodox or secular, tend to encourage

enterprise at the fringes (the selling of holy relics or psychedelic jewelry). We could say, for instance, that the multi-billion-dollar life insurance business serves as a commercial development of the Christian spirit. Certainly a cash profit can be made out of decent instincts, to protect loved ones, etc. Some critics feel that life insurance extracts damaging sums from struggling family men, who might use these amounts to enrich their lives in some better way.

Now . . . the Cryonics Movement may at some point have vast commercial possibilities. Science-fiction writer Frederik Pohl estimates the potential profits from freezing and storage in trillions of dollars. At present, churches, life insurance companies and mortuaries (the cryonics people expect to cooperate with these institutions) can count on grossing a virtual infinity of receipts from death. Will they go about this "honestly?" The answer depends on the nature and quality of your faith. Behind the production of more ornate and longer-lasting caskets is the idea that when resurrection teams come around you had better be in good enough condition to get up and walk. A super-stainless coffin will make a better impression on the officials than an old crate. The cost of burning candles, reciting masses, maintaining eternal flames, laying wreaths on graves, and all that sort of thing, derives from the implicit promise—whether or not dressed in symbolic terms—that you can come back.

The Cryonics Societies do not go so far as to make this promise. What they do maintain is that freezing immediately after the pronouncement of death offers a fair bet for survival; in Ettinger's phrase, "a chance of debatable magnitude, but nevertheless some chance," and as of now the only chance. Or as Curtis Henderson, president of the New York society, said: "No matter how slim the chances are today, they are better than the worms or the crematorium are going to give you."

To arrest our impending decay in frozen capsules and

hold mortal humanity in a suspended state, actually planning for bodily resurrection, can hardly avoid being a revolutionary concept. Yet it sometimes appears to be a limited sort of revolution. Ettinger, for example, seems not to visualize the program shaking present-day social and business structures.

Thus he has expressed the belief that: ". . . No real vested interests should be damaged by it—not religion, not morticians, not cemeterians, not physicians, certainly not lawyers or businessmen; all of these, in fact. can benefit from it. (It is true, however, that some people may *imagine* their business interests threatened, and that many will bristle at the psychological threat— the undermining of their carefully constructed philosophical castles of sand.) "

We have a curiously disturbing vision. Piled-up bodies in frozen "dormantories" wait for rebirth; outside life goes on much as before, except that instead of burying our dead we stow them away. In hundreds of laboratories scientists are working to liberate the race from its mortal condition while the suspended bodies multiply in capsules all over the world. Prudently insured men and women walk about, half-liberated from their fear of extinction, hoping . . .

In 1947 Ettinger came across the report of experiments performed by Dr. Jean Rostand in which the French biologist successfully preserved frog sperm using glycerol as a cryoprotective agent to prevent freezing damage. He instantly saw the application of this new development to preserving human life, having our bodies frozen immediately after death with the hope that they could be revived at some later time. But for more than thirteen years after this insight, he made no attempt to pursue the matter. "I thought surely, before long, better qualified people would take up the idea," he explained in an interview with Saul Kent, editor of *Cryonics Reports*.

When no one did, he made a tentative start. "Finally, in 1960, I felt I had to do something on my own," he told Kent. "I summarized the thesis on one page, emphasizing the life insurance aspects, and sent this to a couple of hundred people selected at random from *Who's Who*. Only a few responded, and it was clear that a long dissertation was needed to make such a revolutionary proposition, with so many apparent difficulties, seem plausible."

While an instructor in physics on the faculty of Wayne State University in Michigan (more recently he has taught at Highland Park College), Ettinger wrote the first draft of his proposal for a cryogenic approach to eternal life, and in 1962 had it privately printed.

A revised version of *The Prospect of Immortality* was published by Doubleday in 1964. Although the book went into a second edition, it did not make an exceptionally strong showing considering the boldness of Ettinger's theme. The literary and philosophical establishments ignored it. Despite a favorable preface by Jean Rostand, who had belatedly read and approved the thesis originally developed from news of his experiments, the journal *Science* refused to take the work seriously—on the grounds that the successful freezing and thawing of a complex organism such as the human body was beyond reasonable hope for a long time to come.

(Ettinger considers this view utterly irrelevant. The cryonically-suspended are not going anywhere, his counter-arguments runs, and can wait virtually to eternity until the proper techniques *are* developed.)

In October, 1965, science editor Albert Rosenfeld noted in *Life* ("Will Man Direct His Own Evolution?") that "although Ettinger's proposals are highly controversial and most scientists refuse to take them seriously . . . the marvel is that [they] do have a valid base and that they have struck such an instantaneous public nerve."

The argument for cryogenic interment (now changed to "cryonic suspension" for public relations reasons) proceeds from the fact that men do not die all at once but rather succumb to clinical, biological and then cellular death, in that order. *Clinical* death arrives first, confirmed by the cessation of heartbeat and breathing. Within five to eight minutes deterioration normally sets in, culminating in *biological* death, defined by Dr. A. S. Parkes as ". . . the state from which resuscitation of the body as a whole is impossible by currently known means." (Ettinger has extended this definition slightly, describing biological death as "just a critical malfunction incurable by present means." In his own book he finds it "implicit in Dr. Parkes's definition . . . that if we use extreme freezing to prevent deterioration, sooner or later 'currently known means' will be adequate, and the body will no longer be regarded as dead.") Finally, in *cellular* death, all the cells degenerate, suffering irreversible damage.

The critical period for the expiring individual whose heart and breathing have just stopped is that between clinical and biological death. This will always be a time of emergency for suspension teams, since measures needed to preserve the body must be taken quickly. At the point of clinical and legal death, writes Ettinger: "in most cases, the body (including the brain), is still at least ninety-nine percent alive, since only relatively few of the cells have failed. Hence, if we keep the patient out of the clutches of the traditional undertaker and promptly give him instead to a mortician or physician trained in the procedures of cryonics, he can be frozen (by special methods that minimize freezing injury) and preserved indefinitely in his not-very-dead condition, with the hope of future survival and rejuvenation."

Under the best possible conditions—that is, in the right hospital, or at home with the proper equipment and a crew of specialists near by—quick-freezing can certainly be accomplished in a manner that will prevent severe cellular damage during the brief time of clinical death. Also, when the body is placed under low temperatures the period before biological breakdown occurs will be prolonged.

Unhappily, very large numbers of people do not—and will not—die in bed or at a location within five minutes of cryonics equipment. At the First Annual Cryonics Conference in New York (March, 1968), the Society showed a film by Karl Werner depicting a simulated cryonics medical alert. A phone call brought the freezer technicians into action like firemen; a truck careened through the streets; the body was hurriedly but carefully packed into its resting place where it would ultimately be stored at -197°C., the temperature of liquid nitrogen.

But such a procedure requires the best of luck to be successful. The man who has purchased an insurance policy to cover this final moment will almost certainly not obtain full value if, say, he suffers a fatal heart attack while on a summer fishing trip. Even if the end should come in the middle of traffic in New York or Chicago, the likelihood of his being transported across town in time to reach cold storage would be forbiddingly small, unless emergency cryo-capsule parlors were placed like pharmacies on every block.

To deal with such emergencies, the Cryonics Societies have utilized the services of the Medic Alert Foundation. A collect call to Medic Alert will obtain the telephone numbers of specialists in the area prepared to administer treatment to the person who has just died. For five dollars the subscriber receives a stainless steel bracelet, a wallet information card, and an emergency telephone number. On the bracelet he can have stamped urgent instructions, "IF I AM DEAD CALL QUICKLY" or "CALL COLLECT" the designated phone number, which would be that of a Cryonics Society headquarters. Additional lines for 50 cents apiece could provide supplemental information, "IF DEAD, COOL BODY WITH ICE—ESPECIALLY HEAD—

WHILE GIVING ARTIFICIAL RESPIRATION AND CARDIAC MASSAGE. CALL FOR HELP." A wallet information card gives additional instructions.

The record of present-day city dwellers in answering live outcries for help has been dubious enough. Frantic instructions from the clinically dead sprawled on the sidewalk would seem even less likely to receive the attention they deserve, even with a collect phone call guaranteed. What can be the point of pretending otherwise: unless a police, fire or ambulance unit happens to be a short distance away, the departing individual is going to be well into biological death before reaching cold storage.

Ettinger has been well aware of this problem, and *The Prospect of Immortality* contains a brief section on "The Limits of Delay in Treatment." Earlier he prepares the structure of faith essential to the Cryonics Movement. Its first principle is Ettinger's conviction which cannot be abandoned that "the phrase 'irreversible damage' is used much too cavalierly, and really means 'incapable of being reversed by methods so far employed.' "

He concedes that the brain "may certainly" suffer " 'irreversible damage' " from anoxia (the deprivation of oxygen when blood circulation stops), but then, having more or less acknowledged this, he gradually retreats from the unpleasant brute fact by expressing doubt whether, after all, it really is so. The Cryonics faith is built up on a structure of conditionals. Italics, except for *"any,"* are added.

While the brain cells do indeed "die" more quickly than cells of any other kind, we must not therefore come to a hasty pessimistic conclusion. As already indicated, it *may well be* that the most important parts and functions of these cells are not so delicate as the cell as a whole . . . *It is possible,* then, that hope should not be given up so long as *any* of the body cells show life. If the skin, for example, is still alive, then there is *some chance* that the brain cells are also alive, albeit damaged. Removal of the excess lactic acid, adjustment of the fluid balance, and so on, by techniques at the disposal of future science, *may* find them as good as new.

Therefore, unless the body has been exposed for a hopelessly long period, the enthusiasts of the cryonics movement believe that if a handful of cells can be saved by the freezing effort, the gamble is worth while. Looking far into the future, Ettinger imagines that "if brute-force methods are necessary, it is not inconceivable that huge surgeon-machines, working twenty-four hours a day for decades or even centuries, will tenderly restore the frozen brains, cell by cell, or even molecule by molecule, in critical areas."

In September, 1967, seventy-four-year-old Marie Phelps Sweet (Mrs. Russ LeCroix Van Norden), follower of Dr. Ettinger, was frozen by members of the Cryonics Society of California between two and three days after her unexpected and unattended death in a Santa Monica Hotel. During much of the waiting period she was stored in a mortuary at 30° F.—by cryonics standards a relatively high temperature. Acknowledging these unfavorable circumstances, Ettinger maintained, "Yet no one can say for certain that Marie's chance is zero, or even small . . . and no one can prove that truly irreversible damage has occurred."

Miss Sweet had not been able to make provision for her cryonic suspension. This meant that the Cryonics Society had to go through with the perfusion and storage of the body at its own expense. In *Cryonics Reports,* Robert Nelson, author of *We Froze The First Man,* noted that "cost of storage, dry ice replacement and incidental maintenance is approximately $75.00 a week. . . . Because of the prohibitive cost, which we cannot maintain indefinitely, permanent storage arrangements must be made."

Asked: "Why did you freeze her?," Nelson replied: "As one of the pioneers in the cryonics revolution, and in view of her intense desire to be frozen under any conditions, we felt we should honor her wishes."

The decision severely tested members of the cryonics movement, since they had not only to act on their convictions but to pay for them, and possibly continue to pay. This proved not only to be awkward and difficult, but also involved a test of conscience.

A *Cryonics Reports* editorial pointed out that "a pattern of placing full responsibility for the dead upon the living *cannot* be perpetuated. It is simply too expensive —physically, emotionally, and morally."

This expense of spirit may be seen in Robert Ettinger's appeal to the membership: "She did not make adequate arrangements, and so lies stricken and helpless, with only the will and resources of her relatives and friends to save her from the mindless enemy. . . . [there] are the intangible but paramount matters of morale and conscience. Marie is not just a statistic; she is one of us . . . For our own integrity, as individuals and as organizations, we must acknowledge our moral responsibility. A friend and comrad—*simply cannot*—be abandoned."

Today, Marie Sweet rests in an interim frozen shelter, with the permanent disposition of her body still undetermined.

The eminent University of Minnesota surgeon Dr. Richard Lillehei has predicted (Daniel Greene, *The National Observer* 4/29/68) : "Ultimately we'll be freezing organs and keeping them in some kind of bank. . . . If we can reach the stage of freezing organs for transplants, there is no reason why we can't go further and freeze and thaw a whole person."

At the First Cryonics Conference Dr. Armand Karow, Jr. of the Medical College of Georgia and Dr. Ralph

Hamilton of the University of Pennsylvania lectured on developments in cryobiology and the state of the freezing art. "I think," Dr. Karow has said, "in general cryobiologists would have to concede that freezing a human [form] and bringing it back to life is a real possibility," and Dr. Hamilton: "Theoretically, if you can preserve one cell by freezing and thawing, you should be able to preserve any aggregate of cells."

But most researchers agree that those who have been placed in cryonic suspension to date will stay dead. For example, Dr. Roy Walford, Professor of Pathology at UCLA and an advisor to the National Institutes of Health, believes that, unfortunately, "the corpses already frozen in liquid nitrogen will doubtless never be revived . . . they are literally—in the protein sense—like cooked eggs. It's unlikely we'll ever be able to uncook an egg." To which a young biochemist has replied: "Given time enough, of course we'll learn how to uncook an egg."

Time enough remains the key to the faith of all cryonics believers. They stress that for the temporarily lifeless sleepers time is virtually stopped—and if need be they can wait through centuries until all eggs in all sciences have been uncooked. For this reason, the matter of thawing damage does not disturb them. Obviously, they point out, people are not going to be re-warmed until such time as the formation of ice crystals and gas bubbles in and around cells and other adverse reactions have been dealt with by cryobiologists of the future.

The Cryonics Faith can point to a growing body of evidence suggesting that, in purely technical terms, the deep-freeze gambler may not be up against such long odds.

Much is made of the experiment conducted by Professor Isamu Suda, Dr. K. Kito and Dr. C. Adachi in which a cat's brain was perfused with glycerol, cooled to -20 C., and stored for 203 days. After re-warming, an encephalograph reading was registered indicating almost normal electrical brain wave activity. ". . . at this stage," wrote the Kobe

University scientists, "we wish to conclude that brain cells are not especially vulnerable to lack of oxygen. It appears that even nerve cells of the brain can survive and be revived after long-term storage under special circumstances."

May we therefore assume that consciousness will hold intact under extreme cooling? Possibly, although Dr. Karow raises the question whether the encephalograph reading represented *organized* cerebral function—i. e. survival of coherent activity may not have been proved.

Even so, the Suda experiment appears to be one more of many signs pointing toward mastery of the freezing art. Dr. Charles E. Huggins of the Harvard Medical School reports golden hamsters being revived after five hours and twenty minutes at the freezing point of 32° F. Another experiment has shown that memory may not only continue but actually improve in laboratory rats after they have been cooled nearly to the freezing point. The University of Oregon surgeon, Dr. Stanley W. Jacob, found that after being placed under hypothermia white rats, for no known reason, solved mazes with fewer errors than their litter-mates whose vital functions had not been disturbed.

Today, writes Dr. Karow, "it is relatively easy to freeze-preserve life in single cells, cell suspensions, and small specimens of tissue." Frozen blood and sperm cells may also be kept for months or years. But so far only corneas, skin and bone-marrow cells are being held at the National Naval Medical Center, the world's leading bank for frozen tissues.

Being frozen is not cheap. According to *Newsweek*: "The cost for this preparation and indefinite storage comes to about $50,000, more than three times what it was only seven years ago." The magazine quotes "a disappointed official at the Trans Time cryotorium in California as saying: "Acceptance has been much slower than anyone involved would ever have guessed. We thought it would sweep the country."

Naturally a policy set up to cover one's own freezing, amounting to $50,000 or whatever, will subtract that much from what the heirs to an estate might expect. To the families left behind, the suspended bodies of their parents may be likely to represent a dead selfishness entombed in an endless future. Families who feel this way will not want to share the faith, or keep it, and the tendency among many will be to obstruct frozen interment.

Even so, the expectation of the cryonics groups is that freezing will soon become routine—and not confined to the aged. For example, with parental permission, in September, 1968, the Cryonics Society of New York froze the body of a twenty-four-year-old student who had died of complications following surgery. The young man's body was placed in a capsule of liquid nitrogen at Washington Memorial Park Cemetery in Coram, L.I. Members of the Society regard him as a "frozen friend."

Readers of *The Prospect of Immortality* will find that the economic, social, and most important, the emotional consequences of the author's program have only been touched on, sometimes in negligent fashion.

For instance, Ettinger assumes that over the centuries cryonic suspension will be carried out within the framework of capitalism. This leads him to the calculation that a person frozen in our time, taking with him conservative investments yielding only three percent interest, will accumulate seven million dollars during a sleep of three hundred years. "This money is real . . . " he adds, but "I see no reason to expect future generations to be jealous of the bank accounts and financial influence of the frozen."

The supposition—especially when made in these times of upheaval—that money is going to lie around for three centuries, with a bank account growing just as it does now, and that the world three centuries beyond us will have such a unit of exchange as money, illustrates how the cryonics people sometimes advance their views in a vacuum.

Ettinger briefly mentions but does not seem entirely to realize what events would follow if potential immortality became—in a physical, observable way—the privilege of the economically elect. Consider a freezer program with affluent white people (their life insurance policies paid up) lying in neat rows waiting for the trumpet of science to return them to life, while the struggling black and brown masses continue to die as they always have. Do the cryonics partisans dare dream of the black and brown reaction to this final injustice? Not only are the exploiters oppressing us now, but they are planning to come back and sit on the world all over again—and on top of that they will not even die.

This state of affairs would obviously be unendurable, and would result, at the very least, in the unprotected people hosing down and melting the iced-in sanctuaries.

The cryonics groups, neither heartless nor stupid, know that Social Security would be the best administrative framework for their program, with an equal chance of resurrection for everyone. But they see no alternative to private enterprise. Clearly since no government—that of the United States or any other—is about to make freezing possible for everyone, the rich, regrettably, will have to take the lead, allow themselves to be suspended in liquid nitrogen, set the example. Reasonable enough, perhaps, yet the question remains whether the deprived masses would put up with death no longer being democratic for more than a month or two.

Robert Ettinger recognizes—as he must—that already severe problems of over-population would be exacerbated by the addition of millions stowed away in cryo-capsules waiting to return. He argues, not unconvincingly, that with or without freezers, there will soon be increased longevity, and later an indefinite life span, and that "since solutions must be found anyhow, we may as well make them good enough so that our own generation and those immediately succeeding can share the Golden Age."

He then estimates that if it takes three hundred years to reach immortality, there will be forty billion people to revive and relocate. Even these immense numbers can be accommodated, he believes, citing the opinion of University of Chicago Professor Richard L. Meier that as many as fifty billion could survive on the globe, given improved industrial and agricultural techniques, exploration and development of undersea areas, expanses of jungle, deserts and currently infertile regions. Here Ettinger seems uncharacteristically conservative. Indefinite extension of life may be much closer than three centuries away. Further, if it somehow becomes possible for millions to be placed in frozen vaults, with eternity to wait (assuming that future generations kept faith with them), the populations of that time will surely have started to move out to other planets or to artificial "suburban" satellite worlds, somewhat relieving our over-crowded condition.

In the beginning, the strength of a revolutionary group is always difficult to estimate. Despite streams of leaflets, appearances on radio and television, and the like, "the party" intending to change the world, when tracked down, may consist of four men and a dog sitting around a garage printing press. A local officer declares the combined membership of the cryonics movement, including relatively inactive associate members, to be about one thousand persons. The actual number may be considerably less: a hundred or two, or even a few score. But this would not be an insignificant figure. Christ, Hitler and Castro each started with twelve. The psychedelic movement—at least Timothy Leary's part of it—began in Newton, Massachusetts, with a single multi-family of about two dozen, including several children.

The cryonics underground must have its Resurrection. When the first cryonaut comes back through the icicles, after having been frozen for a number of hours or days— only then will the world be changed. Until that time (or when, as with the Space Revolution, a dog returns from the unknown), the movement must perforce remain pre-revolutionary.

A question lingers: whether the cryonics package may not be too bulky, calling for too many hard-to-secure financial arrangements and too much hardware. In view of these and other difficulties, the cryonics way could turn out to be the most roundabout and least passable road to eternal life.

An intensified drive to control the aging process seems far more promising. Along with this, basic research in cryobiology will certainly be essential, and ought to be greatly increased. While not to be ruled out, the immortality-now "put-me-in-the-capsule" approach may offer the smallest yield of all.

The cryonics answer will certainly be that both programs should immediately be put on a crash basis. Perhaps so. A national committee (including poets and artists as well as scientists, and the usual churchmen and company presidents, and the conservative senator) could be appointed to determine the most effective way to engineer our divinity.

In the immortalist view, freezing by itself ought to be seen as no more than a holding action. We are in search primarily of the new rhythms of living that will prevail beyond time. The refined way of making possible "shifts" of humanity, some sleeping some waking—especially pending the colonization of space—will be through some sort of suspended life, or hibernation, rather than the awkward and scientifically inelegant freezing and thawing of life forms.

But the territory to be secured and administered by humanity must be that of the race's own physical body. Only by subduing the processes that force us to grow old will we be able to exempt ourselves from death, the lot of beasts, and assume the status of gods, our rightful inheritance.

XIX

AGING, DEATH AND BIRTH

What shall I do with this absurdity—
O heart, O troubled heart—this caricature,
Decrepit age that has been tied to me
As to a dog's tail?

W. B. YEATS

Senescence is not biologically speaking a very satisfactory
entity.

DR. ALEX COMFORT

Man, it has been said, is DNA's way of understanding itself. If our species has evolved from some such mysterious project, then energy must be judged to have played a trick on its own nature, and until now we have been the victims of this game.

At some point energy either surpassed itself or possibly made a mistake by separating out and spinning off little sub-creations. Practically for ever after, these varied units rhythmically assembled and fell apart—we now say "lived" and "died"—knowing nothing. All this was evidently not pointless. Whatever created life seems to have improved its capability through the living and dying of its separated forms.

Thus, we may see ourselves as a fairly late development in energy's self-improvement program. By way of consolation, some biologists believe death to have been an evolutionary device. Energy's differentiated little subcreations could not remain immortal, or there would have been no advance toward our present condition. Carrying this one step more, we may then be programmed to die so that our descendants will eventually escape mortality and become gods.

Such an arrangement may be convenient for DNA, but unfortunately the master plan must have gone awry so far as *we* are concerned. There has been a serious error in scheduling: we who live now have come down to the end of the river and find ourselves genetically deposited here before our intended time of arrival. This could be DNA's miscalculation: it carried us to the edge of immortality too swiftly. And now the old protective gods are gone. Technologically unready, we have been taken down to a wilderness surrounded by death. Members of the rebel species, refusing too soon to serve any longer as evolution-fodder, back up like a lost wagon train in a small clearing with nowhere to go, with no weapons powerful enough to accomplish anything more than a delaying action against the end.

The error in programming occurred when DNA apparently lost control over the nice balance between man's superstition and his scientific capability. If these forces had been brought down to the late twentieth century more or less evenly, the species could triumphantly have thrown away its protective myths at precisely the time when it learned how to arrest the aging of its own cells. Unluckily this did not happen. It was not foreseen that we would be able to turn consciousness inside out and aspire so early to command and redirect the very processes that made us. "Retribution," one is tempted to say, although of course it has not been retribution but simply bad luck, now seems about to hit mankind very hard.

The problem becomes one of negotiating the hazardous years between now and the time when indefinite living—freedom from inevitably growing old—will be made possible. How to manage this, with the race's powers of self-deception critically impaired?

DNA has chosen to put the idea of the deep-freeze into our heads. The surfacing of this idea at a critical time in history reveals the tremendous force of our determination somehow to become gods. Even though probably trapped, we ought never to underestimate ourselves. The human race is wily. Our transitional generations can be imagined belonging to a lost battalion with no other alternative but to fight. I am not talking about a *gung ho* charge into oblivion. We will be ingenious. What we are about to do, as soon as we assemble our talent and plan properly, is first of all to mount a continuing research-assault on the processes that cause us to grow old and die.

Again we let stand the quickly-passing headlines, and stories:

SCIENCE IS URGED TO COMBAT AGING
Understanding of Biological Causes is Called Near
The New York Times 2/2/66 by John A. Osmundsen

"An understanding of the biology of aging is within reach of this generation," an authority in this field of scientific research said in a speech prepared for delivery at the New York Academy of Sciences last night.
. . . Dr. Bernard L. Strehler of the National Institutes of Health . . . said his belief that the determination of the biological causes of aging "could be achieved within this decade" was based on the provision that "a sufficient

priority in terms of good brains, sound financing, adequate facilities and administrative support is given this undertaking. . . ."

ASKS BIG DRIVE FOR SECRETS OF STAYING YOUNG
New York Daily News 3/27/68

San Diego, March 26—A noted British scientist urged today that the American scientific community join in a concerted drive to find the fountain of youth.

Dr. Alex Comfort, director of the Medical Research Council at University College, London, said the enormous power of American science might uncover the secrets of aging within a decade if sufficient energy were devoted to the task. . . .

SCIENTIST SEES AN END TO NATURAL DEATH
New York Post 6/9/67

Washington (AP)—A much-honored engineer predicts that by 1980 man may be able to choose in advance the sex of his children and slow down his own aging.

Still further in the future, writes Dr. Augustus B. Kinzel in the current issue of *Science* magazine, man may, by controlling hereditary factors, create supermen and abolish death from natural causes entirely. . . .

Can such optimism be justified? Dr. Carroll Williams, Professor of Zoology at Harvard, famous for developing a "juvenile hormone" which has prolonged the life of American Polyphemus moths, is quoted by Robert Prehoda in *The Future and Technological Forecasting* as believing that "the day is not too far distant when we will be able to treat senescence as we now know how to treat pneumonia."

Prehoda also offers Alex Comfort's meticulously qualified prophecy: "Once we get moving, the rate of scientific progress in life extension might conceivably become so rapid that provided one was young enough for treatment, one might hope for a series of life extending bonuses."

Elsewhere, in his book, *The Biology of Senescence*, Dr. Comfort, distinguished also as a poet, essayist and novelist, as well as author of *The Joy of Sex*, briskly sets aside the dream of eternal life: ". . . the character of the wish itself generally changes in the direction of realism, so that most people today would incline to prefer the prospect of longevity, which may be realizable, to a physical immortality which is not . . ."

So does Dr. Strehler in his *Time, Cells, and Aging:* ". . . the evolutionary dereliction is probably so manifold and so deeply ingrained in the physiology and biochemistry of existing forms, including man, that the abolition of the [aging] process is a practical impossibility."

Yet the futurists persist. In an article, "Physics and Life Prolongation," Dr. Gerald Feinberg, a professor of physics at Columbia, projects their conviction:

Things we can think of today as possible, without knowing how to do, are the ones that will be done in a relatively short time. It is these things we cannot yet even imagine that will take longest to accomplish. I am inclined to put two hundred years as the upper limit for the accomplishment of any possibility that we can imagine today.

Application of this view to progress in medical science leads to the conclusion that cures for all diseases that afflict man eventually will be found. This accomplishment would be just a step along the way toward regulating biological processes in living organisms on all levels from molecular to macroscopic. . . .

If one accepts that aging is a particular set of chemical

and physical changes that occur within living organisms, the logic of this argument suggests that it will eventually be controllable and reversible, even if the methods are as yet unknown.

The study of aging (for some reason many specialists prefer the Latin form *senescence*) goes back to alchemy. It is also one of our newer, least-organized sciences. Gerontology has become its proper name, with geriatrics referring to the treatment of debilitating symptoms common to old people. Currently the field—hardly yet a discipline—finds itself in a state of enlightened confusion. The enlightenment, of a negative sort, arises from the awareness that we do not really know our enemy, have not even agreed upon a definition of senescence, and have only the vaguest understanding of its underlying processes.

A dozen or more hypotheses attempt to explain biological deterioration. Few have turned out as yet to be especially useful. Often the theorists seem to be grasping for a suitable metaphor to picture the phenomenon that Yeats described straight on: ". . . things fall apart." In such a competition, the best writers may now and then appear to be advancing the best theory.

Gerontology could almost be said to have been born disorganized. As science reporter Barbara Yuncker put it: ". . . the research pattern is loose to the extent of seeming haphazard. There are virtually no gerontologists, but rather there are psychiatrists, biochemists, sociologists, and so on working in gerontology."

"In delving into the scientific part of aging," says Roy Walford, "you are in a field that historically and today as well is rampant with pseudo-science, quackery, and just not very good (but still legitimate) science."

Part of the difficulty until a short time ago stemmed from a dearth of support. As of 1967, Robert Prehoda reported funding of gerontological research by the Child Health and

Human Development Institute of the National Institutes of Health as amounting to about $3 million a year—this outlay supporting 400 grants explicitly for fundamental studies on biological aging.

(In that year the three leading producers of canned and packaged *dog food* in the United States—General Foods, Ralston Purina, and Quaker Oats—together spent $19.7 million on advertising in all media for this product alone.)

Why should the study of the body's deterioration have been so neglected over the years? Again Dr. Walford: "This is a very underpopulated field. . . . For several reasons: 1) until recently aging was regarded as a kind of Ponce-de-Leon subject and scientists tended to stay away from it because people smiled at them. 2) It takes a long time to do an experiment involving aging—depending of course upon the animal; for insects it can be done very shortly—because mice or rats live 2-3 years; and graduate students doing their theses on something besides, say, insects, won't pick such a long-term uncertain project. Suppose at the end of three years you've got a negative experiment? So they don't often select such projects. And what a graduate student does for his thesis often determines his future course of work. . . ."

A decade later the outlook for aging studies has been greatly improved. Favorable developments for gerontological research began with the U.S. government's creation of the National Institution on Aging (NIA) in 1974.

In an article, "The Ponce de Leon Trail Today," in *BioScience*, Gairdner B. Moment points to ". . . the establishment, in most of the industrial countries of the world, of special programs and institutes for the study of aging in all its aspects."

"This new Institute (NIA)," he continues, "under the National Institutes of Health, has as its nucleus the Gerontological Research Center in Baltimore and the Adult Development and Aging Branch, both parts of the National Institute of Child Health and Human Development. [It] will study the whole spectrum of aging problems from the molecular to the psychological and economic."

A *Science* "News and Commentary" essay by Constance Holden elaborates: "Creation of the NIA . . . marks a commitment by the government to give basic research on the problems and processes of aging the kind of visibility and prestige it has not hitherto enjoyed. . . . Major new initiatives will have to await further expansion of the budget, which is being increased from $17 million to about $26 million in fiscal 1977."

As director of NIA the parent National Institutes of Health appointed 49-year-old Dr. Robert N. Butler, author of the Pulitzer Prize-winning book *Why Survive? Being Old in America.*

Dr. Butler told *Science*, ". . . the very fact we have the NIA is in itself a momentous step. Given half a chance this institute is going to be the best in the world studying the mysterious, fascinating, and implacable process called aging."

As emphasized earlier, gerontology will really start moving when it liberates itself from modest objectives. Needed here is self-administered shock treatment—taking the form of an all-out and unabashed announcement of our determination to put an end to death, giving voice to this hubris without apology.

The industrial chemist and gerontologist, Dr. Johan Bjorksten, pointed out that if all current medical problems were solved—if all known illnesses now, today, could be successfully treated—only about fifteen years would be added to the present life expectancy of a person of sixty. But, he said, understanding and treatment of the chemistry of aging would offer the possibility of incalculably greater results, perhaps increasing the human life span in spectacular fashion.

The freely-avowed goal of seeking to change the human condition, the announced refusal to accept mortality as the race's final lot, would almost certainly help push research beyond its present limitations—not only quickening the professional effort but enlarging the hunter's vision of what can be accomplished. The effect would be similar to that produced by Roger Bannister when he broke through the psychological limit of the "impossible" four-minute mile. Not, of course, that miraculous discoveries would immediately follow. Rather, just as dozens of runners began routinely breaking the four-minute barrier soon after Bannister's feat—thereafter progressively lowering the mark until the mile is now run nearly ten seconds faster—so young scientists in the field of aging will find their way to freer and bolder conceptions once the modest (god-fearing) disclaimer of mankind's ever being able to overcome death has been cast aside.

Announcing such a battle-order is one thing, but even beginning to carry it out another. The study of senescence brings the researcher close to humbling mysteries. From the start, he moves into a jungle of cellular deterioration, not knowing, for example, whether he is hunting for a natural process, a disease, or programmed illness in which our disintegration as individuals has been imposed in the best interests of the species.

In 1957 some of the world's best-known specialists in aging met at Gatlinburg, Tennessee. At the end of their conference Dr. Bernard Strehler summed up the gerontologist's dilemma: "Every single hypothesis which has been suggested at this meeting probably has something to do with the aging process . . . It may be that every one of them contributes a tenth of a percent to the overall results . . . but before any of these theories is treated as established fact . . . one might determine whether the deterioration which occurs is due to errors, due to accidents, or whether it is due to a predetermined debilitating process built into the biological organism."

Two decades later, we still have only the enlightened but contradictory, or at least varying, opinions of learned men to go by. What actually happens, physically within us, to bring about our inexorable decline over the years?

In the course of a lifetime, according to one group of theories, the body falls victim to *accumulated insults and injuries.* Cells fall one by one to specific blows. The late physicist, Dr. Leo Szilard, thought that the insulting agent was ionizing radiation landing chance hits on individual cells. According to his view, random bombardment from deadly democratic rays gradually reduces us.

Dr. F. Marott Sinex of Brookhaven National Laboratories Medical Department has described the aging of an organism as "primarily caused by *molecular changes in nucleic acid and protein* . . . subject to a *variety of insults*—chemical, mechanical and thermal."

Dr. Hans Selye of the University of Montreal considers *stress* the insulting agent. Bernard Strehler elaborates on this approach. Because "an organism's ability to overcome stress decreases linearly with age, the probability that it will encounter a stress great enough to destroy it increases proportionately."

We have also the proposal of Dr. George A. Sacher that senescence results from a *rebounding imbalance:* one physiological malfunction leading to another, which rebounds in turn, affecting other cells and tissues, so that everything starts to degenerate.

Or we can turn to the "clinker" theory, as enunciated by Dr. Albert I. Lansing of the University of Pittsburgh. Studying tiny, multi-celled rotifers, he found significant differences in pigmentation between younger and older animals, and with the passage of time saw being built up "a *glut of insoluble elements* inside the cell incompatible with cell life and reproduction."

Stress and insult: the themes recur in the literature of aging. As Alex Comfort has written: "All concepts based on 'wear and tear' in neurones or other cells postulate a similar sequence: *loss of regenerative power* followed by *mechanical or chemical exhaustion.*"

Skeptically, a psychologist asked: "If you had an individual free of stress, would he live forever?" The problem is unreal, in that, as Dr. Nathan Shock has said, "all environments are deleterious." This includes cellular environments within the organism. Any individual form with moving parts must suffer kinks and strains. Also, the health of that form may depend on a smoothly-flowing turnover of fresh cells being born and worn-out ones dissolving and vanishing, to keep the higher organism going. But when new cells fail to replace the outworn ones fast enough, "enzyme exhaustion in post-mitotics" (Comfort) sends us on the downward slope.

Trouble need not come only from structures in the body falling apart. We may also age and die because too many cells and tissues lock into immobile systems. The *cross-linkage theory* put forward by Dr. Bjorksten and others attributes senescence to the random action or normally present cross-linking agents on proteins and nucleic acids in the cytoplasm so as to immobilize them irreversibly. This creates a "frozen metabolic pool" which finally leaves no space for active molecules. Not only cells but inter-cellular connective tissues appear to be susceptible to such molecular aging. The hardening of connective tissue (among the strongest cross-linking agents: ionizing radiation and tobacco) impairs the delivery of oxygen, nutrients and hormones to the cells. Dr. Bjorksten has held that the only way to control aging will be to find the means to break down, in the cells, the cross-linked insoluble molecules, reducing them to excretable components. We would then rid ourselves of such unwanted stabilization within the body.

Unhappily, as it grows older, the body seems to turn against its own being, rejecting itself. This *disturbed immunological function* has been described by Dr. Sinex, who proposes that as the body ages an auto-immune mechanism is switched on and that with the consequent release of antibodies, we devour ourselves.

An earlier researcher, Dr. Charles Minot, found death to be "the price we are obliged to pay for our organization, for the *differentiation* which exists in us." Things would be simpler if we were all of a piece, consisting exclusively of identical cells. Sea anemones, for example, have shown no evidence of decline after existing for years or decades in a culture, and seem at least potentially immortal.

Ought we to call aging loss? Or decreasing performance with time? "There must be multiple causes," Dr. Shock has said: "It bothers me when people talk about *the* aging process. . . ." The question persists, continuing to frustrate all gerontologists. Dr. Warren Andrew of the Indiana School of Medicine has questioned whether there is such a thing as "normal" aging? Is "the weight loss of an old man, or the wrinkling of his skin, or the graying of his hair, or even his general loss of vigor, a pathological change?" Disease or program, or programmed disease, does aging serve the species by getting rid of its individual members? Dr. Comfort thinks not: "Senescence has no function—it is the subversion of function."

Still, our fragile constitutions seem designed to fall into pieces. In complex biological systems, which we certainly are, different kinds of cells controlled by different genetic projects eventually start interfering with one another. The survival of one type after maturity may depend on precisely the sort of action that destroys another group of cells. A cell lingering after the performance of its original function may, in mutated form, cause damage later on. Dr. T. M. Sonneborn of the University of Indiana gives a hypothetical example: "We might imagine a mutation arising that has a favorable effect on the calcification of bone in the developmental period but which expresses itself in a subsequent somatic environment in the calcification in the connective tissue of arteries. . . ." Taking place here, in Dr. Sonneborn's example, may be "planned obsolescence" involving a progressive *switching-off* of youthful function and, in accordance with a genetic time-table, a *switching-on* of functions that age us.

Another approach extends this analogy, but changes it around. We age and die because of genetic errors. Our switchboard (or its operator) gives out. We suffer an impairment of the ability to transmit or receive instructions. Injuries to DNA—as the result of radiation, wear-and-tear or other causes—disorganize the stored collection of genetic information. The consequent accumulated damage produces accumulated error in the genes of non-dividing cells. DNA and linking RNA fail to pass on the clear, undistorted messages of youth. Information becomes confused or else distorted in transmission and poorly decoded. In younger animals such injuries are quickly repaired, but as the individual grows older repair is slow, or perhaps completely fails; our body cells no longer get the message of survival. Other cells fail to divide properly. Since mutations are constantly introducing errors into DNA, Dr. Sinex explains, the body can only "run down from accumulated natural confusion."

Dr. Howard J. Curtis, senior biologist at the Brookhaven National Laboratories has proposed that it might be possible to control aging by stabilizing DNA, by halting its gradual modification which brings about the diseases typical of old age. Stabilize DNA, the life force itself? This leads back to the molecular memory research of Holger Hydén, and his stimulation of aging laboratory animals' brain cells by injecting fresh DNA into them from the brains of young animals.

It may connect too with startling developments to come in memory transfer research. A few years ago Dr. James V. McConnell of the University of Michigan reported that flatworms ground up and fed to others of their species passed on acquired reactions to those that had eaten them. At Baylor, Dr. Georges Ungar has trained rats to ignore clanging sounds; then injected a broth of their brain tissue into Swiss mice which, similarly, ignored the clamor that would normally terrify them. Dr. Allan L. Jacobson and his colleagues at the University of California injected RNA, ribonucleic acid, DNA's information-carrying molecule, into a control group of rats from trained rats and—across species—from trained hamsters. They found that the RNA-injected animals showed quicker responses to tests than rats which had received no injection.* Probably the best-known scientist in this field, Dr. David Krech of the University of California at Berkeley, has been testing the possibility that boldly defined events impress both structural and chemical changes in brain cells. "The chemical changes may decay with time, but the structural changes should be permanent. [David Perlman, *New York Times Magazine* 7/7/68] . . . the experiments may establish that once the permanent structural changes of memory are fixed —in a rat at any rate—a fresh supply of undecayed 'memory molecules' from another rat may act as a booster shot to revive the signals along the rat's old, inactive memory circuits."

Such booster shots, it would seem, must eventually relate in some way to a transfer and restoration of youthful functions. If a fresh supply of one's own young DNA can be grown culturally in a test-tube—then conveyed to our brain cells, perhaps by artificial viruses—the genetic instructions of youth might be switched on again, and an at least partial restoration of youth made possible.

---

* This experiment remains controversial. Twenty-two scientists from nine research centers reported in a joint communication that they had all failed to duplicate Jacobson's results in 18 similar experiments. One, Dr. William L. Byrne of Duke, later achieved a successful memory transplant experiment in the laboratory.

The processes of development and aging in mammals remain mysterious, but by no means hopelessly so. For instance, in a limited way we already know how to interfere with them. The life span of laboratory animals can be extended by four methods: underfeeding; the inhibition of "free radicals" (oxidizing agents in the body); immunosuppression; poikilothermy (cooling of body temperature).

The classic experiment disproving the inevitability of a fixed life span was performed in 1934, by Dr. Clive M. McCay of Cornell. By subjecting rats to nutritional deprivation—feeding them a proper amount of vitamins, minerals, and proteins but a greatly reduced number of calories—he slowed down their rate of maturing and also extended their life spans. In some instances rats whose growth had been retarded lived twice as long as those maturing on a standard diet.

What may be a remarkable development along the same line of research was announced October 27, 1961, by the Monsanto Chemical Company. Dr. Richard S. Gordon, it was disclosed, had succeeded in arresting the growth of baby chicks and mice *altogether*, suspending their physiological maturation over a period of from six to nine months. When the amino acid, tryptophan, was reduced to 15-25 percent of the normal daily requirement, baby chicks and newly-weaned mice simply stopped developing. As soon as the imbalance was corrected, they returned to normal growth processes, maturing without ill effects.

Tryptophan-deprivation in the Monsanto laboratory prolonged life only insofar as it delayed maturity. This avenue of research does allow us to entertain one fantasy. If underfeeding of one kind or another can also indefinitely delay the physical maturing of human beings— while the accumulation of experience and information continues—we might conceivably produce a grouping of "immortal" boy-men and girl-women, held indefinitely on the brink of adolescence, with formidable, ever-growing intelligences and the bodies of children. For such an elite group, of course, once its members chose to release themselves from the biological suspension, the onset of maturity would mean rejoining the human race—and an irrevocable commitment to the mortal life span.

At the University of California, Berkeley, Dr. Paul E. Segall and Professor of Physiology Paola A. Timiras have for a number of years been pursuing research in administering tryptophan-deficient diets to a strain of Long-Evans female rats for periods ranging from a few months to nearly two years.

In a 1976 paper, "Patho-Physiologic Findings After Chronic Tryptophan Deficiency in Rats: A Model For Delayed Growth and Aging," they reported:

Growth was interrupted during the period of tryptophan-deficiency, but when the animals were returned to a complete diet they gained weight and grew to normal size. *Ability to reproduce,* as indicated by litter production, *was present at 17-28 months of age in rats which had been deprived of tryptophan,* whereas no rats (in the control group over *17* months of age produced any offspring. (Author's italics)

Other signs of delayed aging in the experimental group included, at advanced ages, greater longevity, as well as later onset in the appearance of obvious tumors, and better coat condition and hair regrowth.

To extend this example of advances being made by only two of a growing number of researchers in life-extension, a letter from Dr. Segall states:

. . . We know caloric restriction can delay death from aging. We have shown that rats place on the Tryptophan-Minus diet at 21 days of age for 13 months, then place on a normal diet, can continue to reproduce as late as 28 months, when most rats become infertile at approximately 16 months of age. Thus we can drastically interfere with reproductive aging as well.

We also know that we can take a normal rat at 13 months, place it on the T-Minus diet until 26 months and then feed it normally. One month later, it grows back a youthful-looking coat of hair with rich shiny colors instead of a mottled, dull coat generally associated with that age. However, a few months later the coat deteriorated and the animals died.

There is no doubt that these diets can drastically alter the process of aging. . . . Unfortunately, at present they may weaken the animals' endocrine and immune systems, thus impeding really long-term survival.

Therefore, there are hints that not only may aging be retarded, but possibly at some time in the future even reversed. Obviously, because of the many problems, finding the exact methods to employ will take much more work and money.

However, the possibility of aging arrest and reversal looks even greater with each new research insight. . . .

Biochemist Denham Harman of the University of Nebraska Medical School has called attention to a "striking" prolongation of life among male mice fed with an antioxidant chemical, butylated hydroxytoluene (BHT). The median life span of a short-lived strain of mice was extended 53 percent by this diet. Harman thinks that oxydizing agents in the body known as "free radicals" bring about aging changes such as hardening of the arteries. The addition of similar chemicals to a man's diet, he believes, may become "an acceptable, practical means of significantly increasing his useful life."

At the 10th International Congress of Gerontology held in Jerusalem (June 1975) Dr. Roy Walford, with his UCLA colleagues M. Gerbase-DeLima, R. K. Liu, and G. S. Smith reported in a paper, "Immunological Engineering":

Marked prolongation of the lifespan of a long-lived strain, particularly of the longest-lived survivors, can only be achieved by tampering with the basic aging process itself.

Manipulation of the diet (particularly caloric undernutrition during childhood) in rodents and (lowering) of the body temperature (hypothermia) in poikilotherms does significantly prolong lifespan. Biochemical data, including for example, collagen solubility confirm that the rate of aging of animals subjected to these two regimes is significantly slowed.

The lifespan of annual fish can be greatly prolonged by retaining them at a slightly lower environmental temperature than the control population. . . . The favorable effect on lifespan of a hypothermic regime may operate via mitigation of a spontaneous autoimmune response. Recent preliminary studies by one of us (R. W.) in India suggest that certain yogic techniques can temporarily lower body temperature by $\frac{1}{2}$ to $1°$ C. Furthermore, some cave or forest dwelling yogis subsisting on meager (400-500 calorie) diets may be semi-permanently hypothermic by as much as 3 or $4°$ C (and probably hypometabolic).

Other experiments classifiable as "immunologic engineering" include reconstitution with lymphoid cells, and attempts at immune rejuvenation by treatment with polyribonuceotides, thymosin, or other agents.

Today gerontology appears to be a science waiting for its Einstein, someone who will establish a structure of agreed-upon first principles. Or possibly, even more important, a sudden advance may be achieved in the study of aging by a researcher like Sir Alexander Fleming, happening to notice mold growing in a container on the window sill or laboratory shelf. Perhaps, too, a young Korzybski will be needed to help pin down the biochemical-semantic content of each new theory, to determine how much it really differs from all the others.

The student of aging, engaged in a combined fight for life and bounty hunt, will find good reasons to become discouraged. The human body turns out to be such an unstable repository of ills. Moving out from what he imagines to be a secure base of understanding, he encounters one mystery after another. Everywhere he finds impossibilities. From all sides voices warn, caution and discourage him. Now and then he passes by the encampments of older specialists, who are shaking their heads in bafflement. All over the jungle blind men seem to be feeling an elephant, and this immense mystery of the slowly dying body endures.

Still, he will keep on. In time, he will have new weapons more powerful and precise than the laser or electron microscope. Sooner or later, with persistence, he can practically count on luck. Somewhere inside the tangle of speculation and error a researcher is going to stumble across a clue.

The young gerontologist must not let himself be intimidated. He will, of course, listen to his seniors and learn from them, but will also find that they contradict one another, have not discovered very much, and need him. As Alex Comfort said at the Gatlinburg Conference: "The more we beat the drums of senescence to students, the more we will find out."

Future successes in this field will come from willingness to take chances and carry out independent lines of study. Can aging possibly be turned off? The researcher may find something, or nothing; he may chance on a slightly different line of action, or abandon his approach for an entirely new idea. He will perhaps feel as miserable and baffled as Wilbur and Orville Wright only two years before they put their craft in the air at Kitty Hawk, North Carolina:

The experiments of 1901 were far from encouraging . . . we saw that the calculations upon which all flying-machines had been based were unreliable, and that all were simply groping in the dark. Having set out with absolute faith in the existing scientific data, we were driven to doubt one thing after another, till finally, after two years of experiment, we cast it all aside, and decided to rely entirely upon our own investigations. Truth and error were so intimately mixed as to be indistinguishable.

Established laws of physics, of course, held good for the Wright Brothers, and later, amended by Einstein, for the scientists who developed atomic energy and procedures for rocketing into space. As yet no such principles are available to guide our researchers in aging. Hence, any national crash effort devoted to gerontology would, in the beginning, involve basic biological research rather than the development of technology—and would (still searching for first principles) encounter harder going and move at a slower pace.

Even though emergency action is needed—for the race's emotional health depends on it—advances toward the ultimate prevention of death are bound to be tentative and slow. Barring extraordinary good luck, help will arrive too late for everyone alive.

The frozen casket does hold out a faint promise, and currently the only promise, of survival. Another remote hope might be that of regenerating a person some day from the preserved snipping of his own flesh. But these offer faraway prospects, with the present chance of our returning to consciousness as remote as can be. In the face of unadorned death, now or tomorrow, how will we content ourselves?

First, we must live one day at a time and hope for one piece of good luck at a time. This means looking forward to the prolongation of life. It means going after, perhaps for peace of mind even counting on, the "series of life extending bonuses" cited by Alex Comfort. These certainly are not out of reach; some, in crude form, we already have with us, such as the implanting of new hearts and in time all of the body's major organs—eventually without fear of tissue rejection. Progress in this field has already moved beyond the euphoric expectations of, say, five years ago. For instance, the recent recommendation by a special faculty committee at Harvard that the medical community redefine death in terms of irreversible brain damage, even though the heart continues to beat, will undoubtedly help clear the way to the routine transplantation of "live" organs.

By such means, the eventual growing of duplicate organs for each of us *in vitro*, elimination of substances that quicken aging (such as Denham Harman's "free radicals") from the every-day diet, and by other measures that—if the past is any indication—will unexpectedly be revealed at some forthcoming medical conference, we may arrive at a legitimate hope.

Intensified research can prolong life and buy time for everyone. Whenever you buy time, you buy a new geometric progression of medical advances. The prolongation of life buys discoveries not yet known. Over two or three decades, in fact, you will probably find yourself living in an entirely new medical frame of reference. In successive decades your life may have been saved by sulfanilimide, penicillin, cortisone, reserpine . . . Today, if you can buy fifty years, you may look forward to more than a prayer of buying eternity. Even fifteen to twenty-five, with good luck, could provide booster shots well into the twenty-first century. And at some time, just beyond a horizon that is no longer receding, extensions of life will, with luck, merge into an immortal present.

Then we will have nothing less than the self-created mutation of a species achieved by its own members who refused to be victims of a master design. Man's disguised drive to immortality will at last have prevailed over his biological destiny. Born to die, the rebel will have taken a stand against his own nature, said "No!" to his own faulty cells, and countermanded the lower-level evolutionary orders that consigned him to oblivion. The simulated death and rebirth rhythms moving through all the life we know may be seen in retrospect as those of a species in labor, giving birth to a divine form of itself.

XX

THE ENGINEERING
OF DIVINITY

The resurrection of the body is a social project facing mankind as a whole, and it will become a practical political problem when the statesmen of the world are called upon to deliver happiness instead of power. . . .

NORMAN O. BROWN

. . . death, thou shalt die.

JOHN DONNE

The pursuit of death's secret should not be undertaken glumly. We will press on, but avoid crabbed fanaticism, hunting down the quarry with exuberance, and above all with relief that our disguised desire has come out in the open. The primary source of our fears, and of all evil and meanness afflicting the human spirit, has been acknowledged and publicly identified. It was death all the time, and nothing else. What a fabulous liberation not merely to know but to realize that! Anxiety falls away (though fear remains). The main point is that understanding what we fear, we may perhaps act less violently against one another and direct our aggressions against death itself.

The false gods to whom the immortality-hunter formerly bowed down will be reduced to artifacts. He will no longer injure his fellow men in the struggle for the gods' imaginary favors. The Computer of Excellence will have vanished, and the pathetic and vainglorious competition to ring up scores for the record will come to an end. The old Mathematics of Retribution will stand exposed as an empty threat of our own making. Meaninglessness—the state of mind that currently renders humanity either inert or vicious—will make no more trouble.

We will have something to do. Our mission will be simply, first, to attack death and all of its natural causes, and, second, to prepare for immortality, or the state of indefinite living, which is the divine state. To become divine will mean at last the freedom to play eternally beyond death's shadow—and if the play palls, the privilege in one's own good time, not pushed by fear, of ending the game with a graceful suicide.

But there remains the catch: members of the transitional generations will almost surely not live to experience the immortal state. Knowing this, we will have to psych ourselves, like athletes, into a superior performance. We can begin with a self-congratulatory religion rather than a humbling one, spreading abroad a new faith honoring our race instead of punishing it for an imaginary primal crime. Through our efforts we honor the human species by helping to turn it into the divine species. We may fairly consider ourselves the heroes and heroines of the evolutionary process. Our grandchildren and great-grandchildren will look back and know that we, the last of the old mortals, held the world together even in the full knowledge that death was waiting for us. We did not blow our minds after all, nor, out of frustration and forsakenness, blow up the planet, destroying their inheritance. We showed the grace not to take revenge for our own permanent loss by imposing suicide on mankind. These will be reasonable enough grounds for self-worship, and permit us all indulgences so that during the final hours of the hunt we may enjoy every pleasure that mortal life has to offer.

What we are hunting, and hoping to secure for our grandchildren, is really nothing less than the long-promised kingdom of heaven. In dark moments, thinking of ourselves, we can try to have faith in the long chance that John Donne's prophecy will be fulfilled soon. The Gospel According To Matthew—which may be accepted as an evolutionary foretelling—warns that the Kingdom of God will come as a thief in the night. "Watch therefore," Matthew counsels us, "for ye know not what hour your Lord doth come."

He will arrive in a caravan with certain precious medicines. Meanwhile we may at least start planning the utopia to follow.

XXI

NOTES ON A UTOPIA
BEYOND TIME

The mistaken and unhappy notion that a man is an enduring entity is known to you. It is also known to you that man consists of a multitude of souls, of numerous selves. . . .

. . . I was living a bit of myself only—a bit that in my actual life and being had not been expressed to a tenth or a thousandth part. . . .

HERMAN HESSE

. . . a profound longing enters into that dream that our souls shall pass from star to star through the vast spaces of the heavens, in an infinite series of transmigrations.

UNAMUNO

It is said that men and women will go mad in the face of eternity and, with infinite time ahead of them, lie around like lotus-eaters, succumb to indolence and despair, give up work projects, cease to love because there is no urgency and, finally, kill each other through sheer boredom.

Alan Watts has bemoaned the "terrible monotony of everlasting pleasure," and conjectured that "there would be no joy in being alive save in relation to the awesome prospect of death." Berdyaev refers to "evil infinity." These fears are understandable, but based on old-style temporal thinking. They arise from the surprisingly Western assumption, for Watts, that scarcity and urgency are required to make people do anything. True, with death the fact, men have organized their activities to race the sunset, hoping to rise above the human condition and escape judgment. With death no longer the fact, another kind of man will evolve whose nervous system (after a period of adjustment) will have been freed of anxiety. Having no clock to race and nothing to prove, this divine man will be free to play, with no more fear of meaninglessness than a football or baseball player, an actor, a lamb or a puppy.

Besides, in the Immortalist State the citizens of eternity will be living on different levels of time, taking part in one historical game or another as they please. Since endless existence on a single plane would indeed be a bore, the utopia beyond time will extend the Hindu conception so beautifully adapted to Western concerns in Herman Hesse's *Steppenwolf*: that each of us can, if we try, lead many lives in one. Most men, like the Steppenwolf of the novel, live out only a tiny portion of their potential existence. The Hindu model, following Buddha's journey, provides for a life in which the traveler plays successive roles: that of student, youthful explorer in the wilderness, rake and wastrel, merchant, family man, hermit and finally beggar and holy man. Through these stages the soul progresses toward the unknowable, and one day (it is pretended), with luck, will escape the eternal return.

In the immortalist view, this is an elaborate fake: the eternal return is desperately wanted. It can be made possible in our world beyond death and time by a system of *designed sleeps* and *programmed reincarnations.* Techniques of freezing or administered hibernation will permit us to rest for designated periods in between an endless variety of lives and careers. In eternity—always excepting the possibility of accident—men and women will have the chance to live out all the unlived lives and travel the untraveled paths that they wish they had explored.

Assuming that the aging of cells and tissues has been arrested, and can be reversed during the period of sleep, the body may be returned to whatever age the person desires—presumably this side of puberty, since a return to physical childhood might well prove to be impossible. The individual may rest in peace for ten, twenty, seventy-five years, or for centuries, before being wakened to his new existence.

By such means each of us may pursue lost dreams and careers, becoming doctor, space explorer, artist, athlete, scientist—fleshing out in free play all of the myths that have ever occurred to mankind; being in our turn Apollo, Dionysius, Loki, Gilgamesh, Helen, the Wife of Bath and Isadora Duncan. And if we lack the talent to carry off one role or the other—being, say, a mediocre athlete or actor a hundred years from now as well as today—well then, we will have had our try, and perhaps failed, but the penalty for failure will not be annihilation from the world's memory as we now fear. There will always be fresh chances to project our being in new ways.

There will no longer be one linear history of the species. History will not be going anywhere in particular. Instead, we will live in a mosaic of histories, crossing over from one to another in each incarnation. "Side-by-side" lives will go on in separate frames of reference like circus acts under the same tent. Executing their mythic patterns, people will be in different phases of exploration and different blocks of time. Imagine a group of friends—

one in his voluptuary stage, another scientifically ob-
sessed, a third mystical and contemplative, a fourth all
business. A century later they might meet and find their
roles interchanged. Or an individual dedicated to ex-
ploits in his last incarnation might seek to rest and
reflect. Arising from his cool sleep, he might then enjoy
an interlude as teacher and scholar, and devote himself
for the next fifty years to tending, watching over and
guiding the lifelines of others.

Part of the population will be playing these varied
world-games, another part hibernating, and a third en-
gaged in some sort of training, briefing or de-briefing, in
between lives. The one who has just "waked up" will
not, of course, be a child, but in his new surroundings—
decades or centuries later—he will be *as* a child, requiring
reeducation for the new scene he has been born into. The
reorientation will not only acquaint him with Utopia's
current ground rules, cultural and scientific develop-
ments that have taken place since he went to sleep, and
news of this sort; it will also be designed to prepare him
for new emotional settings in the lifetime to come. Eter-
nity will contain many kinds of time and possibilities for
action, as each rebirth confronts the traveler with different
game-values. Each time he will have to care about new
things; even if there is no death, he should not feel com-
pletely secure. For men turned into gods, stress and anxiety
in reasonable amounts must be provided—like artificial
gravity in a space ship.

Our present-day faith in games should carry us
through. For divine people the question of why we are
here, why we exist, will be unimportant. Once we have
learned to move in and out of different kinds of time at
will, the "meaning of life" becomes our business, not
that of a cosmic authority which has refused to reveal
itself. As gods, we no longer ask about meaning; we deter-
mine it. We make the rules, and *are* meaning. Life has

become our sport, like football, which simply is, and has no reason why. In their ontological significance, comets, rocks, dust and solar flares do not concern us, except as matter to be controlled. We, the individual forms through which the river of energy passes, are responsible for our own significance. With the conquest of aging-to-death, we will have qualified to become our own deities, lords of creation by default, fully able to dictate life's meaning as we see fit.

Still, without the pressure of time passing and the idea of only one life to live, might not our drive to create, learn and explore wither for lack of urgency? Perhaps so. Conceivably, with life ending in a temporary slumber rather than in death, we would not try as hard as so many of us do now—pushing for salvation achieved by scores registered on the imaginary Cosmic Machine. But trying hard, in itself, is not an absolute virtue, nor progress an eternal ideal. Immortality has always been the ultimate goal of progress. Once death has been rendered obsolete for our species, the journey along that old road will be unnecessary, except for pleasure. Beyond time and death, all creative play will be gratuitous and accomplishment in any field, or in any game, an act of exuberance rather than a duty. There will be no moral need to create, learn or explore any more than we need to go skiing or skin-diving. Yet think how many make a virtual religion out of these forms of free play.

It is true that we could eventually grow tired of our games, but not for many lifetimes. Meanwhile a greater danger to the utopia beyond time will be likely to come from a lingering physiological disorientation: for many centuries the body may not realize that parabolic aging to death is no longer a threat. It may continue reacting to the human condition that doesn't exist any longer. During this period liberation from death may make our nervous systems uneasy. Vestigial fears and reactive aggressions may contend in the individual's dreams. Under this kind of stress cosmic delinquents may go so far as to attempt a disruption of paradise and even try to bring back death, perhaps by means of random murders.

The immortalist view is that the early feeling of disorientation in eternity would not lead to such evil extremes, or in any event that incidents of this kind would probably be rare. Since, so far as we know, the desire to injure others relates to one's own fear of death, most rebels beyond time would stop short of killing. (By this time, of course, chemical control of personality will be possible, but we are assuming or hoping that in the Immortalist state it would be used sparingly, only to upgrade intelligence or, as a last resort, prevent psychopathic violence.)

To be on the safe side, facsimiles of conflict must be devised for nervous systems temporarily disoriented by the abolition of death. Nervously aggressive individuals should be encouraged to compete in tournaments, offered dangerous assignments, for example, in exploration, and permitted to take part in institutionalized blood-letting. If the risk of death attracts these people, so be it. Let there be chivalric games with dragons and artificial evil introduced into them.

For less extreme but still normally competitive men and women the illusion of ratings will continue to be essential. Reflexively showing off before the old gods, even though immortality has been won, they may come back in all their incarnations—playing a succession of human seasons within the divine framework—as athletes return year after year to play in the National and American Leagues, with the ups and downs of their career averages and their Standings in the Sky recorded through eternity by our utopian statisticians.

Coordinators of the world societies will be restricted to one term, one lifetime of authority, so that a self-perpetuating bureaucracy can make no bid for eternal power. The trust assigned to them will be to keep watch over all wheels of being. They will make sure scientists do not interfere with one another, and that space rugby teams will not drop the ball amid flocks of sheep. The governing cadres must serve as spiritual traffic consultants and guardians of the eternal return; as educators and keepers of every history. They will maintain a record of all developments, advances and setbacks. Most important, they are to be charged with creating simulations of bygone events that the newly-awakened voyager might want to reexperience as part of his education during the next time around.

In a world beyond death there will probably be more nonconformists than ever before. Great numbers of such people may choose to live outside of history altogether, and spend their days gardening, weaving and tending animals. Others will reject eternal life, preferring to mature and die in the old way, and certainly no attempt will be made to change their minds. With severe overpopulation problems likely in the earlier years, the more citizens who opt for mortality, the easier it will be for everyone else.

Children will be treated as immigrants, requiring visas to be admitted to the new society. This should cause no great hardship for anyone. After all, we have children mainly to perpetuate genetic repetitions of ourselves in eternity, to "keep the family going." Now, when we can move into an indefinitely extended future ourselves, in person, the longing to have children may, for many couples, be moderated. And if the aging process has been stabilized, why hurry? With indefinite time ahead, the parents-to-be can well afford to wait their turn until the attrition of the accidental-dead leaves an opening.

In these circumstances children will become a welcome and beloved minority treated with great tenderness by everyone. Born free of time and death, the newcomers will probably form a slightly different class, having no memory of the old days when people fell sick and died. The veterans who knew time and death and barely escaped it will regale these beautiful and fortunate young people with tales of that bygone purgatory.

In the Immortalist State, the nature of love as we know it will almost necessarily change. Already in transition today, love will have nothing much to do with social contracts nor have a form supposed to last forever. All erotic events can take place free of time and last indefinitely. In fact, some people might choose to spend an entire incarnation in one stupendous erotic event. Andrew Marvell's vision summoned up for his coy mistress: "Had we but world enough and time, this coyness, lady, were no crime . . ." will suddenly come true, and it will be possible for our love to grow "vaster than empires, and more slow."   •

If love—especially romantic love—has been attempting to share consciousness in a simulated eternity, what will happen to it in *real* eternity? If love now serves to stop time, what will be its role when time and aging have in fact been stopped? If love has conveyed a longing for rebirth out of time, how will it fare when rebirth into many successive lives is routinely guaranteed? More often than not, the individual will probably pursue a new way of loving. Hence, if marriage in its present form should survive the conquest of death (which it very well may not), the best arrangement will probably be for the contract between husband and wife automatically to terminate after each existence. This offers no problem to the couple who have been happy together in their last incarnation: a simple renewal of marriage vows can unite them as young man and woman together again a lifetime later.

The young man coming down the road may be one's

grandfather, and the old man nearing his time of sleep one's son. In eternity—assuming that members of the family still want to communicate with each other—the son and grandson will sometimes be "older" than the reborn father. With reference to a given incarnation, they may be more experienced and wiser, and therefore unhesitatingly counsel the fledgling parent. The old lament: "if youth knew, if age could . . ." will be forgotten, and since no man and woman will really be older than another, traditional authority, in and out of the family, will give way to brotherhood. But sooner or later the small unit that we know now will be likely to break apart. Expanded families of twenty or more persons, increasingly common among younger people, may become the rule. Still, though we go on to live in different blocks of time, family records will be carefully maintained through the centuries—to avoid an orphaned feeling and to prevent inbreeding.

Even when we no longer age and die, the need to worship some sort of mystery will undoubtedly remain. What symbols then will represent the Essential Mystery? This is impossible to forecast, but the children of eternity may worship variations of Luck, or That Which Cannot Be Controlled. There will be no point in worshipping anything else, since they will have everything else. Or if they do not possess it, they will have endless time to try. But Luck will be different: the only thing that can kill them, and for this reason they may go down on their knees before it.

The philosopher will revere the principle of indeterminacy. Others may conduct ceremonies before the future equivalent of a giant slot machine or roulette wheel. This curious and enigmatic element, the mystery of luck containing through all eternity the chance of death—perhaps, beyond time, offering the mathematical certainty of a terminal accident—will probably, as suggested earlier, fascinate many members of the race and tempt them into strange deeds daring annihilation. This in no way contravenes immortalist principles, since it is the once unavoidable passage through aging and illness into oblivion that will have been rendered obsolete, not the voluntary risking of death if the spirit so pleases itself.

Berdyaev has suggested that "the crowning point of world creation is the end of this world. The world must be turned into an image of beauty, it must be dissolved in creative ecstasy."

This hardly seems desirable or necessary. Why should the world be dissolved at all? Because the writer himself is going to die—for no other reason. *Götterdämmerungs* need not be invoked, no matter how beautiful. True, in the Immortalist state death might occasionally be summoned. It is conceivable that an older traveler tired of his divinity—after having lived out dozens of lives and explored every desire—could slip from personal to general consciousness, and drift into his long-sought nirvana with eyes.

The individual would give himself up and simply rest. He would not be a fixed person anymore, and he would care only to sleep. A sweet weariness might pervade his being. Then his eyes would close, not in forced death but in voluntary leave-taking because he had lived enough.

Such an ending gives mystical satisfaction. But the prospect is also that this sweet suicide might never appeal to him. He could perfectly well live on and on without apology or contrived abandonment of himself—and, after each life cycle and period of sleep, look forward to beginning again, always to begin again.

APPENDIX

A NOTE ON POPULATION CONTROL

The crisis of world overpopulation will reach emergency stages long before personal immortality has been made possible. Famine, it has been freely predicted, will threaten underdeveloped parts of the world by 1980. In his lengthy essay on the need for cooperation between the United States and the Soviet Union, the Soviet nuclear physicist Andrei D. Sakharov cites "a prognosticated deterioration of the average food balance in which localized food crises merge into a sea of hunger, intolerable suffering and desperation, the grief and fury of millions. . . . "

This forecast may be in need of revision, at least for part of the globe. Extraordinary advances in food production were reported in 1968 from large areas of Asia. According to the United Nations Food and Agriculture Organization (FAO): ". . . the world food and agriculture situation is now in a state of transition and hope." In September, Secretary-General U Thant stated: "Record wheat crops and unparalleled yields of rice and maize during the last year prompted predictions that the race between food and population could be won."

In his article published in *American Forests,* Charles J. Hitch, former president of the University of California and currently president of Resources for the Future, Inc., notes:

Even the relatively dour prophets of the Club of Rome state in its latest report that "neither food, nor energy, nor mineral resources appear from a technological viewpoint to be seriously critical for the next 25 years. . . .

Thomas T. Poleman, professor of international economics, New York State College of Agriculture and Life Sciences, Cornell University, Ithaca, writes in *Science*:

a revival of the fear, periodic in its emergence, that the world is running out of food, and that some cataclysmic Malthusian solution will shortly be upon us.

He points out:

We sometimes forget how great has been the change of the past 25 years. The real product of the world perhaps trebled, so that on a per capita basis we are on the average twice as well off as we were in 1950. Change, to be sure, has been concentrated in the developed countries, but not exclusively. The explosion in education and literacy has been world-wide. . . . Famine, if not entirely eliminated, has come to be localized and to reflect political failings more than anything else. . . .

We learn as well in *Science* that

. . . there is about twice as much land on which to produce food as is now used: 3.2 billion hectares vs. 1.4 billion. . . . Though there will be costs to develop this land, it certainly is feasible. More important, land becomes less important as food production methods improve. Yield increase has accounted for 60% of production increases in the world, in the last few years.

We have then some evidence that population control rather than food production will become the more immediate problem for a world in which life has been greatly ex-

tended—death from "natural causes" being put off or some-
day virtually abolished altogether.

Medically and technologically, and in biochemical
terms, the world no longer confronts a hopeless birth-
control problem. We need only look at recent birth-rate
statistics to discover markedly reduced population pres-
sures in the industrially advanced countries. Inexpensive
intrauterine devices and oral contraceptives have helped
bring down the United States birth rate to 15 per 1000 in
1974, a drop from 19 in 1965.

A study prepared by the Population Reference Bureau,
Inc., a non-profit educational organization under contract
to the Agency for International Development (AID) re-
ported that more than two-thirds of the world's popula-
tions lived last year (1975) in countries with birth control
programs of some kind. Birth rates world-wide dropped
from 34 per 1000 people in 1965 to 30 in 1974, and could
drop as low as 20 per 1000 in ten years. These figures indi-
cated more slowly increasing populations in the near future.

Specifically, the population programs cited in the study
had "a marked effect on the most populous nations: China,
India and Indonesia . . . and also in South Korea, Taiwan,
Hong Kong, Cuba, Costa Rica, Jamaica."

Within a relatively few years, it would seem, wherever
simple and inexpensive means of contraception become
available on the mass-market, the threat of overpopulation
ought logically to diminish. Even the most severe religious
authority will eventually come to terms with contraception.
For example, popular Roman Catholic resistance to the
edict of Pope Paul VI affirming once again the sinful nature
of chemical or mechanical means of birth control indicates
that the Church can no longer enforce this prohibition.
What the Roman Catholic Church cannot do, no other
authority can hope to manage—in other words, it is prac-
tically impossible to prevent large numbers of people from
making use of contraceptives once they have legal access to
them.

Not every savant detects an overwhelming emergency in this regard. "Fortunately," wrote R. Buckminster Fuller a few years ago, "population explosion is only the momentary social hysteria's cocktail conversation game. Real population crisis is fundamentally remote. There is room enough indoors in New York City for the whole 1963 world's population to enter, with room enough inside for all hands to dance the twist in average night-club proximity. There is ample room in the New York streets for one half of the world's population to amble about, leaving room enough inside buildings for the other half to lie down and sleep. . . ."

We must assume that something rational is going to be done to relieve world population pressures before the year 2000, if only because the nations have no choice. A common prediction is that in the twenty-first century birth control can be achieved by contraceptive agents in foodstuffs. As explained by Dr. John R. Platt, acting director of the University of Michigan's Mental Health Research Institute, to the American Institute of Planners in Washington, D.C.: "Any couple that really wanted to have a baby would have to go down the street and buy untreated food from the 'other store.' But this wouldn't necessarily be a bad thing. It would mean every child a wanted child." Although beyond our technological capability for the time being, Dr. Platt said, the process, once perfected, could be as simple as putting vitamin D in milk or adding iodine to salt.

Finally this must be the Immortalist view, and there can be no getting around it. Not enforced sterilization for people with "too many" children. Nor, necessarily, approval of regulations such as the one recently laid down by Prime Minister Indira Gandhi to Indian civil servants: no more than three children in your family. Rather, very simply, no serum without population control. No life-extending or -preserving elixir for those who choose to have more than x children, whatever number may be deemed reasonable.

Thus the confrontation: extension of your life versus, let's say, excessive parenthood—a critical and most interesting choice for the orthodox.

Once the chemical and technological means to limit population are made available to everyone, the problem of birth control comes down to apprising women in villages around the world of their human right not to exhaust themselves in the production of enormous families. If they can be persuaded not to cooperate with excessive *machismo* or neurotic nationalist drives for more babies, the battle against overpopulation will be won. The best means of education, we know, will be by example. When three or four village women accept the intrauterine coil, and no evil consequences ensue, the word gets around and others tend to be less reluctant to protect themselves in the same way.

Meanwhile during the decades before the year 2000 the race's disguised drive to immortality will continue to bring our gerontologists closer to the secrets of aging. Humanity's push toward the utopia beyond time will not be slowed down by the warnings of demographers. Too much pressure has been built up behind it. Research is not going to be called off. The day will arrive when somebody wearing glasses and a sterilized apron will run through a laboratory yelling wildly and waving a test tube. Provided that the species refrains from destroying itself, there will be no way for this not to happen.

NOTES

Epigraph
Miguel de Unamuno, *Tragic Sense of Life* (New York, Dover, 1921/1954), p. 39.

I Presentation of the Immortalist Argument

PAGE	LINE	
4	6	Blaise Pascal, *Pensées,* Pensée #414 (New York, Modern Library, 1941), p. 131.
6	16	Reinhold Niebuhr, *The Nature and Destiny of Man,* Vol. I (New York, Scribner, 1941), p. 178.
7	13	Pascal, *Pensées,* Pensée #194, p. 67.
	27	Paul Tillich, *The New Being* (New York, Scribner, 1955), pp. 170, 172.
9	20	Erich Fromm, *Escape from Freedom* (New York, Avon, 1965), p. 110.
	27	Norman O. Brown, *Life Against Death* (New York, Vintage Books, 1961), p. 6.
	29	*Ibid.,* p. 4.
	32	*Ibid.,* p. 284.
	33	*Ibid.,* p. xii.
11	9	Feodor M. Dostoevsky, *The Possessed,* quoted by

PAGE	LINE	
	5	Jung, *op. cit.*, p. 116.
26	26	*Ibid.*, p. 113.
27	5	From *The Works of Plato*, Vol. III, *Phaedo*, trans. by Benjamin Jowett (New York, Tudor, 1954), p. 203.
	9	St. Augustine *Confessions*, in *Reincarnation: An East-West Anthology*, ed. by Joseph Head and S. L. Cranston (New York, Julian, 1961), p. 38.
	14	The Koran, *ibid.*, p. 56.
	18	*The Book of the Dead* (Egyptian), *ibid.*, p. 23.
	28	The Zohar, *ibid.*, p. 29.
	37	Brown, *Life Against Death*, p. 215.
28	4	Friedrich Nietzsche, "The Seven Seals," from *Thus Spake Zarathustra*, in *The Philosophy of Nietzsche* (New York, Modern Library, 1954), p. 257.
	9	Voltaire, in *Reincarnation*, p. 202.
	15	Marquis de Sade, *Dialogue between a Priest and a Dying Man*, in *Selections from His Writings*. Chosen and trans. by Paul Dinnage (New York, Grove, 1953), p. 87.
	22	Henry David Thoreau, *Walden Pond and Other Writings*, ed. by Brooks Atkinson (New York, Modern Library, 1950), p. 221.
	31	Unamuno, *Tragic Sense of Life*, p. 5.
29	1	Watts, *Nature, Man and Woman* (Mentor), p. 47.
	6	_____, *Nature, Man and Woman* (New York, Pantheon, 1958), p. 71.
	8	_____, *Psychotherapy East and West* (New York, Pantheon, 1961), p. 98.
	21	Unamuno, *op. cit.*, p. 11.
	31	Alan Watts, *Myth and Ritual in Christianity* (New York, Vanguard, 1954), p. 70.
30	9	André Ferdinand Herold, *The Life of Buddha* (New York, Albert and Charles Boni, 1927), p. 57.

PAGE	LINE	
	34	*The Bhagavad-Gita,* in *Reincarnation,* p. 3.
31	6	Chwang Tzu, *ibid.,* p. 19.
	10	Gandhi, *ibid.,* p. 10.
	20	Sigmund Freud, "The Attitudes of Psychoneurotics toward Death," quoted in Choron, *Modern Man and Mortality,* p. 40.
	27	Walter Bromberg and Paul Schilder, quoted in Choron, *ibid.,* p. 40.
32	24	Unamuno, *op. cit.,* p. 133.
39	22	Dr. Elizabeth Kubler-Ross, as quoted by Kenneth Woodward, "There Is Life After Death," *McCall's,* August, 1976.
40	31	Albert Camus, "The Myth of Sisyphus," in *The Myth of Sisyphus and Other Essays,* p. 3.
41	13	Edwin S. Shneidman and Norman L. Farberow, "The Logic of Suicide," in *Clues to Suicide,* ed. by Shneidman and Farberow (New York, Mc-Graw-Hill/Blakiston Division, 1957), p. 32.
	17	*Ibid.,* p. 33.
	21	Herbert Hendin, M.D., *Suicide and Scandinavia* (New York, Grune and Stratton, 1964), p. 21.
	36	Don D. Jackson, "Theories of Suicide," in Shneidman and Farberow, *op. cit.,* p. 13.
42	19	C. A. Wahl, "Suicide as a Magical Act," *ibid.,* p. 28.
43	6	*Writers at Work: The Paris Review Interviews,* ed. and with an Introduction by Malcolm Cowley (New York, Viking, 1959), p. 139.

III   We Must Have Done Something Wrong

Epigraphs

44   Jung, *Collected Works,* Vol. VII, *Two Essays on Analytical Psychology* (1953), p. 156.

Thomas à Kempis (1953), *Imitation of Christ.*

Nietzsche, "The Religious Mood," from *Beyond*

PAGE   LINE

Good and Evil, in *The Philosophy of Nietzsche*, p. 433.

46   17   George Orwell, *How the Poor Die*, in *Shooting an Elephant* (New York, Harcourt, Brace & Co., 1945), p. 25.

47   18   Sir James Frazer, *The Golden Bough*, Part VI: *The Scapegoat* (New York, Macmillan, 1951), p. 302.

34   *Ibid.*, p. 303.

49   1   The *Bhagavad-Gita* (3, 10–16).

50   22   Thomas à Kempis, *op. cit.*

51   4   Thomas Bailey Aldrich, *The Story of a Bad Boy* (OOP).

25   Nikos Kazantzakis, *Report to Greco* (New York, Bantam Books, 1966), p. 169.

52   8   Thoreau, *Walden Pond*, p. 148.

25   Brown, *Life Against Death*, p. 266.

53   13   Herbert Marcuse, "The Ideology of Death," in Feifel, *The Meaning of Death*, p. 73.

34   St. John of the Cross, *The Dark Night of the Soul* (New York, Benziger, 1917), pp. 20–21.

54   10   Brown, *Life Against Death*, p. 31.

IV   The Disguised Drive to Become Divine

Epigraphs

58   Albert Camus, *The Rebel* (New York, Vintage Books, 1956), p. 24.

Jung, *Collected Works*, Vol. XI, *Psychology and Religion: West and East* (1958), p. 454.

65   30   Unamuno, *Tragic Sense of Life*, pp. 49–50.

V   Satan, Our Standard-Bearer

67   *Epigraph*

Feodor M. Dostoevsky, *The Brothers Karamazov* (New York, Harper & Bros., 1960), pp. 720–721.

PAGE	LINE	
68	10	Jung, *Collected Works,* Vol. X, *Civilization in Transition* (1964), p. 140.
	26	The Koran, quoted by Giovanni Papini, *The Devil* (London, Eyre & Spottiswood, 1955), p. 133.
69	3	R. B. Anderson, *Norse Mythology* (Chicago, S. C. Griggs and Company, 1879), p. 398.
	12	Sir Thomas Browne, *Religio Medici* (New York, Everyman's Library/Dutton, 1906), pp. 43–44.
70	1	Lord Byron, *The Poetical Works of Lord Byron* (London, Oxford University Press, 1904), pp. 513–14.
71	7	Milton, *Paradise Lost.*
73	9	Albert Camus, *Notebooks 1935–1942* (New York, Knopf, 1963), p. 37.
74	15	Kurt Seligmann, *The Mirror of Magic* (New York, Pantheon, 1948), p. 219.
	28	*Ibid.,* p. 222.
75	1	Watts, *Nature, Man and Woman* (Mentor Books), p. 25.
76	17	Papini, *op. cit.,* p. 14.
	18	Nicholas Berdyaev, *Freedom and the Spirit* (New York, Scribner, 1935), p. 169.
	23	De Rougemont, quoted by Seligmann, *op. cit.,* p. 219.
77	3	Dostoevsky, *op. cit.,* p. 732.
80	9	Erna Fergusson, *Dancing Gods: Indian Ceremonials of New Mexico and Arizona* (New York, Knopf, 1931), p. 31.
	17	*Ibid.,* p. 49.
	25	*Ibid.,* p. 51.
	34	*Ibid.,* p. 53.
81	26	Ramona and Desmond Morris, *Men and Snakes* (New York, McGraw-Hill, 1965), p. 72.
83	23	Papini, *op. cit.,* p. 89.
84	1	Dostoevsky, p. 724.

PAGE   LINE

86   7   Martin Buber, *I and Thou* (New York, Scribner, 1958), p. 52.

VI   Conditional Immortality for the Elect

Epigraphs

91   Franz V. M. Cumont, *After Life in Roman Paganism* (New Haven, Yale University Press, 1922), p. 111.
         Ibid., p. 114.

    1   Unamuno, *Tragic Sense of Life,* p. 250.

94   23   Browne, *Religio Medici,* p. 63.

    34   *Ibid.,* p. 63.

96   2   Vergil, *Bucolia,* Eclogue IV.

    31   F. B. Jevons, *The Idea of God in Early Religions* (Cambridge, Cambridge University Press, 1960), pp. 104–5.

97   6   C. G. Jung and C. Kerenyi, *Essays on a Science of Mythology,* Bollingen Series (New York, Pantheon, 1949), p. 212.

    14   Robert M. Grant with David Noel Freedman, *The Secret Sayings of Jesus* (New York, Doubleday, 1960), pp. 109–10.

99   22   Cumont, *op. cit.,* p. 111.

105 19   Ernest Renan, quoted by Kazantzakis, *Report to Greco,* p. 179.

VII   Showing Off Before the Computer
         of Excellence

Epigraphs

106   Jung, *Collected Works,* Vol. XI, p. 87.

         Jacques Maritain, "The Meaning of Contemporary Atheism," in *The Manse of Reason* (New York, Scribner, 1952), p. 171.

111 14   Holmes Welch, in "The Chinese Art of Make-Believe," *Encounter* (May, 1968), p. 9.

PAGE   LINE
        23   Seligmann, *The Mirror of Magic,* p. 69.
        26   Frazer, *The Golden Bough,* cited by Seligmann, *op. cit.,* p. 71.
        32   *Ibid.,* p. 164.
113   12   Lorenz, *On Aggression,* p. 261.
        25   St. John of the Cross, *The Dark Night of the Soul.*
114   8   Jung, *Collected Works,* Vol. V, *Symbols of Transformation,* quoted in *Psychological Reflections: An Anthology of the Writings of C. G. Jung,* ed. by Jolande Jacobi, Bollingen Series (New York, Pantheon, 1953), p. 150.
115   5   Martin Heidegger, *Being and Time* (New York, Harper & Row, 1962), p. 165.

        VIII   Four Styles of Consciousness in the Face of Death

                Epigraphs
116   Alfred Adler, *Understanding Human Nature* (New York, Greenberg, 1927), p. 215.
                Jung, *Collected Works,* Vol. XIII, *Paracelsus as Spiritual Phenomenon,* quoted in *Psychological Reflections,* p. 143.
                Maritain, *Christian Humanism,* in Evans and Ward, *The Social and Political Philosophy of Jacques Maritain,* p. 167.
                Charles Baudelaire, "Le Goût du néant," from *Les Fleurs du mal.*
121   25   Adler, *op. cit.,* p. 74.
        33   *Ibid.,* p. 72.
126   33   Sade, *Selections from His Writings,* pp. 147–48.
129   14   Heidegger, *Being and Time,* p. 165.
131   17   Thoreau, *Walden Pond,* quoted by Will Durant in *Mansions of Philosophy,* p. 575.

PAGE   LINE

132   17   Unamuno, *Tragic Sense of Life*, p. 52.

       28   Thoreau, *op. cit.*, p. 26.

IX   Emotional Mathematics

Epigraph

134   Unamuno, *Tragic Sense of Life*, p. 52.

142   34   Martin Buber, *Good and Evil* (New York, Scribner, 1953).

X   Love and Evil

Epigraph

146   José Ortega y Gasset, *What Is Philosophy?* (New York, Norton, 1960), p. 172.

            Berdyaev, *Freedom and the Spirit*, p. 160.

147   17   Leo N. Tolstoy, *Anna Karenina* (New York, Modern Library, 1950), p. 475.

148   3   Watts, *Myth and Ritual*.

       6   Watts, *Nature, Man and Woman* (Mentor Books), p. 162.

       11   Jung, *Collected Works*, Vol. XVII, *The Development of Personality* (1954).

       32   De Rougemont, *Love in the Western World* (New York, Anchor Books, 1957), p. 8.

149   19   D. H. Lawrence, *Women in Love* (New York, Viking Press/Compass Books, 1960), p. 178.

       33   De Rougemont, *op. cit.*, p. 36.

150   3   *Ibid.*, p. 297.

154   22   Buber, *Good and Evil*, p. 131.

       25   Berdyaev, *op. cit.*, p. 103.

       29   Unamuno, *Tragic Sense of Life*, p. 213.

155   11   Buber, *Good and Evil*, p. 46.

156   25   *Ibid.*, p. 103.

       32   Tillich, *The New Being*, pp. 172–73.

PAGE   LINE

XI   Shared Consciousness

Epigraphs

158   Ortega y Gasset, *What Is Philosophy?*, p. 116.

             Unamuno, *Tragic Sense of Life*, p. 213.

      6   Jung and Kerenyi, *Essays on a Science of Mythology*, p. 122.

      8   Ortega y Gasset, *op. cit.*, p. 157.

159   1   *Ibid.*, p. 161.

    18   Unamuno, *op. cit.*, p. 7.

163   16   Bertrand Russell, *The Basic Writings of Bertrand Russell*, ed. by Robert E. Egner and Wester E. Denonn (New York, Simon & Schuster, 1961), p. 567.

    24   Tolstoy, *Anna Karenina*, pp. 469–70

XII   The End of Philosophy

Epigraphs

169   Jean Jacques Rousseau, quoted in Unamuno in *Tragic Sense of Life*, p. 53.

             Papini, *The Devil*, p. 14.

170   23   From *The Works of Plato*, Vol. III, *Phaedo*, p. 194.

    36   Unamuno, *op. cit.*, p. 47.

171   9   Niebuhr, *The Nature and Destiny of Man*, Vol. I, p. 185.

172   13   Pascal, *Pensées*, Pensée #194, p. 71.

    15   Buber, *I and Thou*, p. 5.

    18   Niebuhr, *op. cit.*, Vol. I, p. 177.

    21   Watts, *Myth and Ritual*, p. 73.

    25   Evans and Ward, *Philosophy of Jacques Maritain*, pp. 22–23.

    28   Berdyaev, *Freedom and the Spirit*, p. 37.

    30   St. Augustine *Confessions*.

PAGE	LINE	
	33	Jung and Kerenyi, *Essays on a Science of Mythology*, p. 213.
	34	Jung, *Collected Works*, Vol. XI, p. 88.
173	1	Brown, *Life Against Death*, p. 104.
	4	Hegel, quoted by Brown, *ibid.*, p. 104.
	7	Lord Keynes, quoted by Brown, *ibid.*, p. 107.
	11	De Rougemont, *Love in the Western World*, p. 311.
174	17	Buber, *I and Thou*, p. 64.
175	4	Niebuhr, *The Nature and Destiny of Man*, Vol. I, p. 178.
	8	*Loc. cit.*
	33	Watts, *Myth and Ritual*, p. 148.
176	4	Tillich, *The New Being*, p. 56.
	28	Heidegger, *Being and Time*, p. 308.
177	2	Sade, *Dialogue between a Priest and a Dying Man*, in *Selections from His Writings*, p. 89.
	16	Ortega y Gasset, *What Is Philosophy?*, p. 174.

XIII   The End of Art

Epigraph

181		Crane Brinton, *A History of Western Morals* (New York, Harcourt, Brace & Co., 1969), p. 100.
183	7	Brown, *Life Against Death*, p. 61.
184	9	Aldous Huxley, *Island* (London, Chatto & Windus, 1962), pp. 243–44.
	30	From *The Works of Plato*, Vol. IV, *Republic*, Book X, p. 396.
	34	*Ibid.*, p. 378.
185	2	*Ibid.*, p. 386.
186	12	Brown, *op. cit.*, p. 60.
188	18	Shakespeare, *As You Like It* II. vii. 139.
192	14	Norman Mailer, "The White Negro," in *The Beat Generation and The Angry Young Men*,

PAGE   LINE

ed. by Gene Feldman and Max Gartenberg (New York, Citadel, 1958), pp. 342–43.

193   11   Brown, *ibid.,* p. 175.

29   Claude Brown, "An Introduction to Soul," *Esquire* (April, 1968), p. 79.

XIV   Time and Games

Epigraphs

195   Berdyaev, *The Beginning and the End,* p. 206.
John von Neumann and Oskar Morgenstern, *Theory of Games & Economic Behavior* (Princeton, Princeton University Press, 1953), p. 49.

197   36   Timothy Leary, from "How to Change Behavior," in pamphlet entitled *"Visionary Experience"* by Aldous Huxley and *"How to Change Behavior"* by Timothy Leary, reprints from *Clinical Psychology* (Copenhagen, Muksgaard, 1962), p. 57.

XV   The Great Defiance

Epigraph

202   Karl Barth, *Deliverance to the Captives* (New York, Harper & Bros., 1961), pp. 146–47.

4   *Ibid.,* p. 147.

203   35   Watts, *Psychotherapy,* p. 4.

204   10   Pascal, *Pensées,* Pensée #210, p. 75.

15   Leo N. Tolstoy, *Ivan Ilyitch and Other Stories* (New York, Crowell, 1887), p. 51.

18   *Ibid.,* p. 66.

20   *Ibid.,* p. 76.

206   7   . Barth, *op. cit.,* pp. 118–19.

17   Evans and Ward, *Philosophy of Jacques Maritain,* p. 167.

207   8   Marcuse, "The Ideology of Death," in Feifel, *The Meaning of Death,* p. 67.

PAGE	LINE	
	30	Watts, *Nature, Man and Woman* (Pantheon), pp. 46–47.
208	23	William Butler Yeats, "In Memory of Major Robert Gregory," from *Collected Poems of W. B. Yeats* (New York, Macmillan, 1960), p. 131.
	24	Ernest Renan, quoted in Choron, *Modern Man and Mortality,* p. 161.
	34	Marcuse, "The Ideology of Death," in Feifel, *op. cit.,* p. 72.
209	8	Marcus Aurelius, *Meditations.*
	31	Maritain, *The Meaning of Contemporary Atheism,* from Evans and Ward, *op. cit.,* p. 177.
210	9	*Loc. cit.*

XVI   The Future of Unnatural Man

Epigraphs

213		Ludwig Binswanger, *Being-in-the-World* (New York, Basic Books, 1964), p. 235.
		Heidegger, "The Way Back Into the Ground of Metaphysics," quoted in Walter Kaufmann, *Existentialism from Dostoevsky to Sartre* (New York, Meridian, 1957), p. 214.
214	11	Jung, *Collected Works,* Vol. XI, p. 105.
	16	Choron, *Modern Man and Mortality,* p. 135.
	16	Arthur Schopenhauer, *The World as Will and Idea* (London, Routledge and Kegan Paul, 1883), pp. 286, 306.
	22	Daqué, quoted in Choron, *op. cit.,* p. 203.
	23	Brown, *Life Against Death,* p. 82.
	25	Buber, *I and Thou,* p. 25.
	28	Watts, *Psychotherapy,* p. 29.
215	26	Goethe, *Fragment of Nature,* quoted in Watts, *Nature, Man and Woman* (Mentor Books), p. 113.
216	10	Russell, *What I Believe,* in Egner and Dennon, *The Basic Writings of Bertrand Russell,* p. 573.

XVII State of the Biomedical Arts

Epigraphs

XVIII The Cryonics Underground

Epigraphs

PAGE	LINE	
236	31	Ettinger, from a talk before a meeting of Science Fiction Authors, Los Angeles, quoted in Nelson, *op. cit.,* p. 80.
	34	Henderson, quoted in the *National Observer* (April 29, 1968).
239	9	Dr. Parkes, quoted in Ettinger, *op. cit.,* p. 16.
	12	Ettinger, quoted in Nelson, *op. cit.,* p. 8.
	13	Ettinger, *op. cit.,* p. 84.
	24	Ettinger, quoted in Nelson, *op. cit.,* p. 8.
241	15	Ettinger, *op. cit.,* p. 28.
	19	*Ibid.,* p. 39.
242	4	*Ibid.,* p. 40.
	10	*Ibid.,* p. 37.
	24	*Cryonics Reports* (October, 1967).
	33	Nelson, in an interview with Saul Kent, *Cryonics Reports* (October, 1967).
243	16	Ettinger, *Cryonics Reports* (October, 1967).
244	3	Drs. Karow and Hamilton, quoted in the *National Observer* (April 29, 1968).
	13	Walford, in a letter to the author dated April, 1968.
	10	*Nature* magazine (October 15, 1966).
244	23	Dr. Karow, *Cryonics Reports* (November, 1966).
245	30	*Newsweek* (August 16, 1976).
246	28	Ettinger, *op. cit.,* p. 107.
248	9	Richard L. Meier, *Science and Economic Development,* cited in Ettinger, *op. cit.,* p. 107.

XIX   Aging, Death and Birth

Epigraphs

251	Yeats, "The Tower," from *The Collected Poems of W. B. Yeats,* p. 192.
	Dr. Alex Comfort, *Ageing: The Biology of Senes-*

PAGE	LINE	
		cence (New York, Holt, Rinehart & Winston, rev. ed., 1964), p. 271.
254	28	Robert Prehoda, *The Future and Technological Forecasting,* cited in *Cryonics Reports* (January, 1967), p. 4.
	32	Prehoda, quoted in *Cryonics Reports* (December, 1966), p. 4.
255	8	Comfort, *op. cit.,* p. 270.
	14	Dr. Bernard Strehler, *Time, Cells, and Aging* (New York, Academic Press, 1962), p. 225.
	22	Dr. Gerald Feinberg, "Physics and Life Prolongation," in *Physics Today* (November, 1966).
256	21	Yeats, "The Second Coming," *op. cit.,* p. 184.
	26	Barbara Yuncker, "Is Aging Necessary?," New York *Post,* November 18, 1963.
	30	Walford, letter to the author dated April, 1968.
	35	Prehoda, *op. cit.,* quoted in *Cryonics Reports* (February, 1967), p. 5. [See also Prehoda, *Extended Youth* (New York, Putnam, 1968).]
257	5	Leading National Advertisers Incorporated, *Annual Report 1967.*
	12	Walford, letter to the author dated April 29, 1968.
	30	Gairdner B. Moment, "The Ponce de Leon Trail Today," *BioScience,* No. 10, October, 1975.
258	6	Constance Holden, "News and Commentary," *Science,* Vol. 192.
	17	Dr. Robert N. Butler, *Why Survive? Being Old in America* (New York, Harper & Row, 1975).
259	29	Dr. Bernard Strehler (ed.), *The Biology of Aging,* a symposium held at Gattlinberg, Tennessee, May 1–3, 1957 (Washington, D.C., American Institute of Biological Science Publication No. 6, 1960), p. 95.
260	14	Dr. Sinex, in *The Biology of Aging,* p. 268.
	19	Strehler, *Time, Cells, and Aging,* p. 112.

PAGE	LINE	
	36	Comfort, *op. cit.*, p. 190.
261	5	Dr. Shock, in *The Biology of Aging*, p. 11.
	13	Comfort, *op. cit.*, p. 218.
262	4	Dr. Charles Minot, "The Problem of Aging, Growth and Death," *Popular Science Monthly* (71, 1907), quoted in Strehler, *Time, Cells, and Aging*, p. 205.
	13	Shock, quoted by Yuncker, *loc. cit.*
	17	Dr. Warren Andrew, in *The Biology of Aging*, p. 80.
	22	Comfort, *op. cit.*, p. 270.
	33	Dr. T. M. Sonneborn, in *The Biology of Aging*.
263	23	Bruce Frisch, quoting Dr. Sinex, in "Genetics" (*loc. cit.*).
266	16	Paul E. Segall and Dr. Paola S. Timiras, "Patho-Physiologic Findings After Chronic Tryptophan Deficiency in Rats: A Model for Delayed Growth and Aging," *Mechanics of Ageing and Development*, 5(1976), 109–124.
	22	Denham Harman, in *The Gerontologist*, Vol. VI, No. 3 (1966), p. 12.
	35	Harman, quoted by *Time* magazine (June 21, 1968).
268	1	Segall, in a letter to the author dated June 30, 1976.
269	21	Comfort, in *The Biology of Aging*.
	32	"The Wright Brothers' Aeroplane," *Century Magazine*, Vol. LXXVI, No. 5 (September, 1908), quoted in Elsbeth F. Freudenthal, *Flight Into History: The Wright Brothers and the Air Age* (Norman, University of Oklahoma Press, 1949), pp. 38–39.

XX   The Engineering of Divinity

Epigraphs

| 272 | | Brown, *Life Against Death*, p. 317. |

PAGE   LINE

John Donne, "Death Be Not Proud," from Louis
Untermeyer (ed.), *A Treasury of Great Poems*
(New York, Simon & Schuster, 1955), p. 368.

XXI   Notes on a Utopia Beyond Time

Epigraphs

275   Herman Hesse, *Steppenwolf* (New York, Modern
Library, 1963), p. 216.
Ibid., p. 227
Unamuno, *Tragic Sense of Life,* p. 183.

276   1   Watts, *Myth and Ritual,* p. 227.

       4   Berdyaev, *The Beginning and the End,* p. 230.

282   15   Andrew Marvell, "To His Coy Mistress," from
Untermeyer, p. 484.

284   7   Berdyaev, *op. cit.,* p. 174.

Appendix: *A Note on Population Control*

285   8   Sakharov, text as published in the *New York
Times,* July 22, 1968.

      16   FAO statement, as reported in the *New York
Times,* September 13, 1968.

      18   U Thant, as reported in the *New York Times,*
September 13, 1968.

286   1   Charles J. Hitch, in *American Forests* (April,
1976).

       8   Thomas T. Poleman, in *Science,* Vol. 188 (9 May
1975).

287   21   *New York Times,* April 20, 1976, p. 35, col. 7.

288   1   R. Buckminster Fuller, *Ideas and Integrities: A
Spontaneous Autobiographical Disclosure,* ed. by
Robert W. Marks (Englewood Cliffs, N.J., Pren-
tice-Hall, 1963), p. 248.

      21   Platt, quoted by Rudy Abramson in the New
York *Post,* October 3, 1967.

INDEX